EVERYTHING UNDER THE BLUE MOON

For my wife Sarah and son Harry . . .

Love is not a big enough word.

EVERYTHING UNDER THE BLUE MOON

The Compete Book of Manchester City FC – and More!

DAVID CLAYTON

MAINSTREAM
PUBLISHING
EDINBURGH AND LONDON

Published in Great Britian in 2002 by
MAINSTREAM PUBLISHING COMPANY (EDINBURGH) LTD
7 Albany Street
Edinburgh EH1 3UG

ISBN 1 84018 687 9

Typeset in Gill Condensed and Janson Text
Printed and bound in Great Britain by
Mackays of Chatham

ACKNOWLEDGEMENTS

You can't write a book and do it completely alone, so I'd like to thank the following people for their support during the summer of 2002. First, Shirley Clayton, my mum, for believing in me all these years and taking me to Platt Lane to watch the team train in snow and rain. It was never too much trouble for her and I'm forever in her debt.

My brother Rowan, for taking me to my first game – a boring 0–0 draw with Leicester City, but I'd been bitten and that was the end of it – and also for suggestions of what should and shouldn't be included, and, no, Rowan, I didn't include 'Behind the Scenes'.

Thanks also to Dad, Kath, Wend, Julie, Neil and all the kids for their support and love.

To Graeme Blaikie at Mainstream for help, support and advice and, of course, to Bill Campbell for allowing me the chance to realise a dream – I knew Bobby Kennedy would swing it, Bill!

A big thanks, too, to Radio 1's Marc Riley and Mark Radcliffe for writing the foreword for me – keep skinning the competition . . . alive!

It would have been impossible to make the deadline if Phil Noble hadn't checked that all the dates, facts and figures were correct and he also provided me with some rarely seen photographs. Thanks, Phil.

Finally, to my wife Sarah and my baby son Harry – I know Sarah's felt like a one-parent family at times. For her support and love, I thank her from the bottom of my heart.

Finally, little Harry for keeping me sane by giving me kisses and hugs when I needed them most. I love you, son, and you *will* support City.

FOREWORD

From the castigated to the celebrated – they're all to be found in David Clayton's commendable *Everything Under the Blue Moon*, in short, an A–Z of Manchester City Football Club.

It's an overdue (and obviously *under*priced) tome, generously published to assist loyal Blues unlock certain parts of their much-loved club's history in their minds, which, due to either old age or in many cases the 'selective memory' process, they seem to have forgotten.

How easily does the score 5–1 spring to mind . . . and with it years of reference and reverence? A drunken September evening of celebration and pride that seems to have lingered for the past 13 years. But what familiarity does the (not radically) *different* scoreline of 5–0 bring with it? Do you know? We can't even remember!

How to use the book? Well it's alphabetical – as all good A–Zs should be – and you start at the beginning and read through to the end. Unless, of course, you're using it as an informational tool rather than simply for a good night in. Let us explain . . .

If, for example, you're at a loss as to why the words 'beleaguered', 'brow-beaten', 'good humoured' and 'war-torn' are all too often used to describe supporters of Manchester City Football Club, then leaf through the pages to the letter 'P', where – if Clayton has done his job properly – you will find the section headed 'Patronising Gits', followed by a written savage attack on, among others, Alan Hansen, Mark Lawrenson and Trevor Brooking. In among the P's you will also find 'Glyn Pardoe', 'Penalty Shoot-outs', 'Promotion' and 'Pubs', though, at the risk of being critical, the last two should really be found within the same paragraph . . . anyway, we digress.

Be warned, though, this publication can be fraught with frustration if used by a non-City supporter. Should, let us say, you wish to find ex-City legend Robert ('Didn't he do well against us at Wembley?') Taylor – *don't* head towards the 'T' section – for there you will be met only by disappointment. Instead, head for the 'B' section where you will find the portly player, not under B for *Bob* Taylor, but B for *Big* Fat Bobby Taylor.

It's easy once you get the hang of it, and if you find any of the information contained in this foreword to be either confusing or misleading, well, we wouldn't be at all surprised.

Enjoy.

Marc Riley and Mark Radcliffe – Radio 1

INTRODUCTION

When I was first asked to write this book, I wondered if I could actually manage to do it alone. I didn't tell Bill Campbell at Mainstream that I was unsure because it represented a challenge to me and, if I had been faltering badly in the early stages, I would have come clean and told him so. But I didn't need to. The research was tough and, at times, painstaking but still enjoyable, if that makes any sense. Discovering facts about players and events that I had little knowledge of made me feel closer to the club I've supported since I was a kid. I toyed with the idea of a post-war A–Z but, as I trawled through various books, newspapers and programmes, I realised that every player that had ever pulled on a City shirt from all periods of time deserved to be written about, even if he only had half a game.

Of course, such a work would resemble *War and Peace* and, personally, weighty books have always put me off, so I had to solve the dilemma of who was to be included and why. I came to the conclusion that a broad representation of all the ingredients that have made the club what it is today would be the best solution. Therefore, most of the great players are in the following pages, but not all; many of the lesser-known stars are included, but not all; most of the meaningful facts and figures are present, but not all – you can probably see a pattern forming.

There's no hard or fast rule as to how much I've written about each alphabetical entry, either. I wrote more about some players than I have others – I don't see the point of padding information out if it becomes boring to the reader, I just want the book to be entertaining to read and that's not so bad, is it? As you read through the players records you may notice the odd * on certain players. This indicates that that record was up to date as of 16 August 2002.

Now, to the subject matter in hand. It's safe to assume that, if you have bought this book or have been given it by a friend, you are a Manchester City fan, so I know I'm among friends.

Our team is a unique and wonderful club with – and I don't care if it's becoming a cliché – the very best supporters in the world. I've never been anything but proud to be among fellow Blues, home or away, and there are still moments when I'm a little in awe of you all. The club is, at last, on the verge of great success with Kevin Keegan in charge and a solid board behind him. In fact, I have great confidence that when my son Harry is old enough to go to school, the Blues will be playing Champions League football. Laugh if you want to, but it's what I believe.

I sincerely hope you enjoy reading *Everything Under the Blue Moon* as much as I did writing it. Like the song says, there *really* is only one City.

David Clayton
Manchester
August 2002

A

ABANDONED MATCHES

There have been 19 abandoned matches since the club first formed and City were losing in only one of those games – typical of the 'luck' that has sometimes dogged the Blues throughout their history. There have been several particularly galling halts to proceedings but none more so than the time Denis Law, a raw but deadly young striker fresh from Huddersfield Town, scored a double hat-trick – six goals – as City ran riot away to Luton Town. Leading 6–2 with only 69 minutes on the clock, the conditions became unplayable and referee Ken Tuck (brother of Friar?) decided to end Luton's misery by abandoning the game. Come on, referee! The lad had scored six times and suddenly the British weather becomes a problem?

The home players and fans went home breathing a huge sigh of relief – when they had dried out – but how young Law must have rued his misfortune after such an awesome display of finishing. A theme that will run throughout this book – something along the lines of *this could only happen to Manchester City* – was illustrated perfectly when the game was rearranged a few days later and City lost 3–1! The scorer? Denis Law – who else!

Only two games since 1969 have been abandoned and ironically they have both been against Ipswich Town at Maine Road, with excess surface water being the reason each match ended before the 90 minutes were up. The first occasion, in 1994, saw City leading 2–0 in a crucial Premiership game and the decision understandably infuriated the home fans. Fortunately, the Blues won the revised fixture 2–1. Then, in December 2000, Paul Dickov clawed City level in a Worthington Cup tie with the same opponents. Referee Graham Poll had seen enough and, with the water almost ankle-deep, took the players off. This time, Ipswich were the victors when the tie was rearranged, winning the game 2–1 in extra time.

The total record for how the abandoned games stood is:
Winning: 5 Drawing: 13 Losing: 1 For: 23 Against: 12
The record for the rearranged fixtures is:
Won: 10 Drawn: 3 Lost: 6 For: 25 Against: 23

AGE – YOUNGEST AND OLDEST

It's hard to see either of the records for youngest or oldest City player ever being broken, especially in today's game, where youngsters are rarely pitched in at the deep end and most footballers retire around the age of 34. Glyn Pardoe still holds the current record for being the youngest player to play first-team football for City. He made his debut aged 15 years and 314 days old on 11 April 1962 (after his paper round) and he went on to play a total of 374 times for the club. The oldest player to turn out was the legendary Billy Meredith, who was just 120 days short of his 50th birthday when City played Newcastle in a 1924 FA Cup semi-final. Sixteen-year-old Tommy Caton and thirty-nine-year-old Stuart Pearce were other notable names from the more recent past from both ends of the age spectrum.

AGGREGATE SCORES

The highest aggregate scores for City in cup competitions, both domestic and European, are as follows:

LEAGUE CUP

9–1 – Notts County (1998–99) 1st leg: (a) 2–0 2nd leg: (h) 7–1
6–0 – Torquay United (1983–84) 1st leg: (h) 6–0 2nd leg: (a) 0–0
6–0 – Burnley (1999–00) 1st leg: (h) 5–0 2nd leg: (a) 1–0

DIVISION TWO PLAY-OFF SEMI-FINAL

2–1 – Wigan Athletic (1998–99) 1st leg: (a) 1–1 2nd leg: (h) 1–0

EUROPEAN CUP-WINNERS' CUP

8–0 – SK Lierse (1969–70) 1st leg: (a) 3–0 2nd leg: (h) 5–0

UEFA CUP

5–2 – AC Milan (1978–79) 1st leg: (a) 2–2 2nd leg: (h) 3–0

FULL MEMBERS' CUP

3–2 – Hull City (1985–86) 1st leg: (a) 1–2 2nd leg: (h) 2–0

ALLEN, CLIVE – 1989 TO 1991

Appearances: 43 + 25 as a substitute
Goals: 21
Position: Striker
Born: Stepney

One of the most instinctive goal poachers since Jimmy Greaves, Clive Allen joined City for £1.1 million in July 1989 from French club Bordeaux. Mel Machin wanted a proven marksman with experience at the highest level to spearhead the Blues' attack on their return to the top flight and Allen fitted the bill perfectly. He took five games to find the net for his new club but his solitary effort against one of his former employers, QPR, proved to be the only goal of the game.

He spent much of the season in and out of the side, and when Howard Kendall arrived in December to replace the sacked Machin, Allen's future at the club was thrown into further doubt. With the questionable purchases of Wayne Clarke from Leicester City and Adrian Heath from Aston Villa, when Allen did start a game he was inevitably substituted. The City fans felt many of the withdrawals were unjust and a strong bond between supporters and player began to form. Clarke and Heath were largely ineffective and, with a total of six goals in 61 League games, plus another 31 substitute appearances between them, it wasn't hard to see why they were viewed with mild derision by the fans.

Allen finished his first season with City with 10 League goals from just 23 starts. The 1990–91 season began disastrously for him with only 11 appearances as substitute from the first 21 games. Things had hardly improved when Peter Reid took over from Kendall in November 1990 and Allen was completely omitted for a number of matches.

With the recently-signed Irish international Niall Quinn and David White forming an impressive partnership up front, the writing was on the wall for Allen, who was finally given a first-team run by Reid early in the New Year. He was dropped for the final two months but was still at Maine Road for the start of 1991–92 campaign. Reid brought him on as substitute against Notts County and Allen struck twice to inspire a 3–1 win. He ran to the City fans kissing the club badge to express his feelings of frustration but he was merely preaching to the converted. Two months later, tired of being the odd man out, Allen was a Chelsea player. Such is football.

ALLISON, MALCOLM
Manager from 1972 to 1973 and 1979 to 1980
League Record: Games: 83 W: 23 D: 25 L: 35 F: 96 A: 137

In July 1965, City manager Joe Mercer approached upcoming Plymouth Argyle boss Malcolm Allison and offered him the position of coach at Maine Road. He accepted and so began one of the most successful management teams English football has ever seen. 'Genial Joe' and 'Big Mal' were a perfect match even though their personalities were like chalk and cheese. In their first season together they steered the Blues to the Second Division Championship and two years later, it was the First Division Championship trophy being held aloft by skipper Tony Book.

Seldom, if ever, had a club's fortunes been turned around in such dramatic fashion and there was much more to come. Allison was often in trouble with the authorities for his touch-line outbursts and was banned time and time again by the FA, who must have viewed him as a pain in the backside. Good on him. He just couldn't keep his mouth shut!

He was constantly being chased by other clubs and was linked with Leeds, Juventus and Coventry City before in 1972 he was offered the job he most coveted – manager of Manchester City. Allison felt he deserved more than just being coach, and after Joe Mercer left for Coventry, he was given his chance.

Yet, nine months down the line, City's flamboyant champagne-drinking, cigar-smoking manager had left for Crystal Palace, Fedora and all. He believed he could no longer motivate the City players and it was probably the right decision to leave. He worked in Turkey and the USA before Peter Swales invited him back to the club in July 1979, exactly 14 years since Joe Mercer had done the same thing. The old adage 'you can never go back' was ignored and Allison's Second Coming was nothing short of a disaster.

He tore the heart out of a side that had consistently challenged for Europe throughout the 1970s and replaced them with an assortment of teenagers, unknowns and million-pound flops. In October 1980, Allison was sacked and returned to Crystal Palace. It would be his last high-profile job in English football, despite a number of other appointments as diverse as non-league Willington to spells in Kuwait and Portugal.

It was in his glory days that City fans like to remember Allison, who once said: 'I used to shout that I was the greatest coach in the world.' Few, especially the players and fans who were around in the late 1960s, would disagree.

ALLSOPP, DANNY – 1998 TO 2000
Appearances: 4 + 27 as a substitute
Goals: 6
Position: Striker
Born: Melbourne, Australia

A £10,000 purchase from Port Melbourne Sharks, Danny Allsopp was a raw, powerful teenager who was in the wrong place at the wrong time while at Maine Road. Instinctive, with a keen eye for goal, Allsopp may well be one of the players who will come back to haunt City in future years – the numbers of such individuals are legion. His tally of six goals from four starts is impressive enough – even with 27 substitute appearances included.

A former Golden Boot winner at the World Under-17 championships, Allsopp was loaned to Notts County and Wrexham in an effort to impress Joe Royle but despite a plea to battle for first-team football, he was allowed to join Notts County permanently in 2000. He has been top scorer for the Meadow

Lane club for his first two seasons and Premiership clubs have been watching him closely.

AMATEURS

A total of 11 players have represented City while still amateurs. The most famous in the list is legendary winger Billy Meredith, who turned professional after three months of the 1894–95 season. Sam Ashworth is one of only three amateurs to collect an FA Cup-Winners' medal after City beat Bolton Wanderers 1–0 in the 1904 final. The full list is:

> Billy Meredith 1894–95
> Sam Ashworth 1903–04
> Horace Blew 1906–07
> John Willy Swann 1909–12
> George Webb 1912–13
> John Brennan 1914–22
> Stan Royle 1917–22
> Max Woosnam 1919–25
> Jim Mitchell 1922–26
> Derek Williams 1951–55
> Phil Woosnam 1951–54

ANELKA, NICOLAS – 2002 TO PRESENT
Position: Striker
Born: Versailles, France

In early June 2002, French superstar Nicolas Anelka became City's record signing with a whopping £13.5 million paid to French club Paris St Germain (PSG). The talented young forward first hit the headlines as an 18-year-old wonder kid for Arsenal shortly after manager Arsene Wenger had signed him for just £500,000 from PSG. He would soon become the subject of transfer deals that – to date – total more than an incredible £59 million. He left Highbury for Real Madrid for £23 million – a world-record fee at that time – and returned to Paris for a further £22 million.

Beset by problems off the pitch, the talented youngster went to Liverpool for several months on loan and proved to be hugely popular with the Anfield crowd. Yet, Liverpool boss Gérard Houllier decided against making the deal permanent resulting in a verbal volley from Anelka, who claimed that Houllier 'imagined future problems and imagined the worst'. Kevin Keegan, who had been tracking Anelka's progress, moved swiftly to secure the services of the lightning-paced attacker.

Only time will tell if the move will prove right for the club and the player but all indications are that, despite the price, if the French superstar can rediscover the form that made him a sensation while in north London, the Blues have a bargain on their hands. He scored his first goals for the club in a 4–3 pre-season win at Bury in July 2002 and looks a class act.

ANGLO-ITALIAN CUP

City played in this odd competition on only one occasion in September 1970. The winners of the League Cup met the winners of the Italian Cup on a two-legged basis but whoever dreamed up the bizarre collaboration and why are not common knowledge. City played Bologna away in the first leg, losing 1–0 in front of a 28,000 crowd. The return leg ended in a 2–2 draw at Maine Road in front of a respectable 25,843 fans and that was the sum total of the Blues' involvement. Travel costs and poor crowds eventually saw the demise of the cup but it did make a brief reappearance a couple of years back, only to encounter the same difficulties as before – and the Intertoto Cup gets bad press!

ANGLO-SCOTTISH CUP

Another cup that most definitely did not cheer, the Anglo-Scottish Cup, was little more than a pre-season warm-up for the majority of clubs involved and particularly for the Blues. Formerly known as the Texaco Cup, it consisted of three group games with the winners meeting Scottish opposition. City lost 1–0 to both Blackpool and Blackburn and beat Sheffield United 3–1 at Maine Road, failing to qualify. The 11,167 gate for City's only home game spoke volumes for the future of this doomed tournament.

APPEARANCES: RECORD-HOLDERS

All-time City record appearance holders:

	PLAYER & POSITION	DURATION	APPS	SUB	GLS
1	Alan Oakes (HB)	1958–76	665	4	34
2	Joe Corrigan (GK)	1966–83	592	0	0
3	Mike Doyle (HB)	1962–78	551	7	40
4	Bert Trautmann (GK)	1949–64	545	0	0
5	Eric Brook (W)	1928–40	494	0	178
6	Colin Bell (MF)	1966–79	489	3	152
7	Tommy Booth (CB)	1965–81	476	4	36
8	Mike Summerbee (F)	1965–75	441	2	67

| 9 | Paul Power (MF) | 1973–86 | 430 | 9 | 35 |
| 10 | Willie Donachie (FB) | 1968–80 | 421 | 5 | 2 |

Joe Corrigan, who played 198 League games without a break between 8 November 1975 and 23 August 1980, holds the record for consecutive appearances. Winger Eric Brook made 165 consecutive senior starts between November 1929 and October 1933, and Steve Redmond, Eric Westwood, Alex Williams and Billy 'Spud' Murphy have all cleared 100 without missing a match. Frank Swift made 195 successive appearances following his debut and Joe Fagan clocked up 121 successive games from his Blue baptism, but these two players are the only ones who have achieved the feat from their debuts onward.

ARDWICK FC

When the skipper of Gorton Football Club, a sturdy lad by the name of McKenzie, discovered an ideal patch of ground for his team to make their home on, they upped sticks and moved lock, stock and one smoking barrel to Ardwick. It was agreed that it made sense to change the name from Gorton FC to Ardwick FC and so a new club was formed. Consequently, the profile of the team began to rise. The League was still in its embryonic stages and teams appeared and disappeared at an alarming but understandable rate. Ardwick twice won the Manchester Cup, beating Newton Heath 1–0 in 1891, who were soon to become across-town rivals Manchester United.

Beset by financial problems, in 1893–94 the club was forced into bankruptcy and in 1894 the phoenix that arose from the ashes of Ardwick FC was Manchester City Football Club, thanks in no small way to secretary Joshua Parlby. City would at least continue to play in Ardwick until 1923, at Hyde Road.

ASHWORTH, DAVID

Manager from 1924 to 1926
League Record: Games: 58 W: 20 D: 13 L: 25 F: 112 A: 117

David Ashworth arrived at City with the highest of pedigrees. He had steered Liverpool to the Division One title in 1921–22 and the season after looked set to repeat the feat – only to join bottom club Oldham Athletic in February 1923. A year later and he was succeeding Ernest Mangnall as manager at Manchester City, who were now playing at their new Moss Side stadium, Maine Road.

Ashworth's tenure was fairly uneventful and City finished mid-table in his first season, though the Blues were equal top goal-scorers with 68. The club were struggling badly by autumn the next season and Ashworth resigned as boss. The Blues still went on to be runners-up to Bolton Wanderers in the 1926 FA Cup final but lost their First Division status a week later on the final day of the season.

ATTENDANCE – HIGHS AND LOWS

The 1934 FA Cup tie between Manchester City and Stoke City still holds the record for the biggest crowd in a competitive English match. An amazing 84,569 people crammed into Maine Road to see City win 1–0. Ten years earlier, City's new home was packed with 76,166 fans to watch City draw 0–0 with Cardiff City. As late as 1956, two crowds of 76,129 and 70,640 watched the Blues take on Everton and Liverpool respectively in the FA Cup. City would win the trophy that season having no doubt been buoyed by the tremendous support they were receiving. The record League crowd is 79,491 against Arsenal in February 1935 with the Gunners holding out for a 1–1 draw. Two weeks earlier 50,000 fewer fans watched City as they thrashed Middlesbrough 6–2, complete with two opposition own goals – you usually can't buy entertainment like that!

The lowest crowd on record is 3,000 in 1924 when Nottingham Forest were the visitors and they took full advantage of the depressing atmosphere by beating City 3–1. A year later a gate of 7,000 watched the Blues take on Sheffield United and again lose, this time by 4–2. In 1964, Middlesbrough proved to be a great draw for the Manchester public as 8,053 saw Derek Kevan score the only goal of the game. A poor City side attracted even fewer when only 8,015 attended a Second Division clash with Swindon Town. Twelve months on and only 394 more were at the final game of the same season against Charlton Athletic, a 2–1 win for the Blues.

AUSTIN, BILLY – 1924 TO 1931

Appearances: 172
Goals: 47
Position: Winger
Born: Arnold, Notts

Following in the footsteps of City legend Billy Meredith was nigh on impossible but Billy Austin ('Sam' to his teammates due to his Christian name being Samuel) gave it his best shot. The right winger, with an uncanny resemblance to comic hero Stan Laurel, was signed from Norwich for £2,000 plus a game at Carrow Road! Skilful with good control, Austin was at Maine Road for seven years and always had a fair return of goals for a winger – slightly better than one every four games. He won one England cap with City and played in the 1926 FA Cup final team that lost to Bolton. He is also remembered as the player who missed a vital penalty during a 3–2 defeat at Newcastle United – a game that City needed only a point from to avoid relegation. He left the club for Chesterfield in 1931, having made only four appearances in the previous three years. Obviously, somebody held the poor lad accountable for the club's relegation!

AUSTRALIA

City have had several connections with Australia over the years. Danny Tiatto became the first Australian to play for City and after a slow start to his career, the utility man and former Blues' Player of the Year 2000–01 is now a full 'Socceroo' international. Striker Danny Allsopp was signed from his hometown team Port Melbourne Sharks in 1998 but left for Notts County a couple of years ago to seek first-team football and Simon Colosimo played a couple of games for the club during 2001 before being released. The Australia national team toured in November 1984 and a sparse crowd watched them beat City 3–1 at Maine Road. Fourteen years earlier in 1970, the Australians went down 2–0 to the Blues as they visited Maine Road for the first time. The year before, City had toured Down Under for the first and only time, winning six and drawing one of their unbeaten month-long tour. There are several City Supporters branches in Australia, too.

AUTO WINDSCREENS TROPHY

City's record in this competition is easy enough – played one, lost one. Arguably the lowest point in the club's history, City played Mansfield Town at Maine Road and lost 2–1. The game itself was unimportant and the trophy meant nothing to City fans; most of them saw it as little more than an embarrassment to how far the team had slipped since the glory days of the late 1960s.

With just over 3,000 fans bothering to turn up, supporters had voted with their feet and the message was loud and clear. Incredibly, a national tabloid, in an amazingly poorly judged article, decided to mock the club and the fans by showing empty stands at Maine Road from the Mansfield game. The pictures, however, merely showed stands that weren't even opened on the night! Alongside the picture from City was a packed Old Trafford photo, with United having played in a Champions League game the same evening.

The article, quite rightly, invoked fury among City fans and didn't exactly enamour the tabloid with club officials, either. Many supporters vowed never to buy the paper again and, in an unfortunate incident, a writer from the newspaper – not *the* writer of the offending piece – was punched on the nose at the next home game City played. The offender was subsequently banned. A lot of history for one match.

AWAY – BEST AND WORST

BEST AWAY WINS:
9–3 v Tranmere Rovers (26 December 1938) Division 2
7–0 v Reading (31 January 1968) FA Cup 3rd round (replay)
7–1 v Derby County (29 January 1938) Division 1
6–0 v Burnley (9 March 1999) Division 2
6–1 v Wolves (21 March 1904) Division 1
6–1 v Manchester United (23 January 1926) Division 1
6–1 v Clapton Orient (6 March 1926) FA Cup 6th round

WORST AWAY DEFEATS:
2–10 v Small Heath (17 March 1894) Division 2
1–9 v Everton (3 September 1906) Division 1
2–9 v West Bromwich Albion (21 September 1957) Division 1

HIGHEST SCORING DRAW:
4–4 v Chelsea (3 February 1937) Division 1

Most away wins in a season: 12 in 2001–02 (Division 1)
Fewest away wins in a season: 0 in 1986–87 (Division 1)
Most away defeats in a season: 16 in 1958–59 (Division 1)
Fewest away defeats in a season: 4 in 1898–99 and 1902–03 (both Division 2)
Most away goals in a season: 51 in 1936–37 (Division 1)
Fewest away goals in a season: 8 in 1986–87 (Division 1)

AWAY KIT
A strange incident occurred on 15 December 1990 when Tottenham Hotspur were the visitors to Maine Road. Spurs turned up to play in their usual yellow away kit but with heavy fog descending over the pitch, the referee ordered the Blues to wear their change strip of maroon so he could tell the teams apart. It is believed to be the only time the Blues have played in an away kit at home, but it didn't do any harm as City won 2–1, with goals from Steve Redmond and Mark Ward.

City once wore an all-yellow strip for the opening fixture of the 1994–95 season at Arsenal. The Blues ran out to the sound of silence when even the club's own fans didn't recognise them. The strip drew many comments from the supporters and hardly helped the side perform any better and a 3–0 defeat made sure the kit was confined to the city dump. Where the kit came from is still a mystery.

B

BACUZZI, DAVE — 1964 TO 1966

Appearances: 59 + 1 as a substitute
Goals: 0
Position: Full-back
Born: Islington

Former Arsenal full-back Dave Bacuzzi arrived at Maine Road in 1964 for £14,000. It was a particularly depressing time to be a City player as manager George Poyser's outfit struggled with life in Division Two. Even the hordes of loyal Blues couldn't be tempted to watch the mediocre football on offer – 8,015 was the paltry figure that came to watch a 2–1 home defeat to Swindon Town – and Bacuzzi's first season ended disappointingly with a mid-table finish. At least he could have salvaged some comfort in playing in all but one of the games.

There was talent in the side – Neil Young, Dave Connor and Derek Kevan – as well as the emerging Mike Doyle, Bobby Kennedy, Johnny Crossan and youngster Glyn Pardoe. Unbeknown at the time, it was the beginnings of a glorious side. Poyser was replaced by former Aston Villa boss Joe Mercer the next season. One of the new manager's first observations was that wing-half Bobby Kennedy would be better utilised as a full-back and so Bacuzzi was gradually phased out of the side. He would only play 15 games plus another appearance from the bench. Not content to play a bit-part he moved to Reading in September 1966 on a free transfer.

BADGES

The badge City currently wear on their shirts was introduced at the same time as the new laser blue strip was released in 1997. The golden eagle with the traditional ship and three stars above replaced the round badge with ship and Lancashire red rose in the middle. Up until the late 1960s there was no badge on the shirts at all, unless the club appeared in a cup final of some kind, when the traditional coat of arms was proudly stitched on. Many City fans like to wear small metal pin badges on jackets and shirts to subtly announce their allegiance.

BAKER, GRAHAM — 1982 TO 1987
Appearances: 129 + 6 as a substitute
Goals: 19
Position: Midfielder
Born: Southampton

That Graham Baker played as many games as he did for City may surprise many City fans, but he was unfortunate to play in a pretty dismal period for the club. Not much happened of any real interest from 1982 to 1987 and they happened to be Baker's years at the club. John Bond signed the lightly-built midfielder but the flamboyant boss would later resign halfway through the season.

City had begun with four wins from their first five games and sat proudly on top of Division One in his first season. Baker's amazing lob at Tottenham was one of a double strike on the day and the Blues won 2–1 to stay at the summit. It was, unfortunately, a false dawn and soon after the gaping holes began to appear in the paper-thin squad and without the quality to replace several injured or out-of-sorts first-team players, the Blues went into free-fall.

Confidence was low and the Blues conceded four or more goals on eight occasions and were relegated at the end of the season by a dramatic Raddy Antic goal for Luton Town. Baker settled to life in Division Two well and had a good season for the 1983–84 campaign – his first under new boss Billy McNeill. His return of eight goals from 36 games placed him as third top scorer, but the Blues missed out on promotion by one place.

Injuries meant that Baker played only 29 of the 1984–85 season as City won promotion back to top-flight football after finishing in third place. His appearances were even scarcer for the following term (1985–86) and he played just nine games. Even so, he battled on and played 13 times in 1986–87, scoring three under yet another new manager, Jimmy Frizzell. However, for the second time in his career with the Blues, he was part of a relegated side. It was hardly surprising that when his hometown club Southampton offered him the comparative sanctuary of a return to The Dell, he jumped at the chance.

BALD
Bald players have been few and far between at Maine Road and looking back at shots of Bobby Charlton and Ralph Coates with their 1970s wraparounds hanging down one shoulder, we should thank God for small mercies. Basil Fawlty look-alike Barry Siddall (1985–86) and midfield hard man Steve McMahon (1991–95) were both thin on top, as was German full-back Michael Frontzeck (1995–97), but there just aren't that many bald players around these days. Back in the 1950s and 1960s it seemed almost mandatory to have at least three or four in each side.

BALL, ALAN

Manager from 1989 to 1990
League Record: Games: 41 W: 10 D: 11 L: 20 F: 35 A: 61

In July 1995 Francis Lee's search for a manager ended when he appointed his old mate Alan Ball as manager of Manchester City. The move bemused most City fans who had been expecting the likes of former Arsenal boss George Graham to come and manage their club. It's a fair bet that England World Cup hero Ball would have registered few – if any – votes had the supporters been canvassed at the time.

Ball's track record in management left much to be desired but Lee maintained he'd found the ideal man to lift the club to new heights and predicted exciting times ahead. Yet, Ball's City side lacked cohesion and they were often tactically naive and City made an awful start to the season, drawing twice and losing nine, scoring just three goals and conceding 21. He was fortunate to have inherited a talent like Gio Kinkladze, who more often than not helped erase a dismal defeat with a piece of individual magic.

Almost perversely, City enjoyed an unbeaten November 1995, resulting in Ball being awarded the Manager of the Month, but some of his signings were unbelievably ill-judged – none more so than the deal that saw the popular Paul Walsh leave for Portsmouth and Gerry Creaney arrive at City. Ronnie Ekelund, Martin Phillips, Nigel Clough and Michael Frontzeck were all signed with little effect and by the end of Ball's first season, City were relegated having never recovered from their awful start.

The fans were unhappy with events on and off the pitch and after two defeats in the first three games of the 1996–97 campaign, they'd had enough. Ball was booed and jeered by both sets of fans after a 2–1 defeat at Stoke City, where he was equally as popular! He was dismissed shortly after. The Blues had won just 10 of the 41 League games during his tenure.

BALLET ON ICE – CITY 4, SPURS 1 (9 DECEMBER 1967)

The famous 'Ballet on Ice' – as the press later dubbed it – was, on the face of it, no more than a Division One match between City and Tottenham on a snow-covered pitch. However, those present and viewers of *Match of the Day* all agreed they had seen something very special on a cold, wintry Saturday afternoon back in 1967.

Joe Mercer decided to let his players warm up an hour before kick-off to acclimatise to the slippery conditions and it proved to be one of his many managerial masterstrokes. The Blues came out and played with sure-footed grace that had Spurs on the rack virtually from the word go.

Despite falling behind to an early Jimmy Greaves strike, City stormed back in almost blizzard-like conditions to score goals through Colin Bell, Mike

Summerbee, Tony Coleman and Neil Young. City, destined to win the League Championship that season, were described after the match by the legendary striker Dixie Dean as one of the best sides he had ever seen. High praise, indeed.

BANANAS

Inflatables would be perhaps a more suitable home for this entry but seeing as it was the inflatable banana that brought City supporters to the attention of the national media, Europe and then the world, bananas win the contest.

There are various reasonable claims as to how it all began but it is difficult to pin the source down to the founder of probably the most endearing and genuinely funny trends City or any football club have introduced over the years. The defunct fanzine *Blue Print* seemingly played a large part in the arrival of our bendy yellow plastic accessories, and if it is indeed the case, Bill Borrows and Frank Newton take a bow.

One school of thought is that former City striker Imre Varadi played a major role in this urban legend, with theorists reckoning that some City fans chanted 'Imre Banana' on the Kippax as a variation to his name. He was around at the right time so maybe it's possible, but it's more likely the name adaptation occurred after the arrival of the yellow perils.

Matchdays during the 1988–89 season were a colourful affair, especially on the Kippax or at away grounds and the Blues' faithful were rightly praised by the media for bringing some much-needed humour back to a bit of a dull period for the club and football in general. Who could forget the fights between the inflated Frankenstein and the green Dinosaur? The blow-up doll, ET, a giant claw-hammer and a hundred other variations. Particularly impressive was the pink pterodactyl (ahem!) but I can't imagine who owned that.

The craze caught on and supporters at other clubs had their own varied themes, one of the best being Stoke City and their legions of Pink Panthers, Grimsby Town and their 'Harry the Haddocks' and Norwich City with their yellow canaries. The losers in the imagination stakes were Manchester United and their inflatable forks. Please . . .

BARKAS, SAM – 1934 TO 1938 AND 1945 TO 1947
Appearances: 195
Goals: 1
Position: Full-back
Born: Wardley

Costing £5,000 from Bradford City, Sam Barkas would stay with City for 13 years and was one of many footballers of that era to have his career interrupted by the Second World War. A stylish left-back, Barkas was no kick and rush defender – he liked to play the ball out with purpose and his reward was five full England caps.

Though he was 38 when League football resumed in 1946, he was in excellent shape and captained the Blues to the Division Two Championship. He left shortly after promotion had been achieved and became manager of Workington Town. He returned to Maine Road in 1957 as a scout and, as many Main Stand regulars will be only too aware, he has a bar named after him under H Block!

BARLOW, COLIN – 1956 TO 1963
Appearances: 189
Goals: 80
Position: Winger/Forward
Born: Manchester

Colin Barlow's record is as impressive as the business acumen he would pick up later in life. Signed as a schoolboy, he turned professional in December 1956 and made a scoring debut against Chelsea in 1957. A right winger by trade, his return of 17 goals in 39 appearances was nothing short of a revelation, particularly in his first season. He had an almost identical record for the following season ending with 17 goals from 38 games played.

Barlow was unusually consistent and his third full season as a professional was almost a carbon copy of the previous two; the 1959–60 season ended with Barlow having scored 19 goals from 39 starts. There was no international recognition for this exciting discovery and his fourth season at Maine Road produced yet more of the same – 17 goals from 33 games. If anything, he was getting better.

Yet, the final two seasons for Barlow yielded much less for the talented winger and he would play 30 games and score eight times from 1961 to 1963. He moved to Oldham Athletic in August 1963 and finished his career with Doncaster. In 1994 he returned as part of Francis Lee's consortium that won control from Peter Swales in February 1994 and, for a period, became the Blues' first-ever managing director.

BARNES, HORACE — 1914 TO 1924
Appearances: 235
Goals: 125
Position: Inside-forward
Born: Wadsley Bridge

City have enjoyed the privilege of some outstanding forwards throughout the club's history and Horace Barnes is right up there with the best of them. Possessing a fierce left-foot shot, the £2,500 signing from Derby County would eventually form one of the Blues' most lethal partnerships with another legend, Tommy Browell.

The First World War was sandwiched in the middle of Barnes' career and during the war years he scored an amazing 73 goals in 73 games! He once missed a day's work at a munitions factory to play for City against Stockport and was promptly fined by local magistrates. He was also the first City player to score a goal at the new Maine Road stadium.

Barnes continued to score freely after the war, and by the time he left for Preston North End in 1924, he'd scored 125 times in just 235 games. Add the unofficial wartime statistics and his record is 198 goals in 308 games. He scored four hat-tricks in the League and a further seven during the war. It's a fantastic record by an excellent servant of the club.

BARNES, KEN — 1950 TO 1961
Appearances: 283
Goals: 19
Position: Half-back
Born: Birmingham

Ken Barnes, father of '70s City star Peter, was famously known as 'the best uncapped defender who ever played in English football', as christened by goal poacher *par excellence* Denis Law. Signed from Stafford Rangers, Barnes would take four years to break into the first team. Once established, however, he would rarely miss a game in the first team and appeared in both the 1955 and 1956 FA Cup finals. He moved to Wrexham in 1961 and became player-manager of the Welsh team, guiding them to promotion in his first year. He returned to City in 1970 as trainer/coach before becoming chief scout and discovered many youngsters who went on to play for the first team. Ken finally got his first England cap when, in June 1977, his son Peter handed over the honour after appearing for his country against Italy.

BARNES, PETER – 1972 TO 1979 AND 1987 TO 1988
Appearances: 149 + 12 as a substitute
Goals: 22
Position: Winger
Born: Manchester

Peter Barnes was one of the best out-and-out wingers to ever play for Manchester City. He was part of a successful 1970s team that loved to attack and was influenced by the likes of Mike Summerbee and Rodney Marsh, whom he had watched from the terraces as a boy. Teenager Barnes burst on the scene and quickly earned a reputation as a tricky left winger with an ability to cross the ball from seemingly impossible angles.

He made 149 starts for City – a handful of these during his second, and best forgotten, spell at the club – and enjoyed successful stints at West Bromwich Albion and several other clubs, including Leeds United. Barnes still had much to offer at the time he was first transferred from Maine Road but was part of Malcolm Allison's 'culling' policy, which saw many established stars leave the club in a relatively short space of time. He won 14 full England caps and 9 at Under-21 level while with City.

BEAGRIE, PETER – 1994 TO 1997
Appearances: 58 + 7 as a substitute
Goals: 5
Position: Winger
Born: North Ormesby

Peter Beagrie didn't like to beat defenders once, he liked to beat them at least three or four times in the same attack. A nightmarish prospect for any full-back to face, the former Stoke City hero was an unusually gifted player who was surprisingly overlooked at international level. His peak at Maine Road was when he was supplying Paul Walsh, Uwe Rosler and Niall Quinn with perfect crosses that often were more difficult to miss. If he had one fault, entertaining though it was, it was his over-elaboration.

Beagrie had enjoyed successful spells at the Victoria Ground and Everton before he joined City for £1.1 million, but it is doubtful that he ever quite matched the heights he managed at Maine Road. There were times when he was simply unplayable, but alas injury kept him out of the first team for the best part of two years. Famed for his spectacular back-flip scoring celebration, though he only managed five in total, he eventually joined Bradford City, playing a big part in their promotion to the Premier League. He is now with Third Division Scunthorpe United.

BEARDSLEY, PETER – 1997 TO 1998
Appearances: 5 + 1 as a substitute
Goals: 0
Position: Midfielder/Forward
Born: Newcastle

Frank Clark's decision to bring former Liverpool and England star Peter Beardsley to Maine Road on loan from Bolton was widely regarded as an intelligent move, considering City's perilous position at the time, but Clark was sacked just hours after arranging the deal. With the Blues heading towards Second Division football for the first time in their history, Beardsley was effectively signed to fill in for the injured Kinkladze but many felt he was, if anything, underused in his brief spell with the Blues.

With Kinkladze often the target of roughhouse tactics from opposing sides, who had (correctly) singled out the Georgian as City's main threat, many felt the more resilient Beardsley would have been a more effective attacking foil for the fight against the drop. His best performance for the Blues was in the 3–1 away win at Huddersfield Town when he rolled back the years to inspire City to a crucial victory.

In what had been a pretty awful season, it seemed that City hoped to avoid relegation by having Beardsley's talent on board to steer the rudderless ship away from the rocks. Mystifyingly, the former England star was allowed to leave Maine Road by new manager Joe Royle after just one month at the club and the Blues won only two more out of the remaining ten, earning a place in football's third tier for the first time in their history.

BELL, COLIN – 1966 TO 1979
Appearances: 489 + 3 as a substitute
Goals: 152
Position: Midfielder
Born: Hesleden

It is unlikely there will ever be a footballer to match Colin Bell – the king of Maine Road. With his limitless energy, skill and all-round ability, he was the beating heart of the most successful Manchester City side ever. He was, quite simply, probably the most complete City player of all time and a tremendous athlete. Bell was signed by Joe Mercer from Bury on 16 March 1966 after the club finally managed to raise the necessary £45,000 asking price. It took Malcolm Allison's constant criticism in the stands at Gigg Lane to put off the hordes of scouts watching the youngster, as England's most respected coach reeled off one made-up deficiency about Bell after another. It worked and he went straight into the side that won the Second Division Championship and, from there on, he made the No. 8 shirt his own from 1966–67 to mid-November 1975.

A testament to his ability during those nine years is that Bell only failed to score less than ten League goals per season on three occasions – a record many strikers would not be able to match. 'Nijinsky', as he was also known (after another famous thoroughbred, this time a racehorse), went on to win 48 caps for England – a record for a City player – and also scored a memorable goal against World Champions Brazil in Rio. He was in his prime when he suffered a serious knee injury during a Manchester derby, when United's Martin Buchan clattered him on the edge of the box. Bell stated that he had been in three minds as to whether he was going to cut inside, shoot from a distance or go around Buchan. He chose the latter and has regretted it ever since.

The tackle itself has been the subject of much discussion over the years but the end result was severe damage to Bell's knee ligaments. He somehow battled back to play a handful of games for the Blues and after his testimonial in December 1978 – a Manchester v Merseyside match – he was forced to retire in August 1979. He is a Maine Road legend in every sense of the word.

BENARBIA, ALI – 2001 TO PRESENT
Appearances: 42*
Goals: 8*
Position: Midfielder
Born: Oran, Algeria

Voted French Player of the Year in 1999 and installed as captain for the 2002–03 Premiership campaign, Algerian International Ali Benarbia's career before joining the Blues was exclusively in France, where he played for several top sides. Kevin Keegan learned of the Paris St Germain star's availability and moved quickly to sign the skilful midfielder over lunch at City's training ground after Sunderland failed to secure his services. The Blues boss was well aware of Benarbia's exciting talent after he had twice scored against Keegan's Newcastle while at Monaco.

Blessed with almost telepathic vision, striker Paulo Wanchope claimed: 'He can see you when you can't even see yourself.' Benarbia is probably City's best ever piece of business in the transfer market. Signed on a 'free', Ali was unanimously voted Player of the Year by the City fans after a string of incredible performances in midfield and he was the creative genius behind many of the Blues' 124 goals scored during the 2001–02 campaign. A joy to watch and a fantastic footballer.

BENNETT, DAVE – 1976 TO 1981
Appearances: 55 + 9 as a substitute
Goals: 15
Position: Forward/Midfielder
Born: Manchester

Dave Bennett joined City from school and soon progressed into the youth team, scoring six goals in the FA Youth Cup in his first year. The skilful striker made steady progress and was promoted to the reserve team, where he played a vital role in the Blues' 1978 Central League-winning squad – the first time the Blues' second string had won the trophy. He eventually broke into the first team and made his debut as substitute in April 1979 – a 0–0 draw with Everton. He also finished top scorer for the reserves that season, where he had formed a formidable partnership with Roger Palmer.

Malcolm Allison was installed as manager in late 1979. As he cleared out many of the experienced, established stars, the door opened for many of the club's younger prospects and Bennett was given his full League debut in a 3–0 win at home to Coventry on 22 September 1979. Allison felt the silky skills of Bennett may be better utilised in midfield and he gave the youngster a sustained run in the first team. Bennett played well in the 1981 FA Cup final but the replay against Spurs would surprisingly be his last match for City. The exciting young striker was allowed to join Cardiff City and later Coventry City spotted Bennett's potential. He joined the Highfield Road club and enjoyed several successful seasons with the Sky Blues.

BENSON, JOHN
Manager: 1983
League Record: Games: 17 W: 3 D: 2 L: 12 F: 13 A: 32

It would be easy to be harsh towards John Benson, the assistant manager promoted to the hot-seat following John Bond's hasty departure in February 1983. He was thrown in at the deep end and, sadly, was engulfed by the murky waters as City lost a dozen of the 17 games he took charge of. He seemed incapable of motivating a team that was still full of quality and experience, and the Blues lost seven of his first nine games, drawing the other two. In interviews with the press and television, he constantly claimed that 'the lads know what they've got to do', but the question being asked by supporters was, did Benson know what he had to do?

He had no money to spend and with one game to go, the Blues, who had sat proudly on top of the first published table of the season, needed a draw to stay up. Luton Town, City's opponents, needed a win. With the tension unbearable, five minutes from time the ball came to Raddy Antic on the edge of the box. His low drive deceived Alex Williams and ended up in the net for an almost predictable winner. City were relegated for the first time in 20 years. The Blues had entered the bottom three for the very first time that season – the only time when there was nothing that could be done. Very bad timing. Benson was sacked a couple of weeks later.

BERKOVIC, EYAL – 2001 TO PRESENT
Appearances: 25 + 6 as a substitue*
Goals: 6
Position: Midfielder
Born: Israel

Israeli international Eyal Berkovic soon became a firm favourite with City fans after a series of outstanding midfield displays since arriving for a bargain £1.5 million from Celtic in 2001. A world-class star, it is a travesty for the talented play-maker that he hasn't been able to perform on a global stage because Israel has never qualified for a major tournament. Berkovic arrived in England with Southampton and quickly established a reputation as a skilful attacking midfielder. He was soon on the move to West Ham United, where he spent two successful seasons and became a huge crowd favourite.

A training-ground spat with teammate John Hartson speeded his departure from Upton Park and he joined Glasgow Celtic for £5 million. He failed to settle in Scotland and became a target for the Parkhead 'boo-boys' before Kevin Keegan rescued him during the summer of 2001. He managed only 25 starts in his first season at Maine Road due to hamstring and ankle injuries, but he maintained a high standard of performance when he did play. He has won almost 90 caps for his country and formed an impressive, hugely creative midfield partnership with Ali Benarbia.

BERMUDA
The beautiful British colonial island of Bermuda has a strong link with City, thanks entirely to the Blues' Bermudian striker Shaun Goater. 'The Goat' was even honoured with his own tribute day – 21 June 2001 – officially named 'Shaun Goater Day'. Thousands turned out to watch his motorcade drive through the capital's streets. The local press follows his progress keenly throughout the season and the islanders watch City's games on cable television whenever they can. They can occasionally be spotted in the laser blue of City – especially when Goater goes home for his holidays! Shaun runs an annual training camp for youngsters with fellow international David Bascam.

BEST START

City's best start to a season was made at the beginning of 1914–15. City won seven and drew four of their opening fixtures before Sheffield Wednesday spoiled things with a 2–1 away defeat. City finished fifth in Division One and would have probably won the League but for an awful run-in of just three wins from the final 14 fixtures.

BIG FAT BOBBY TAYLOR

At the insistence of Mr Marc Riley, one half of Radio 1's finest, Mark and Lard, an entry for the great Robert Taylor who briefly played for the club on their way to promotion to the Premiership in 2000. Actually, there is a more formal entry for Super Bob further on in the book but seeing as Marc mentioned this section in the foreword, here it is. No offence, Bob, and cheers for the goal against Birmingham City.

BISHOP, IAN – 1989 TO 1990 AND 1998 TO 2001

Appearances: 83 + 33 as a substitute
Goals: 7
Position: Midfielder
Born: Liverpool

Graceful midfielder Ian Bishop enjoyed two spells at City during the 1990s with a seven-year stint at West Ham United sandwiched in-between. Mel Machin signed him in 1989 for £700,000 from Bournemouth after he'd almost played a part in the Blues missing out on promotion when City, needing a win from their penultimate game at home to Bishop's Bournemouth, let slip a half-time lead of 3–0 to draw 3–3. Long-haired, skilful and a great passer, the young Liverpudlian stood out for the Cherries and Machin made his mind up there and then that this was a player his team could be built around.

In November 1989 Machin was sacked after a series of poor results and little over a month since City demolished Manchester United 5–1 – a game in which Bishop was superb and scored a terrific diving header cementing his place in Blue hearts for life. Howard Kendall became the new manager and had once told Bishop to cut his hair when the player was a youngster at Everton. Kendall sold Bishop from the Toffees and with Kendall signing dogged defenders and midfielders to shore up a leaky City defence, it became clear that Bishop's days at Maine Road were probably numbered.

He was finally sold to West Ham in exchange for Mark Ward and left the pitch against Norwich City allegedly in tears. Arguably, he had his best years at Upton Park but returned in 1998 for three highly productive seasons with the Blues before deciding to move to Miami Fusion in the States. He recently joined Barry Town in the Welsh League after Miami went bankrupt and later signed for Rochdale.

BOGEY TEAMS

City have had several 'bogey teams' over the years. Wolves and Chelsea have left Maine Road with maximum points on many occasions and the Blues haven't won against Arsenal at Highbury since 1975. Even worse, the Blues have failed to win at Old Trafford since 1974 when Denis Law's back-heel sealed United's relegation. Wimbledon have proved a tough side for City – as emphasised during the 2001–02 season when the Dons won 4–0 in Manchester and then won the return 2–1 and in doing so became the only side to do the double over the champions.

Middlesbrough and – wait for it – Stockport County also seem to hold the Indian sign over the Blues, whereas Oldham Athletic rarely get beaten at Maine Road but then City rarely lose at Boundary Park. Weird.

BOND, JOHN
Manager from 1980 to 1983
League Record: Games: 97 W: 39 D: 26 L: 32 F: 128 A: 123

John Bond breezed into Maine Road in October 1980 to pick up the pieces of Malcolm Allison's whirlwind second stay as City boss. Having achieved success at Bournemouth and Norwich City, the steady, but flamboyant Bond left the tranquil surrounds of Carrow Road for the crisis-torn Blues. Within weeks, Bond had turned the club upside down.

Few managers have had such an instant effect on the team and with City lying bottom with no wins in 12, the mere fact that his arrival was imminent seemed to inspire the Blues to a stirring 3–1 win over Spurs. The standards had been set and what had been a dismal season full of doom and gloom became a fantastic adventure that, with a little more luck, would have brought both domestic cups back to Maine Road.

City finished a respectable 12th and only a linesman's flag denied them a place in the League Cup final, but, then, only a coat of paint saved Tottenham Hotspur in the FA Cup final. Bond's signings had included Gerry Gow, Bobby McDonald and Tommy Hutchison, who combined to play the best football of their careers and inspire the rest of the side to greater heights.

The following campaign saw the arrival of Trevor Francis for £1.2 million and caused great excitement among supporters. Here was an England international full of class, and by 28 December of the 1981–82 season, City topped the First Division and many believed the seemingly impossible might just happen. It didn't, and a dramatic slump in form would eventually see City finish tenth.

Bond lasted just over five months of the 1982–83 season with his magic aura fading by the week and he resigned after a 4–0 FA Cup fourth-round defeat at Brighton and Hove Albion. His shattered and shocked side pitched and rolled under his assistant John Benson and the Blues were relegated on the last day of the season. Bond's tenure had, in reality, merely been a stay of execution.

BOND, KEVIN – 1981 TO 1984
Appearances: 122 + 2 as a substitute
Goals: 12
Position: Defender
Born: West Ham

Life was never easy for Kevin Bond at Maine Road. Signed by his father, John, in 1981 from Seattle Sounders for £350,000, his every move was under the scrutiny of supporters and the media as the time-old question was asked, 'Is he playing on merit or because he is the manager's son?'

To his eternal credit, Kevin Bond just got on with his job and seemed to be unfazed by events. Many City fans saw him as a threat to local hero Nicky Reid and during one home game many fans had a sit-down protest against Reid's exclusion from the first team. Bond junior was the culprit as far as some were concerned and for a time he became the subject of the notorious Maine Road 'boo-boys' – not a new teen band but a section of support that made their displeasure vocally known.

During his second season at City, his father quit and assistant John Benson took over. Nicky Reid was now playing less and Bond more, but this time nobody could accuse him of being picked solely because of blood ties. He grew in stature and despite the club being relegated at the end of the 1982–83 campaign, Kevin Bond had won the respect of the majority at Maine Road and was paid the ultimate tribute by the fans by being voted Player of the Year.

He was no blood and thunder defender, had a certain grace about him and was good on the ground and in the air, though speed wasn't one of his greatest assets. Under new manager Billy McNeill, Bond formed a decent partnership with first Tommy Caton and later Mick McCarthy. Nicky Reid had moved to the USA. He also scored two penalties in two minutes at home to Huddersfield Town in April 1984. City had missed out on an automatic return to Division One and Bond played just three games of the 1984–85 season before transferring to Southampton, ironically to be replaced in defence by Nicky Reid, who had returned from America.

BOOK, TONY – 1966 TO 1974 AND MANAGER FROM 1974 TO 1979
Appearances: 306 + 3 as substitute
Goals: 5
Position: Full-back
Born: Bath
League Record as manager: Games: 210 W: 88 D: 60 L: 62 F: 310 A: 241

Tony Book, better known as 'Skip', joined City from Plymouth Argyle in 1966 for £17,000. Malcolm Allison, who had managed Book at both Bath and Plymouth, persuaded Joe Mercer that, despite Book being 30 years old, he was one of the finest defenders in the country. All this from a player who had just two years earlier been playing for non-league Bath and bricklaying part-time. He would turn out to be an inspired signing and became captain of City's greatest-ever team.

Book was the recipient of the first ever Player of the Year award in 1967 as City consolidated promotion, and he missed just one League game all season. He was one of the quickest defenders around and George Best is quoted as listing Book as his most difficult opponent. He overcame a serious injury in late 1968, when he damaged his Achilles'. Many thought that Book's career was over, but six months later, he was holding the FA Cup aloft at Wembley. He was also voted joint Footballer of the Year that same season as his fellow professionals acknowledged his tremendous achievement.

Malcolm Allison said Book was one of the best defenders he'd ever seen and few who saw him play would disagree with that view. Tony captained City to many trophies, including the European Cup-Winners' Cup, before retiring in 1974. He later became assistant manager to Ron Saunders and then became manager shortly after, taking City to League Cup glory at Wembley in 1976 and within a point of the First Division title in 1976–77, before being replaced, ironically, by Malcolm Allison in 1979. He later became part of the backroom staff at Maine Road for several more years. As a captain and as a manager, Book gave the Blues tremendous service, which stretched over an incredible 30 years.

BOOKS
There have been several books of note on the Blues that are worthy of mention – nowhere near the amount published about our much-loved neighbours but as an editorial director of a local Wilmslow-based publisher once said to the writer of this book, 'We prefer United, if the truth be told. We don't really do City because there's not much interest.' Hang your head in shame.

Andrew Ward and Ray Goble produced *Manchester City: A Complete Record* (Breedon Books) in 1987 and updated it in 1993 – an indispensable work for anyone writing about the Blues. In 1990 Gary James and Steve Cawley released *The Pride of Manchester* (Polar) and two years later John Creighton wrote *Manchester City: Moments to Remember* (Sigma).

Alec Johnson's *The Battle for Manchester City* (Mainstream, 1994) charts the bitter take over by Francis Lee. Gary James was responsible for the excellent *Football with a Smile: The Authorized Biography of Joe Mercer* (Polar, 1993) and the equally impressive *Manchester – The Greatest City* (Polar, 1998).

Among the earlier written works were Mike Doyle's *Manchester City – My Team* (Souvenir Press, 1977), and John Harding's *Billy Meredith* (Breedon Books, 1985). Of late, there has been Ian Penney's *Maine Road Encyclopaedia* (Mainstream, 1995) and Mark Hodkinson's superb *Blue Moon* (Mainstream, 1999).

There have been several other works plus a couple on former City players: *Priceless* by Rodney Marsh (Headline, 2001) and *Bowles* (Virgin, 2002) by Steve Bidmead. More will follow, so keep an eye on that blue shelf in your local bookshop.

BOOTH, TOMMY – 1965 TO 1981
Appearances: 476 + 4 as a substitute
Goals: 36
Position: Centre-half
Born: Manchester

Manchester-born Tommy Booth spent 16 years at City and, like fellow local-boy Mike Doyle, he was at the club during the glory days of the late 1960s and early 1970s. His most productive period at City was between 1969 and 1974 when he was a first-team regular. During this period, Booth famously scored the last-minute goal in the FA Cup semi-final against Everton in 1969 to send City on their way to winning the trophy.

The towering defender refused to buckle following Dave Watson's big-money signing in 1975, and though he was seldom guaranteed a regular spot from then on, Booth's career outlasted many of the centre-backs that joined the club while he was a player. He even adapted to a useful midfielder when circumstances demanded and became a pivotal part of City's 1981 FA Cup run, scoring the only goal of a sixth-round tie at Peterborough United. Later that same year, Tommy joined Preston North End for £30,000 and brought a distinguished City career to an end.

BOWLES, STAN — 1965 TO 1970
Appearances: 17 + 4 as a substitute
Goals: 4
Position: Forward
Born: Moston

One of football's true entertainers and most naturally gifted footballers, Stan Bowles began life as a junior at Maine Road and went on to play for the first team, though in a limited capacity. There was no denying Bowles had tremendous ability but Joe Mercer was reluctant to pitch the youngster into a side that was sweeping all before them and Bowles eventually grew tired of waiting for his chance and joined Crewe Alexandra in 1970.

Yet his debut could not have been more promising. The teenager burst into the first team with two goals on his debut against Leicester City in the League Cup and then bagged another two against Sheffield United just three days later. Deputising for his good friend Tony Coleman, Bowles was left out of the team for the next match and must have felt there was no justice in football.

He was reinstated for the next two, but didn't score. The arrival of Francis Lee meant Bowles would play only one more game during the Championship season. Dogged by off-field problems and what was regarded as a lax attitude to training, Bowles had a disagreement with coach Malcolm Allison in a Manchester nightclub. Things were beginning to go wrong for the lightly built youngster and he only played one full League match during the 1968–69 season.

After missing a flight to Amsterdam to play a friendly with Ajax, Bowles claimed he had turned up but the plane had just gone. The plane, in fact, had been delayed for four hours and Bowles, who had been lying low at a friend's home, was in even more trouble with the management.

He managed 11 League and cup appearances for City in his final season but failed to score a single goal. He began missing training, failing to turn up for matches and had another altercation with Allison in a nightclub. All things considered, it was hardly surprising when the club sacked him in 1970. He was picked up by Bury, who also terminated his services shortly after. After joining Crewe, he fared better and being away from the bright city lights couldn't have done him any harm, either. Later, Bowles would become a star at QPR and he is remembered as one of the game's original mavericks.

BOWYER, IAN — 1966 TO 1971

Appearances: 57 + 12 as a substitute
Goals: 17
Position: Midfielder
Born: Ellesmere Port

By the time young Ian Bowyer left for Orient in 1971, chances are that both he and many others were relieved. Bowyer wasn't a bad player – far from it – but for one reason or another it just didn't happen for him at City. He was a young footballer and no more than a squad player who came in and out of a very successful side, and was only ever replacing established favourites such as Neil Young, Tony Coleman or Mike Summerbee – all flair players and big boots to fill.

He'd been signed as an apprentice from school aged 15 and was no more than a raw teenager when he made his debut in a 1–0 defeat at Newcastle. It was a difficult season for City as defending champions and they finished in 13th place. Bowyer had a happier second season by making 33 starts and scoring an impressive total of 12 goals in the League. He also played in every round of the League Cup, replacing Summerbee in the final and collecting his first winner's medal. The following term he collected his second winner's medal in the European Cup-Winners' Cup final against Gornik, again as a substitute, but instead of kick-starting his career, Bowyer hardly played during the 1970–71 season and left for Orient in the close-season. He went on to play for Brian Clough's Nottingham Forest and played a major role in the club's many successes, clocking up over 600 appearances in a distinguished career at the City Ground.

BOYS IN BLUE, THE

City released the classic 'The Boys in Blue' in 1972 on to an unsuspecting record-buying public. The song, on the RCA label, was penned by none other than Kevin Godley and Lol Creme – half of the hugely successful 1970s Mancunian band 10cc, and was definitely one of the better football tunes of the time. Though it failed to chart, it became the anthem of Saturday afternoons spent at Maine Road for over 20 years. The much-loved tune is still played every now and then, and is almost certain to get an airing for the final game at Maine Road in April 2003.

BRADBURY, LEE – 1997 TO 1999
Appearances: 40 + 6 as a substitute
Goals: 11
Position: Striker
Born: Oswestry

Dubbed – a little cruelly – Lee 'Badbuy' by some supporters, Lee Bradbury's career at Maine Road never really took off. The former Portsmouth man arrived at City for £3.5 million as a promising but largely unproven forward. His confidence seemed fragile from the first game he played for the Blues and the weight of the huge transfer fee seemed to have a negative effect on his game.

Frank Clark's judgement in the market was suspect at best and it quickly became apparent that Bradbury was no £3.5 million striker. His form was patchy and his total of seven goals in his first season was not the kind of return the club had expected from their expensive investment. City were also relegated to Division Two.

With Joe Royle's arrival and Shaun Goater joining the Blues from Bristol City, the former soldier's future looked bleak and he would add just 11 more League appearances and 3 goals before moving back to Portsmouth for around £1 million. He has since developed an annoying habit of scoring against City when the two clubs meet.

BRIGHTWELL, IAN – 1985 TO 1998
Appearances: 337 + 45 as a substitute
Goals: 19
Position: Midfielder/Defender
Born: Lutterworth

If ever the name 'Mr Versatile' fitted anybody, it was Ian Brightwell. An unsung hero, Ian was a dependable professional who slotted into whatever role he was required to play with minimum fuss. He began life at Maine Road as a midfielder and ended as full-back and, being the son of two Olympic athletes, he was supremely fit. A product of a highly successful youth policy, the highlight of his long City career was undoubtedly the 30-yard rocket he scored at Old Trafford in February 1990 – one of the best ever goals in a Manchester derby by a City player.

With the Blues falling behind a minute earlier, the ball came to Brightwell on the right-hand edge of the United box. Without delay, he cracked an unstoppable shot into the top left-hand corner, sending the City fans behind the goal wild. 'I just wellied it!' he said later. A solid member of the City side for 13 years, Brightwell finally left the club in 1998. He played for several clubs after leaving and now plays for Port Vale. His brother David also played 42 first-team games for City.

BROOK, ERIC – 1928 TO 1940
Appearances: 494
Goals: 178
Position: Winger
Born: Mexborough

Eric Brook joined City in a double deal with Fred Tilson for £6,000 from Barnsley. It would prove to be a fantastic piece of business by the club as the pair plundered an incredible 310 goals between them over an 11-year period. Brook was an unorthodox outside-left who often popped up in the centre-forward position if the occasion demanded. Standing at 5 ft 6 in. tall, the England international also possessed a thunderous shot and was the natural penalty-taker for the team. He rarely missed a game and, with 178 goals for the Blues, he has remained at the top of the goal-scoring chart for 62 years – a record that may well remain for many, many years considering the nature of the modern game. Eric retired in 1940 following a motor accident and sadly passed away in March 1965.

BROTHERS
There have been 18 brothers that have represented City at one level or another, including trialists. The first pair that played for City in the same match was Albert and Peter Fairclough, who signed from Eccles Borough on the same day in 1913. George Dorsett played for the club for six years before his brother Joe arrived at Maine Road in 1910. Paul and Ron Futcher, who were also twins, joined the Blues in 1978.

Manchester lads Dave and Gary Bennett represented the Blues at most levels and Darren and Jason Beckford worked their way through the ranks and into the first team, though neither ever gained a sustained run. Peter Barnes' brother Mike was on the club's books for a couple of years and both Paul Lake's brothers, Mike and Dave, were on trial with City in 1985 and 1988 respectively. There was also Ian and David Brightwell, Jeff and Jim Whitley, Nick and Anthony Fenton and, of late, Shaun and Bradley Wright-Phillips.

The full list is:
Barnes – Peter and Mike*
Beckford – Darren and Jason
Bennett – Dave and Gary*
Brightwell – Ian and David
Broad – Jimmy and Tommy

Caton – Tommy and Paul*
Cookson – Jimmy and Sammy
Corbett – Frank and Vic
Cunliffe – Bobby and David
Dorsett – George and Joe
Fairclough – Albert and Peter
Fenton – Nick and Anthony*
Futcher – Paul and Ron
Hynds – Tom and John
Lake – Paul, Mike* and Dave*
Moffatt – Robert and James
Ross – Frank and George
Whitley – Jeff and Jim
Wright-Phillips – Shaun and Bradley*
* Never played for the first team

BROWELL, TOMMY – 1913 TO 1926
Appearances: 247
Goals: 139
Position: Striker
Born: Walbottle

Tommy Browell was one of City's greatest ever strikers and still sits proudly in the all-time top 10 some 76 years after leaving the Blues. As with many of the players from around that time, there are several stories about how careers began or events that took place along the way. In Tommy Browell's case it was two Hull City directors rowing across a river to secure his signature in his parents' cottage!

The 18-year-old Browell tied up the deal with the Hull officials and later that year he scored a treble against Stockport, leading a journalist to famously write that 'ten men and a boy beat Stockport County' and Tommy's nickname of 'Boy' was born. It wasn't long before Everton had spotted his talent and signed him for £1,650 and his return of 12 goals from 17 games very nearly won the title for the Merseyside Blues. City moved in with a bid of £1,780 shortly after and it proved to be an excellent investment for the club.

Browell made a scoring debut in a 2–1 home defeat to Sheffield Wednesday and bagged 13 from 27 starts in the 1913–14 season. Shortly after, Horace Barnes signed for £2,500, though the two strikers hardly played together during 1914–15. Then the war meant another enforced gap before Browell played for City again during the 1919–20 season. At last, the Barnes and Browell partnership exploded with 22 goals each. The following season (1920–21) saw

Browell hit 31goals and Barnes 17 as City finished runners-up in Division One. The pair then scored a further 41 goals during the 1921–22 campaign.

The B and B partnership had peaked and though Browell scored a total of 28 during the 1925–26 season, he left for Blackpool in September 1926. He had scored eight hat-tricks for City, including all four against former club Everton in a 4–4 draw and five of the eight goals that City put past Burnley in an 8–3 home win. He settled in Blackpool after he retired and became a tram driver, passing away on 5 October 1955.

BROWN, MICHAEL – 1995 TO 2000
Appearances: 83 + 27 as a substitute
Goals: 4
Position: Midfielder
Born: Hartlepool

Big things were expected of promising youngster Michael Brown, the star of City's youth teams of the early to mid-1990s. The combative midfielder never quite fulfilled the promise that he had threatened though he was a popular figure with supporters during his time at Maine Road.

He was used sparingly for his first season in 1995–96, clocking up 16 starts and 5 more from the bench. There were no goals and if there was a fault to his game it was failing to find the net more often. In fact, he played 110 times for the Blues, including numerous introductions from the bench, and averaged a goal every 27 games – a poor return for a midfield man.

His career at City just couldn't seem to gather any momentum and it wasn't until Paul Lake's testimonial that he reminded people he was still around. Never one to pull out of a tackle, Brown fairly flung himself around during Lake's tribute match, much to the annoyance of neighbours United and the delight of everyone else!

Of the four goals he did score, his individual effort in an FA Cup second-round replay with Darlington was quite fantastic. He played a major role in helping the club out of Division Two before moving over the Pennines to Sheffield United for £500,000. As always seems to happen, he has scored a couple of goals against City since, one of them, in January 2000 shortly after signing for the Blades, was also the winner.

BUSBY, SIR MATT – 1928 TO 1936

Appearances: 226
Goals: 14
Position: Wing-half
Born: Bellshill, Lanarkshire

It was for Manchester City, not Manchester United, that the great Sir Matt Busby first made his name. The young Scot was all set to emigrate to America with his widowed mother but City boss Peter Hodge persuaded him to stay and changed his life forever. Originally an inside-forward, City moulded him into a classy half-back and he went on to win the FA Cup with the Blues in 1934, having also been a Wembley loser with City the previous year. It was also while at Maine Road that Busby won his solitary Scotland cap against Wales in 1933.

In 1936, after eight years' solid service, Matt Busby was sold to Liverpool for £8,000 and played in one of the Anfield club's best ever half-back lines with fellow Scots Bradshaw and McDougal. He later became boss at Old Trafford and won the European Cup before retiring.

C

CAPTAINS

City have been fortunate to have had some truly great leaders on the pitch. Billy Meredith was the first captain to lift the FA Cup after a 1–0 win over Bolton Wanderers in 1904. Sam Cowan captained City to no less than three FA Cup finals and Sam Barkas led the Blues to the 1946–47 Second Division title. Roy Paul's determination to drive his side to success was in evidence as City returned to pick up the FA Cup in 1956 after being beaten at the same stage a year earlier. Paul had vowed to take his team back and win the trophy just as Sam Cowan had done 22 years earlier.

City's most successful captain was Tony Book. The influential, no-nonsense full-back was inspirational as City won five trophies in four years, including every domestic honour plus the European Cup-Winners' Cup. Keith Curle was a great leader and wore the armband when the Blues achieved their highest finishes in Division One for 14 years – fifth – for two successive campaigns in 1991 and 1992. It would have been difficult for Andy Morrison's personality not to have rubbed off on his teammates when he became captain of Joe Royle's side. The burly Scotsman cut a menacing figure in the centre of defence and he was inspirational as City escaped the Second Division in 1998–99. But for injury, his record would no doubt have been even more impressive.

Stuart Pearce's one season as skipper saw the side break many records and win the Second Division Championship in great style under his impeccable leadership. Algerian Ali Benarbia becomes a member of an exclusive band of foreign players to skipper City after taking the armband for the 2002–03 season. Others, of late, include Bermudian striker Shaun Goater and Dutchman Gerard Wiekens.

CATON, TOMMY – 1979 TO 1983

Appearances: 197 + 1 as a substitute
Goals: 8
Position: Centre-half
Born: Liverpool

Tommy Caton was just 16 years old when Malcolm Allison promoted the promising centre-half from the youth and reserve teams to the senior side. He was an ever-present during his first year – quite remarkable for such a young player – and though he missed part of the following term through injury, he still helped the Blues to the 1981 FA Cup final, playing in both matches against Tottenham aged only 18. He went on to win 10 England Under-21 caps while at Maine Road but would never win a full cap.

In 1982 Caton became the proud recipient of the Player of the Year award, aged just 19 years old – thus becoming the youngest player ever to win the prestigious honour. His progress was being watched enviously by Arsenal, who had obviously been impressed by the two goals he'd previously scored against them in December 1982. Following a bid of £500,000, he was allowed to move to Highbury, enjoying three seasons with the Gunners before joining Oxford United and later Charlton Athletic. A troublesome foot injury meant he had to retire in 1993 and shortly after the popular youngster tragically died of a suspected heart attack. He was just 30 years old.

CELEBRATIONS – PLAYERS

There have been many memorable celebrations by City players over the years but the one most people will remember is Nick Weavers' 'catch me if you can' celebratory run after saving the penalty that won the 1999 play-off final against Gillingham. He beckoned the rest of the squad who were converging to swamp him and then set off on a run that even the cameramen had trouble keeping up with. Eventually the imposing form of Andy Morrison wrestled him to the ground and he was lost from view. In the same match, Paul Dickov's 94th-minute equaliser will live long in the memory. He slid down on his knees and was lost in the emotion of it all for a few moments.

The goal that Darren Huckerby scored against Millwall at the New Den in 2001 deserves a special mention and expressed a point the players were keen to make to the home fans. Due to a history of violent clashes between Millwall and City fans, both clubs took the decision not to allow away fans for each match between the two teams during the 2001–02 season. When Huckerby scored at the end where 4,000 City fans should have been housed, he ran to the empty stand and applauded with his hands over his head as though the supporters were there. Other players joined in and the point was made. It also went down well with the thousands of Blues watching the game on a big screen back at Maine Road. City won 3–2.

Finally, Francis Lee and Mike Summerbee are probably the only two characters that could single-handedly silence 100,000 Polish fans following a third-round European Cup-Winners' Cup defeat. City took a bit of a battering in the first leg and were fortunate to lose only 2–0. As the delighted Gornik Zabrze players celebrated their performance with the vast crowd seconds after the final whistle, Lee and Summerbee began jumping up and down waving their arms in the air looking for all the world like they'd pulled off a fantastic result. They had – but only psychologically. The Polish crowd began to quieten and the Gornik players watched bemused, probably struck with the thought that City had regarded the result as some kind of victory. The Blues won the second leg 2–0 and a play-off 3–1 to progress to the semi-finals of the competition.

CELEBRATIONS – SUPPORTERS

City took around 20,000 fans to Newcastle in 1968 to watch the Blues win 4–3 and win the First Division Championship. Supporters poured onto St James' Park at the end to dance, throw hats in the air and hug each other. Despite the fact that all the fans were mingled together, the crowd was good-natured and appreciative.

Crucial promotion deciders at Bradford City in 1989 and against Charlton Athletic at Maine Road in 1985 saw scenes of wild celebrations but few matched the events spread over a year from May 1999 to May 2000. A 1–0 win over Wigan Athletic in the play-off semi-final second leg at Maine Road caused near hysteria as thousands of City fans spilled onto the pitch at the final whistle. Disbelieving neutrals roundly criticised this outpouring of emotion but it mattered not a jot to the supporters of Manchester City. They were back at Wembley and nobody – nobody – was going to be allowed to put a dampener on things.

The play-off final against Gillingham will be a game no City fan will ever forget. With the Blues trailing 2–0 and 89 minutes on the clock, thousands headed for the exits and a long, miserable journey home. Even Kevin Horlock's strike seconds from the end of normal time was viewed as almost an act of cruelty by the disappointed hordes. Then there was one last desperate attack, Goater's effort deflected to Paul Dickov, who rifled a shot into the Gills' net for the equaliser. The roof nearly came off Wembley Stadium. Seldom, if ever, has the old ground witnessed such scenes of joy and utter disbelief. Those who could take no more raced back in to watch the drama unfold. There was more jubilation after a successful penalty decider confirmed promotion and then a party to remember, apart from the Status Quo records.

A year later and around 15,000 City fans turned Ewood Park into a mini-Maine Road after the Blues' 4–1 win ensured promotion back to the Premiership. The scenes after the final whistle were quite unforgettable and demonstrated how huge and passionate the support is for this wonderful old club. There was also the five goals in the 5–1 win over United in 1989, David White scoring goal number ten against Huddersfield and John Gidman's injury-time equaliser in an FA Cup tie, also against Huddersfield, that are moments of ecstasy that the Maine Road faithful will never forget.

CELEBRITIES – MUSIC

Oasis are probably *the* most famous City followers and the Gallagher brothers were regulars at Maine Road before their careers really took off. Mike Pickering of M People, Billy Duffy from The Cult and iconic guitarist Johnny Marr, formerly of The Smiths and Electronic, are all lifelong supporters.

Damon Gough, better known as Badly Drawn Boy; Jimi Goodwin from Manchester band Doves; and Cornish exiles Haven are yet more fans of the club – imagine the concert that could be held for Blue bands only. Rick Wakeman and ex-Take That member Jason Orange are also City fans.

Rob Gretton, former manager of New Order and part-owner of the Hacienda, was a loyal Blue and season-ticket holder until his untimely death a couple of years ago. City had Rob, United have Tony Wilson and Terry Christian. Enough said.

CELEBRITIES – SPORT

Olympic swimmer James Hickman, England rugby union star Will Greenwood, champion boxers Michael Gomez and Ricky Hatton, plus rugby league star Shaun Edwards all make for an impressive list of sporting fans. There are also several footballers who were boyhood City followers and these include Manchester United's David May, Blackburn star Garry Flitcroft Aston Villa's Peter Crouch, Wolves' skipper Paul Butler, Dean Saunders and Crewe striker Colin Little. There are no doubt many more who have yet to reveal their true colours!

CELEBRITIES – TELEVISION AND RADIO

The most famous City supporters on radio are irrepressible duo Mark Radcliffe and Marc Riley – Mark and Lard – from the afternoon show on Radio 1. Both are season-ticket holders at Maine Road and rarely miss an opportunity to mention their beloved Blues on the show. Bit of class.

Stuart Hall, legendary presenter of *It's a Knockout*, is a lifelong City fan and commentates on the Blues on a regular basis for Radio 5 Live. His wordy and poetic after-match reports owe much to works of the other great Bard, William Shakespeare. Another Radio 5 Live presenter who is an avid Blue is Susan Bookbinder, as is breakfast television presenter John Stapleton.

Roly-poly comedians Eddie Large and Bernard Manning have both followed the club since their childhood days, and Large was even a regular on the City bench for a time during the 1980s, though many thought he could have done a better job than Gerry Creaney. Only joking Gerry . . . Archie Kelly (Kenny Snr) from Peter Kay's *Pheonix Nights* is another City fan.

Soap stars are well represented by *Brookside*'s Tiffany Chapman, *Emmerdale*'s Jeff Hordley and *Coronation Street* has especially strong connections with

Kevin Kennedy, Bruce Jones, Sally Lyndsay, Amanda Barrie and Adam Rickett, who are all proud to reveal their allegiances to the Blues. Craig Cash from BBC's *The Royle Family* supports City, too.

CENTENARY

Ardwick FC had suffered one devastating blow after another and in March 1894 the club was on the verge of extinction. Three crushing defeats – 5–0 at Notts County, 10–2 at Small Heath and 6–0 at Lincoln City – crippling financial problems and a massive turnover of players meant that it would be extremely unlikely that Ardwick FC would return for another season. Ardwick secretary Joshua Parlby had the foresight to form a new club from the ashes of Ardwick and effectively begin from scratch. On 21 April 1894, a week after Ardwick had finished last but one of 14 sides in Division Two, it was announced in the *Manchester Evening Mail* that a new company, namely Manchester City Football Club, was to be formed for the start of the 1894–95 season. On 1 September 1894 Manchester City played and lost 4–2 at Bury and earned their first point two days later against Burton Albion. The Blues had been officially born and were on their way. The club 'celebrated' its centenary in 1994 with a 3–0 defeat at Chelsea on 31 August – 100 years exactly since the first match. Here's to the next 100, but please, City, make this a happier one.

CENTRAL LEAGUE

City's reserve side had been in existence since 1892–93 when Ardwick FC first formed a second eleven for their burgeoning squad. Ardwick's transformation into Manchester City didn't alter the reserve set-up and for 19 years the Blues' second string played in the Lancashire Combination, winning twice and finishing runners-up twice. The Central League was formed in 1911–12, encompassing a larger and more geographically spread pool of reserve sides. Amazingly, it would take 67 years for City to win the Central League when reserve boss Dave Ewing and team captain Ged Keegan successfully guided the side to the title – finally.

They were relegated for the first time in 1981–82 to the newly-formed Central League Division Two. The club's second reserve championship was in 1986–87, which was also, bizarrely, the same year the senior squad was relegated from Division One. The team consisted largely of the exceptional 1986 FA Youth Cup-winning squad and augured well for the club's future. Following sweeping changes to the reserve league set up in time for the 1999–2000 season, the Blues, coached by Asa Hartford, were put into the top division and duly won the title by seven clear points. City's reward was promotion to the Barclays Premiership Reserve League – the highest level a second eleven can play at.

CENTURIES

The Blues have clocked up 100 goals or more in the league on five occasions. The record is 108 set in 1926–27 when finishing third in Division Two and the figure was equalled for the 2001–02 season, with Stuart Pearce missing a last-minute penalty in the final game and blowing the chance of setting a new record and completing his own personal century of goals scored in his career.

In 1927–28 City again reached three figures for a second successive season and this time they won the Division Two Championship. There were 107 strikes during the Division One title-winning season of 1936–37 and in 1957–58 the Blues scored 104 and conceded 100 to finish fifth in the top division! It's never been done before or since.

CHAIRMEN

Of all the chairmen Manchester City have had, nobody made more of an impression than Peter J. Swales. A true Blue in every sense of the word, Swales, promoted to the chair in October 1973, tried everything within his power to re-establish City as a major force in England after the halcyon Mercer–Allison days of the late 1960s.

Within his first year at the helm he had sacked Ron Saunders, appointed Tony Book, seen City lose a League Cup final and watched Law back-heel United into Division Two. Something of a quiet year, then. Yet the 1976 League Cup triumph was all the Blues won in his 20 years in the chair at Maine Road and his reluctance to step aside and let somebody else attempt to steer his beloved club out of the almost constantly turbulent waters they seemed to be in ultimately proved to be his undoing.

As early as 1978, grumblings of discontent could be heard around Maine Road following a home defeat and the pattern continued throughout the 1980s and rose into a crescendo in the mid-1990s when he was finally ousted by former player Francis Lee. Odd managerial appointments and wasted cash undoubtedly added to the fans' mistrust of Swales and his board of directors but the real end began when he appointed Malcolm Allison as manager for the second time in 1979.

Allison was given *carte blanche* to do whatever he pleased and Swales poured cash into the coffers to finance one poor signing after another. Steve Daley, bought for £1,437,500 from Wolves, epitomised the type of deals that were being allowed to go through while established stars like Asa Hartford, Gary Owen, Peter Barnes and Dave Watson were all ushered unceremoniously out of the club within months. Allison's side crashed and burned and so began the managerial merry-go-round that would last over a decade and feature seven new bosses.

When Francis Lee entered the frame and showed a genuine interest in becoming chairman, Swales' grip on the club finally began to weaken. The bitter battle for Manchester City had begun and in 1994 fan-power finally forced Peter Swales out of Maine Road. It was a disturbing time for all concerned and the effect it had on Swales was catastrophic: within two years he had died of a heart attack, aged 62. Despite the bitterness and anger many supporters had shown to Swales towards the end of his tenure, the minute silence held before the final home game of the 1995–96 season against Liverpool was impeccably observed. Ironically, the Blues were relegated later that afternoon.

Francis Lee promised much but delivered little during his reign as City chairman, possibly not realising the magnitude of the job he had coveted for so long. In a strange twist of fate, Lee's managerial appointments were, at best, no improvement on some of Peter Swales'. Alan Ball was hardly the big-name boss City fans expected for Lee's first manager and after just two years under Lee, City were relegated. Steve Coppell became the next man in but lasted only a month and Frank Clark's appointment once again lacked imagination.

Supporters felt cheated and demanded that Lee step down – the whole circus had come full circle and as City slipped into Division Two under Lee's fifth manager in little over four years, Lee walked away from the fans that had hailed him as the saviour of their club.

In 1998, financial director David Bernstein became chairman. The intelligent, successful and quietly spoken businessman preferred to keep out of the limelight and soon won the respect of the City fans with his shrewd managing of the club's business affairs. Debts were painstakingly wiped out, investors brought on board and much of the old regime were replaced with a more dynamic, focused backroom team, including the likes of Chris Bird, Alastair Mackintosh and Dennis Tueart. The financial backing of directors John Wardle and David Makin has allowed the club to breathe again and, at last, challenge on a level footing at the highest level.

Eyebrows were, however, raised when Joe Royle was sacked in May 2001 after City lost their Premiership status after just one season. Bernstein showed he could be tough when he felt he needed to be, showing passion and desire to make the club he supported as a boy into a major force again. His incredible coup of installing Kevin Keegan as boss proved a masterstroke and City won promotion immediately, playing football with the style and panache that Bernstein demanded for the City fans. His tenure as chairman may yet prove to be one of the most fruitful in the club's history.

CHAMPIONSHIPS

City have won two 'old' Division One Championships and had to wait until the last day of the season on each occasion, which is par for the course with the Blues. The historic first was in 1936–37 when an Eric Brook-inspired City beat Sheffield Wednesday and won 4–1 to clinch the trophy. In 1967–68 City travelled to Newcastle United, needing a win to ensure Manchester United and Liverpool could not overtake them on the final day. City won 4–3 and United had to settle for runners-up spot.

There have been seven titles won in the old Division Two. The first was in 1898–99 and then four years later in 1902–03 and again in 1909–10 – the latter two following relegation the previous season. In 1927–28 City pipped Leeds United to the title by two points and in 1946–47 the Blues won the League by four points over Burnley and enjoyed a 22-match unbeaten run along the way. The 1965–66 title was a prelude to the silverware-laden days of Mercer and Allison, and Kevin Keegan's entertainers were crowned the 'new' Division One Champions in great style, ten points clear of West Bromwich Albion.

CHANNON, MICK – 1977 TO 1979
Appearances: 92 + 3 as a substitute
Goals: 30
Position: Striker
Born: Orcheston

When England striker Mick Channon signed for City in July 1977 from Southampton, it was hoped that he would be the final link of a team that had missed out on the First Division title by a single point the previous season. Costing £300,000, Channon had been with the Saints for 11 years and had been part of the side that won the 1976 FA Cup final. The likeable forward had a distinctive goal celebration and would wheel away to the fans with his arm turning in windmill fashion with a big beaming smile. He was a player who would invariably end up on his backside and leave the pitch covered in mud – even during the summer months!

He failed to really settle at Maine Road and the fans never saw the best of him, though he averaged a reasonable ratio of a goal every three games. He eventually returned to the club he regarded as home, Southampton, after just two full seasons with the Blues. The fee was £250,000. Today, he is a successful racehorse trainer and often pops up on television at big race meetings.

CHARITY SHIELD
City have appeared in a total of seven Charity Shield matches but none of the games were played at Wembley Stadium. In 1934 City were soundly beaten 4–0 by Arsenal at Highbury, but three years later a 2–0 win over Sunderland secured the Shield for the first time. A 1–0 home loss to neighbours Manchester United in 1956 was erased in 1968 when the Blues thrashed West Brom 6–1 at Maine Road. Leeds United won 2–1 at Elland Road a year later and, in what was becoming an almost annual event, the Shield once again sat

proudly in the Maine Road trophy room following a 1–0 victory away to Aston Villa. City's final appearance, to date, in the traditional curtain-raiser to the new season was a 1–0 home defeat to Burnley. Francis Lee tops the list of goals scored with three.

CHEETHAM, ROY – 1955 TO 1968
Appearances: 137 + 6 as a substitute
Goals: 4
Position: Half-back
Born: Eccles, Manchester

Roy Cheetham was a loyal and dependable half-back who spent the majority of his career at Maine Road. Manager Les McDowall gave the teenager his debut in 1958 – a 2–1 win away to Luton Town. He was gradually phased into the side by McDowall but the manager never gave him a first-team shirt for keeps. George Poyser saw things differently and made Cheetham his first choice for the 1963–64 season, but, despite 27 starts, the following term he was back to playing a bit-part role in the side.

Joe Mercer's arrival improved things little for Cheetham and over the next three years he would play only 15 full games and a further 5 as sub. His record of 218 appearances for the reserves speaks volumes for his time at Maine Road but gives an insight to how patient and loyal Roy Cheetham remained throughout his time with City. He left for the USA and joined Detroit Cougars in 1968.

CHRISTMAS DAY
Hard as it may be to believe, City have played many times on Christmas Day throughout the club's history. When the players should have been opening presents and carving the turkey, they were representing the club in cold and frosty grounds up and down the country. The last time the Blues played on 25 December was in 1957, when they lost 2–1 at Burnley in front of 28,000 fans.

The complete record is:
Pld: 44 W: 14 D: 11 L: 19 F: 74 A: 86

CITY OF MANCHESTER STADIUM
Manchester City's new home from the start of the 2003–04 season, the magnificent 'City of Manchester Stadium' is widely regarded as one of the best in Britain and Europe. Housing 48,000 supporters, the futuristic design was also home to the hugely successful 2002 Commonwealth Games held in the city. Several top athletes expressed regret that the running track had

been removed and that the stadium was no longer being used for athletics, but without City's commitment to the new venue there would, at best, have been a temporary sporting arena built and then dismantled after the Games.

After the Games finished, the running track was dug up and the playing surface lowered several metres to uncover the lower tiers of each stand, which had been buried under tons of soil. There was one temporary stand in the stadium and this will be rebuilt, complete with the roof, in time for the Blues to take up permanent residence following 80 years at Maine Road.

CLARK, FRANK
Manager from 1996 to 1998
League Record: Games: 52 W: 16 D: 17 L: 19 F: 65 A: 55

There were rumblings of discontent among City fans when Frank Clark was appointed as manager in 1996. Francis Lee's fourth appointment in two years lacked a track record of any substance and few believed he was the answer to the Blues' mounting problems. His record in the transfer market was not too impressive, either – this was the man who had played Jason Lee up front for Nottingham Forest with alarming regularity and signed Tony Vaughan and Lee Bradbury for a total of £5 million. His record at Maine Road was steady but unspectacular and City lacked flair under his reign and his sacking in early 1998 was, sadly, inevitable. He has never managed since.

CLARKE, ROY – 1947 TO 1958
Appearances: 369
Goals: 79
Position: Winger
Born: Newport

Roy Clarke holds one particular record that will surely never be repeated anywhere in League football. His entry into the history books came when he played three consecutive games in three different divisions! Clarke played for Cardiff City in the Third Division for the penultimate game of the 1946–47 season, then joined City and played in the Blues' last game of a promotion-winning season in the Second Division and his first game of the following season was with the promoted City in Division One. An amazing fact and a good question to ask and annoy your mates!

Clarke was an attacking left winger who forged his career at Cardiff City after being a miner. He went on to win 22 caps for Wales and was an important member of the City team that made their way to successive finals in the mid-

1950s. He joined Stockport in 1958 but returned to Maine Road with the social club in the 1960s.

CLEAN SHEETS

Nothing to do with the club's laundry but with how many stop-outs were achieved by City goalkeepers during a season. With 22, Nicky Weaver holds the record achieved during the 1998–99 season. He kept a further 19 in all competitions the following season and both times City won promotion, underlining his value to the side.

CLEMENTS, KENNY – 1975 TO 1979 AND 1985 TO 1988

Appearances: 270 + 5 as a substitute
Goals: 2
Position: Defender
Born: Manchester

A Kenny Clements goal, it used to be said, was rarer than rocking-horse droppings, or words to that effect. It wasn't his job to score goals, of course, he was employed to help prevent them. Like Mike Doyle and Alan Oakes before him, Clements was promoted from the Maine Road ground staff in 1975 and given a contract for football duties instead.

He was a sturdy, physical defender with a big mop of curly hair who began life with the Blues as a right-back. He broke his leg in November 1978 after a clash with Ipswich skipper Mick Mills when he was arguably in the form of his life. He recovered in time for the start of the following season but was surprisingly considered surplus to requirements.

He moved to Oldham Athletic for £250,000 deal – a move that disappointed many City fans. He spent six years with the Latics and played mostly as a central defender and in March 1985 he returned to City, no doubt on the recommendation of former Latics boss and now City assistant manager Jimmy Frizzell. His form for the following campaign earned him the Player of the Year award for the first time in his career. He soon forged a solid partnership with Mick McCarthy before joining Bury in March 1988.

CLOUGH, NIGEL – 1996 TO 1998

Appearances: 38 + 5 as a substitute
Goals: 5
Position: Midfielder
Born: Sunderland

The Nigel Clough that joined City for £1.5 million from Liverpool was far removed from the Nigel Clough that graced the Nottingham Forest midfield for many years. He'd looked slightly lost at Liverpool and positively bewildered at Maine Road.

He played during the final third of the Blues' relegation from the Premiership in 1996 with little effect and meandered through the 1997–98 Division One season with minimal influence on the team. A talented player, he spent much of his time out of the first eleven and his commitment was questioned as he languished in the reserves on a high salary.

It may just have been that his career was on the wane or he wasn't used to the best of his abilities but ultimately he proved little more than a drain on the club's resources. City eventually bought him out of his contract to save further pain to all parties. Clough is now showing promise as a manager at Burton Albion and recently took them to the FA Trophy final.

COACHES

There have been many excellent first-team coaches for City and perhaps none greater than Malcolm Allison, who complemented manager Joe Mercer perfectly. In a familiar pattern, however, great coaches rarely make great managers and Allison is a case in point with both his spells as first-team boss (1973 and again in 1979) ending in failure.

Another great City trainer was Bill Taylor (see *Taylor, Bill*) who worked alongside Tony Book during his spell as manager. The quietly spoken Scot was highly respected within football and was Senior Coach of the England coaching team under Ron Greenwood. Taylor left shortly after Malcolm Allison's arrival and City's fortunes plummeted accordingly.

Former City star Willie Donachie ably assisted Joe Royle for over three years from 1998 to 2001 but left soon after Kevin Keegan's arrival to assist Terry Yorath at Sheffield Wednesday. City currently employ Derek Fazackerley as first-team coach and also now have a conditioning coach, Juan Carlos Osorio. Stuart Pearce has also joined the coaching staff at Maine Road.

COLEMAN, TONY – 1967 TO 1969
Appearances: 102 +2 as a substitute
Goals: 16
Position: Winger
Born: Liverpool

Tony Coleman was signed from Doncaster Rovers for £12,000 after Malcolm Allison convinced manager Joe Mercer to take a chance on the wayward attacker. A tremendous player who played his part in the 1967–68

Championship side to the full, Coleman was once called 'The nightmare of a delirious parole officer', by Allison. Constantly involved in off-field skirmishes, involving alleged bust-ups with Allison, he moved to Sheffield Wednesday in October 1969 but was never to repeat the levels he achieved at Maine Road.

COLOURS

Gorton are believed to have worn black shirts with a large white cross on the front, though it is difficult to be 100 per cent accurate as few records remain from so long ago. Ardwick have been described as wearing mainly white but it was when Manchester City were first formed that the colour blue is first mentioned – and Cambridge Blue at that – plus grey shorts. The shorts were ditched in 1896–97 in favour of white shorts with a plum-coloured change strip.

The favourite and what are believed to be the traditional colours of City – the light-blue shirts – didn't arrive until some years later. There have been numerous change strips in the past and most of them have been since the 1980s when a garish selection of colours and designs were selected for the club's away kit.

The red and black striped shirt from the late 1960s is a firm favourite with fans and is still used as a third-choice kit today. Many consider the luminous yellow and black striped strip from the 1998 Division Two play-off final also to be lucky. The City players now wear laser blue for the home strip and have done since 1997–98. The 2002–03 away kit is a retro design from the mid-1970s – white with a black-and-red slash across the front. Suppliers of the kit have been Umbro, Kappa and Le Coq Sportif.

COMMENTATORS – RADIO

For years, listening to the trusted and excitable tones of Brian Clarke was the only way of keeping up with the Blues away from home. The Piccadilly Radio commentator was *the* voice of Manchester City and even coined the mystifying phrase 'High, wide and handsome', whatever that means. It was also a time when the jingle 'It's a goal!' would send heartbeats racing around Manchester as listeners waited to see if it was City or United who had scored. Likewise with, 'Oh, no!', which mostly seemed to be City conceding a goal. All in all, very happy days.

BBC GMR's Jimmy Wagg presents the best coverage on the Blues with former City MC Ian Cheeseman relaying the live commentary. Former City stars Peter Barnes and Gary Owen act as pundits for GMR and Century FM respectively. The halcyon days of after-match radio was when James H. Reeve and Tommy Docherty formed a charismatic team for several years on

Piccadilly Radio and Reeve is sadly missed on Saturday afternoons, though he does pop up on various stations from time to time. Stuart Hall's after-match reports on City have nothing to do with football, but he's a Blue and entertaining with it.

CONCERTS

It's not only the football team that have played at Maine Road over the years – many major rock bands and artists have used the stadium as a tour venue generating extra cash for the club. The Rolling Stones, Simple Minds, Manic Street Preachers, The Stranglers, Queen, Prince, David Bowie, Pink Floyd and Bon Jovi have all performed on the hallowed turf at some point during the mid-1980s through to the mid-1990s. By far the most popular and critically acclaimed of all the gigs, though, was the 'homecoming' concerts held by City fanatics Oasis. It had always been the intention of the Burnage-born Gallagher brothers to one day play at Maine Road and in 1996 their dream came true.

CONNOR, DAVE — 1962 TO 1972
Appearances: 152 + 12 as a substitute
Goals: 10
Position: Utility
Born: Wythenshawe, Manchester

Dave Connor never really had a position, as such, to call his own. He was more often than not employed as a man-marker and was highly effective in doing his job, much to the chagrin of the poor fellow he was assigned to snuff out. Connor once man-marked Everton's Alan Ball so effectively in a match at Maine Road that Ball sat down on the pitch in frustration at being unable to lose the limpet-like marker. His contribution to City during their glory years cannot be underestimated and though he wasn't one of the stars of the side, he was equally important and much admired by City fans and several other managers who attempted to buy him. He finally left for Preston in 1972 and returned to Maine Road for a season two years later, playing only in the reserves.

COOKSON, SAM – 1918 TO 1928

Appearances: 306
Goals: 1
Position: Full-back
Born: Manchester

Sam Cookson's career with City was not dissimilar to that of Ken Barnes', in that he gave the club over a decade of excellent service, was respected and recognised throughout the game as a player who should have been awarded many international honours – yet was never awarded a single cap. In his time with the Blues, Cookson's only reward was an FA Cup loser's medal from 1926. The stocky full-back formed a tremendous partnership in defence with fellow full-back Eli Fletcher, who was also tagged as one of the best uncapped full-backs of his time. Sam left for Bradford City in 1928 and later Barnsley, where, aged 39, he finally won a Third Division North Championship medal – the only honour of his distinguished career and one that made him immensely proud.

COPPELL, STEVE

Manager: 1996 for 1 month
League Record: Games: 6 W: 2 D: 1 L: 3 F: 7 A: 10

Steve Coppell's 30-day stay as manager of Manchester City was an embarrassment to all concerned. Quite how he could change his mind in such a short space of time will never be known, but it is believed that he felt the position was too stressful and was making him ill. He later admitted that he knows the City fans must have been bemused by the whole situation but he just couldn't carry on. He was afforded a warm welcome by the fans, so whatever the problem was, it was off the pitch, one would assume, rather than on it. Maybe he just wanted the record as the shortest reign a City boss, which he is welcome to have.

CORRIGAN, JOE – 1966 TO 1983

Appearances: 592
Goals: 0
Position: Goalkeeper
Born: Manchester

'Big Joe', as Corrigan was affectionately known at Maine Road, played an astonishing number of times for the club – 592 in all – in a period stretching over 17 years. He signed as a junior and had to fight hard to establish himself as City's number one with the experienced duo of Ken Mulhearn and Harry Dowd ahead of him in the pecking order.

His early days were difficult and he was far from a crowd favourite as he struggled with his confidence, form and weight. His inconsistency led to him being transfer-listed in 1974, but Joe was determined to prove the doubters wrong. He buckled down, lost the excess pounds and improved to such an extent that he was called up to the England squad and would surely have been the England number-one choice had he not been unfortunate enough to have had Peter Shilton and Ray Clemence around at the same time, for whom a succession of national managers just could not see past.

The fans at Maine Road were in no doubt about Corrigan's qualities and they voted the big man Player of the Year in 1976, 1978 and 1980 – a record number of awards. With the emergence of Alex Williams and the lure of a fresh challenge overseas, he left City in 1983 to join Seattle Sounders in the USA but returned to play for Brighton and Hove Albion not long after. On his return to Maine Road with the Seagulls, he was afforded a hero's welcome, with the fans giving him a standing ovation lasting several minutes. He won nine England caps in total but also played ten times for the England 'B' team and represented his county at Under-21 and Under-23 levels. Joe now coaches at Liverpool FC.

COTON, TONY – 1990 TO 1996

Appearances: 193 + 1 as a substitute
Goals: 0
Position: Goalkeeper
Born: Tamworth

Buying Tony Coton from Watford proved to be an excellent deal by Howard Kendall, who had correctly identified City's goalkeeping problem as potentially disastrous. Costing £1 million, Coton patrolled his area with what is best described as a mean attitude. An excellent goalkeeper, 'TC' should have earned many England caps while at Maine Road but was overlooked by numerous England managers. He inspired confidence in his defence and won many points for the Blues, helping them to successive top-five finishes. His heroics led to many injuries and one in particular caused a potentially life-threatening swelling in his leg, which was diagnosed just in time to save his life and career. A troublesome knee problem meant he missed many games in his final year and he was eventually allowed to join Manchester United before reuniting with his old boss Peter Reid at Sunderland.

COWAN, SAM – 1924 TO 1935 AND MANAGER FROM 1946 TO 1947

Appearances: 407
Goals: 24
Position: Centre-half
Born: Chesterfield
League Record as manager: Games: 42 W: 26 D: 10 L: 6 F: 78 A: 35

Sam Cowan served City for 11 seasons in defence and was proud to do so. He captained the side in the 1933 FA Cup final after telling King George V that his team would be 'back next year to win it'. Sure enough, the Blues returned to win the trophy, just as he'd predicted. He once scored a hat-trick of headers for his old club Doncaster and had a taste for attacking football. He left City in 1935 and after playing for Bradford City and Brighton and Hove Albion, settled in Hove, East Sussex.

He became trainer at Brighton and set up a successful physiotherapy practice near to the Seagulls' home ground. City asked if he would like to become the team manager in 1946 and Cowan, though still living near Brighton, accepted. He guided the Blues to the Division Two Championship but his travelling meant the position became impossible for him and he decided to concentrate full time on his practice on the south coast. How successful Cowan might have been as a manager, one can only guess.

CRICKETERS

Many of today's sportsmen are multi-talented and several former City players could have gone on to play different sports professionally. Striker Darren Beckford (1984–87) was a gifted cricketer and basketball player but chose football as his profession. Two former City players that were also first-class cricketers were 'Patsy' Hendren and Jack Dyson. Hendren played 51 Test matches for England and scored over 40,000 runs for Middlesex. The well-built winger played only twice for the Blues during the 1908–09 season. Jack Dyson was a talented all-rounder for Lancashire scoring 4,433 runs and taking 161 wickets between 1954 and 1964. As one sporting season ended, the other began so holidays were a thing of fancy until his retirement from at least one of the sports. He played 72 games for City (1951–61) in all competitions and scored 29 goals, including one in the 1956 FA Cup final. The irrepressible forward also broke his leg twice during the 1957–58 season.

CROSSAN, JOHNNY – 1965 TO 1967
Appearances: 110
Goals: 28
Position: Midfielder
Born: Derry

Following irregularities in a transfer deal taking Johnny Crossan from Coleraine to Bristol City, the authorities slapped a lifetime ban on the talented midfielder. He was left with no other choice but to go to Europe to continue his career. Sparta Rotterdam were impressed by his credentials and he was signed on by the Dutch side before moving on to Standard Liège in Belgium. He also played for Liège in the European Cup. His skill and technique were taking on new dimensions and when the ban in the UK was lifted in 1962, Sunderland moved the quickest and snapped up the Northern Irish international for £28,000.

He was popular among supporters at Sunderland and the trend continued when Joe Mercer made him one of his first signings, paying £40,000 for his services. Mercer saw Crossan as the man who could help knit a talented young side together with his skill and experience. He was made captain, a role he revelled in, and City won the Division Two Championship. Crossan's contribution was huge, missing just two League games all season and netting 13 goals.

Crossan enjoyed life at Maine Road and his delicate skills, flicks and dribbles had the fans eating out of his hand for a time. After being involved in a car crash, he decided not to tell the club and continued playing while hampered by a leg injury. Many mistook injury for laziness and at the end of the season Johnny Crossan was once again on the move, this time to Middlesbrough for £34,500.

CURLE, KEITH – 1991 TO 1996
Appearances: 204
Goals: 13
Position: Central defender
Born: Bristol

Classy centre-back Keith Curle was signed by Peter Reid in the summer of 1991 for £2.5 million – a British record fee at the time paid for a defender. The ex-Wimbledon skipper was immediately installed as captain by Reid and quickly won over any doubters with his leadership qualities and defensive ability. His abundance of skill and lightning pace made life difficult for forwards.

He may not have been as dominant in the air as some central defenders that have played for the Blues, but he was slick, polished and more than a little unfortunate not to have won more than the three England caps that he did (all, incidentally, out of position). 'Curley-Wurley', as the City fans had christened him, eventually joined Wolves in 1996 after five successful seasons at Maine Road and later moved to Sheffield United.

CURSE

There is an old legend that Maine Road was built on a gypsy settlement and the travellers were none too pleased when they were ordered away. The story goes that the gypsies put a curse on Maine Road and announced that no luck would come to the club as long as they stayed there. To a certain extent, the story is quite believable! Maybe they also added that for the next 80 years, every referee would favour the opposition or just act like a complete divot for 90 minutes . . . the power of the unknown is strong.

D

DALEY, STEVE – 1979 TO 1981
Appearances: 53 + 1 as a substitute
Goals: 4
Position: Midfielder
Born: Barnsley

One of City's most infamous signings, Steve Daley joined the club from Wolverhampton Wanderers for £1,437,500 in 1979 to become the most expensive British signing ever. Malcolm Allison saw Daley as the perfect player to build his young side around but things went horribly wrong. It was hardly his fault, but Daley never looked anywhere near like a player worth the fee City had paid. The huge sum seemed to weigh heavily on his shoulders and he soon became the target of discontent from fans who saw him as a waste of precious funds. He had looked an industrious midfielder with ability at Molineux but the move to Maine Road sent his career spiralling into reverse. After 15 months of disappointment for all concerned, he signed for US club Seattle Sounders for a fraction of the fee paid for his services.

DAVIES, WYN – 1971 TO 1972
Appearances : 49
Goals: 10
Position: Striker
Born: Caernarvon

Towering forward Wyn Davies joined City from Newcastle United in 1971, just 12 days before the new season began. Joe Mercer paid £52,500 for the services of the Welshman known as 'Wyn the Leap' and his signing resulted in Francis Lee's best-ever goals haul for the Blues – 33 – in a season many thought should have ended with the League Championship. Davies was one of the best in the country in the air and he proved the perfect foil for Lee.

He contributed with eight League goals in his first season with the club but when Rodney Marsh was signed for the final push for the title, City's style of play changed noticeably from quick counter-attacks to a slower more deliberate build-up that didn't suit the team as a whole. The old adage 'if it isn't broken, don't fix it' was ignored and they eventually finished fourth. Lee scored only four times in the final ten games and Davies none after previously bagging 37 between them in the previous 32 games. Joe Mercer's departure as team boss was bad news for The Leap. Malcolm Allison decided to sell Davies after just five appearances of the following season to neighbours United for a fee of £65,000 – the first deal between the two Manchester clubs for 41 years.

DEBUTS

Every footballer dreams of a debut where everything turns out the way they imagined, whether it be a hat-trick, a match-saving tackle or a wondrous last-minute penalty save – depending on the position the debutant plays in, of course. Few experience such a dream start to their careers but there have been a few notable exceptions. Fred Howard scored all four goals in a 4–1 win over Liverpool in January 1913 and then scored a goal in each of the next two League matches. He then went seven without a goal but added five in the last six games of the season. He also scored three more against Liverpool the next season and then a single goal in each of the next three encounters, making it an amazing ten in six games – the Merseyside Reds must have been sick of the sight of him!

Jimmy Constantine hit a League debut treble against Millwall in 1946, though he had previously played for the club during the war, hitting 25 in 34 in the Football League North and FA Cup. Paulo Wanchope enjoyed a memorable home debut against Sunderland in August 2000 when he struck three of the goals in a 4–2 victory. Many players have managed a goal on their first appearance for City and Niall Quinn is among them. His towering header against Chelsea in March 1990, earning the Blues a valuable 1–1 draw, was the start of many important goals the Irishman scored for the club.

Carlo Nash endured a nightmarish beginning to his career at Maine Road after being forced to pick the ball out of the net four times in the first 35 minutes against a rampant Arsenal in April 2001, though none were his fault and things improved considerably from then on.

DEFEAT – HEAVIEST

City have been on the end of a few thrashings in the past but it makes painful reading at the best of times. Briefly, the worst of the worst are as follows:

    1896 FA Cup 1st round: Preston 6, City 0
    1906 Division One: Everton 9, City 1
    1962 League Cup 5th round: Birmingham 6, City 0

The 1955/56 FA Cup-winning team

Asa Hartford — record Scottish
cup holder and now reserve coach

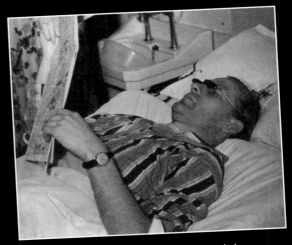

Andy Hinchcliffe — 1985–90.

Bert Trautmann recovering in hospital
after breaking his neck

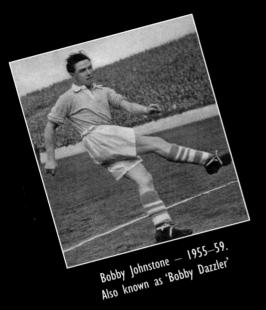

Bobby Johnstone — 1955–59.
Also known as 'Bobby Dazzler'

Ian Brightwell shortly after scoring one
of the best derby goals ever, February 1990

Colin Bell — 1966–79. The
greatest City player ever . . .

Clive Allen — 1989–91. Predator
of the penalty box

Denis Law — confirmed United's
relegation during his second
spell

Derek Jeffries — 1966–73. Utility
player

Eric Brook — City's all-time record
goalscorer with 178 strikes

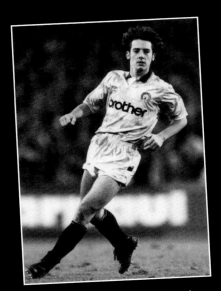

Ian Bishop — stylish midfielder who
returned for a second spell under Joe

Joe Corrigan — 'Big Joe' — kept goal
592 times for the Blues

Joe Hayes — 1953–65. Scorer of the winning
goal in the 1956 FA Cup final

Kaziu Deyna — Polish World
Cup skipper

Kevin Bond — 1981–84.
Worked hard to win over the
City fans

Johnny Crossan — 1965–67.
Mercurial Irish midfielder

Kevin Reeves — 1980–83. Second
million pound player to sign for
the
club

Celebrating the European Cup-Winners Cup triumph at the Town Hall

es McDowall — Manager 1950—63

Malcolm Allison in pensive mood

Meadows, Ewing, Revie and Clarke partake in a pre-season jog

Mercer & Allison — the greatest managerial pairing ever for the Blues

Neil Young scores the opening goal in 1970 ECWC final

Dennis Tueart tucks away a penalty against Sunderland

Niall Quinn — 1990—96.
Hugely popular and skilful
striker

Paul Simpson — teenage
wing sensation, now boss
at Rochdale

Peter Reid — former
midfield war-horse and
manager

Dennis Tueart and Tony Book lift spirits during
extra time with Norwich City, September 1970

Rodney Marsh signs on the dotted line in 1972

Rodney Marsh exchanging pennants at Barcelona,
November 1974

Skipper Roy Paul with the FA Cup, 1956

FA Cup celebrations 1956

Sam Cowan —
1924–35. Former
player and, briefly,
manager

Tony Coleman — City bad boy and
talented winger

Tony Whelan — 1974. Almost made
the grade at Maine Road

Trevor Francis — 1981–82. Classy
striker who played for just one season at
Maine Road

Willie Donachie — 1968–80.
Scottish full-back and former
coach

DEFENSIVE RECORDS

The 1902–03 Second Division Championship season was when City conceded fewest goals in a campaign when just 29 goals were shipped in 34 games, though the 33 conceded in 46 Division Two games in 1998–99 read even better, considering that side played a dozen more matches. The worst season for the Blues' defence was in 1962–63 when 102 goals were leaked and hardly surprisingly, City were relegated.

DERBIES

It's an unfortunate fact of life that the Blues have severely underperformed in the Manchester derby games over the past 20 years. There was a time when City dominated the fixture and, hopefully, they'll be back before long. Favourite derby days include the 4–1 away win for City with Franny Lee notching a hat-trick and, in particular, the 1–0 win at Old Trafford in 1974 which rubber-stamped United's relegation to Division Two. The 1989 5–1 win at Maine Road will never be forgotten by either sets of supporters with Mel Machin's bravehearts ripping the Reds to shreds on a day when everything went right for the Blue half of Manchester.

The 3–3 draw the following season was a hugely entertaining game but a little disappointing all the same having been 3–1 in front. Ian Brightwell's thunderbolt drive in the 1990 1–1 draw at Old Trafford was among the best goals ever scored in this explosive fixture.

Regrets – we've had a few! Somehow a 2–0 half-time lead became 2–3 by full-time in November 1993 and the 2–1 FA Cup fifth-round defeat in 1996 was difficult to swallow – referee Alan Wilkie has still never refereed a game at Maine Road since his mystifying decision to give United a penalty.

Though not as glamorous, derby days with Oldham Athletic, Stockport County, Bury and even Macclesfield Town have all caused a few headaches, with Oldham and Stockport in particular excelling in the Maine Road fixtures. Bolton Wanderers are a sort of derby clash and their supporters' hatred of all things Mancunian is worth attending the games for alone. Save for Bolton, most of these, with respect, minor derbies are likely to be confined to the history books following City's recent renaissance – hopefully!

DEYNA, KAZIU — 1978 TO 1981
Appearances: 38 + 5 as a substitute
Goals: 13
Position: Forward
Born: Starsgrad, Gdansk

There was much excitement among City fans when it was announced that the Blues were on the trail of 102-times capped Polish World Cup captain Kaziu Deyna. Red tape and the player's involvement in the Polish Army would initially delay the deal before a fee of £100,000 was agreed with Legia Warsaw. Despite signing on 11 September 1978, it wouldn't be until 25 November that he finally made his full debut. After almost nine months at City, he finally found the back of the net in his eighth full game for the Blues.

The technique, skill and vision Deyna possessed made him a huge favourite with the City faithful and his first season return of six goals in eleven starts promised even better to come for the following campaign. Injuries put paid to most of the 1979–80 season and his return was six goals in 21 games. Whether the style of play or the team he was in affected him, it is certain that he never reached the heights he did for his former club while at Maine Road. At the end of January 1981, he left for San Diego in the NASL. Tragically, he was killed in a car crash in California in September 1989. His elegance and ability have ensured he is fondly remembered at Maine Road.

DIBBLE, ANDY — 1988 TO 1997
Appearances: 137 + 4 as a substitute
Goals: 0
Position: Goalkeeper
Born: Cwmbran

Andy Dibble joined City from Luton in 1988 and remained with the club for the best part of ten years. Something of a penalty-saving specialist, Dibble's early days at City were without doubt his most impressive when he was at the top of his form. After two years as first choice, a series of injuries and mishaps befell the popular Welshman and disaster struck for Dibble during a crucial League match at Nottingham Forest in March 1990. Labelled 'the Gary Crosby incident', City's keeper had the ball nodded out of the palm of his hand in the full glare of the national media. The pictures of Dibble staring at his empty glove were everywhere in the tabloids the next day and Howard Kendall, apparently furious with the referee's decision, soon splashed out £1 million for Watford's highly-rated goalkeeper Tony Coton. The message to Dibble was clear.

Coton became the archetypal 'immovable object' and Dibble became no more than a bit-part player for the rest of his City career. He was loaned out on five occasions while at Maine Road and has played for around 16 clubs in total.

DICKOV, PAUL — 1996 TO 2002
Appearances: 122 + 59 as a substitute
Goals: 41
Position: Striker
Born: Glasgow

Alan Ball stayed just long enough to see his best signing make his debut away to Stoke City in 1996 and was then sacked by the Blues. The £800,000 capture from Arsenal set about terrorising defenders from the word go and what he lacked in height and natural ability, he made up for in sheer guts and effort. He never really enjoyed the luxury of being an automatic first choice but his attitude did not waver and once he pulled on the laser-blue jersey the 5 ft 5 in. pocket dynamo became like a man possessed, chasing lost causes and wearing down defenders by never giving them a moment's peace.

His part in the revival of fortunes at Maine Road should never be underestimated and many believe that his appearance in the second half of a vital Division Two clash with Stoke City stoked the embers of a team whose flame had been flickering weakly and threatening to go out all together. Dickov chased a ball into the corner with a Stoke defender and clattered into him. The Kippax roared with approval and City's Tony Vaughan made a similar challenge immediately after. City came back from 0–1 to win 2–1 and charged into the play-offs. If this was the catalyst to greater things, the club owes Dickov more than they can ever repay.

It was Dickov who equalised in the first leg semi-final with Wigan Athletic and he changed the fate of City with a last-gasp equaliser against Gillingham in the final. He sealed the promotion-clinching victory at Blackburn Rovers by scoring the final goal in a 4–1 win as City stormed back to the Premiership. The impressive list is endless.

Despite his heroics, his chances became even more limited after Joe Royle purchased George Weah and Paulo Wanchope for the start of 2000–01 Premiership campaign but the tough Scot continued to buckle down and await his opportunity. When Royle left, 'Dicky' was pushed even further down the pecking order and when Leicester City offered a nominal fee in early 2002, Kevin Keegan allowed the player to move on.

He had the chance to say goodbye to the City fans before a midweek home game shortly after and received a rousing ovation from the crowd. He was also invited back to tie the ribbons on the First Division Championship trophy for the final game of the 2001–02 season. A loyal servant and enormously popular player, Dickov's presence and attitude at Maine Road will be sorely missed.

DISTIN, SYLVAIN – 2002 TO PRESENT
Position: Defender
Born: Bagnolet, France

Former Paris Saint Germain star Sylvain Distin joined the Blues for £4 million in June 2002 to become the club's most expensive defensive signing ever. Distin spent much of the 2001–02 season on loan at Newcastle and made 34 appearances in all competitions for them, including a 1–0 win over the Blues in the FA Cup. He was, understandably, believed to be heading for St James' Park this summer after completing a successful spell with the Magpies. However, the French star couldn't agree terms and Kevin Keegan moved swiftly to sign the defender, who effectively had turned his back on the prospect of Champions League football. Essentially a left-sided player, Distin is a quick, powerful player, who at 6ft 4in. is also one of the tallest players to play for the Blues.

DOCUMENTARIES
In 1979 the Blues were the subject of a one-hour documentary simply called *City* and shown by ITV; a fascinating behind-the-scenes look at the Peter Swales and Malcolm Allison relationship with some unforgettable moments between the two. Cataloguing a poor season, the problems that ran to the core of the club were there for all to see in a genuine warts-and-all programme. It culminated with the return of Allison as Crystal Palace coach in an FA Cup match at Maine Road. It was never repeated and today gathers dust in the television archives of Granada.

BBC 1's flagship evening magazine *Nationwide* (a portent of the misery to come?) featuring Sue Lawley made for riveting viewing for City fans as the programme covered the Blues' 1978 Division One campaign. Once again, cameras were granted access to wherever they wished and though each segment was rarely more than five minutes long, it was national exposure for the club and an extra bonus for the supporters.

DOGS
Dogs, 'man's best friend', have not featured too highly in City's history – no surprises there, then. But there is one sad instance that is worthy of mention. On the day after Guy Fawkes Night 1920, the Main Stand at City's Hyde Road ground burned to the ground and with it all the club's records. Worse still, City's faithful hound, 'Nell', also perished in the flames. The cause was not, as first suspected, a firework but a stray cigarette butt. Perhaps the whole sorry episode is the reason why the Blues resisted selling hot dogs at the ground until recently.

Several Moss Side strays have enjoyed a moment of fame by doing a lap of the Maine Road pitch and evading stewards with a feign and burst of pace that would inevitably have the Kippax roaring for the current manager to 'Sign him up!' One cheeky mutt, possibly leaning towards the red side of Manchester, once ran up to the goal posts at the Platt Lane end and promptly cocked his leg up. Barefaced cheek!

DOHERTY, PETER – 1935 TO 1945
Appearances: 133
Goals: 81
Position: Inside-forward
Born: Magherafelt, Eire

Described in revered tones by those who are old enough to remember him, Peter Doherty was among the finest players ever to pull on a Manchester City shirt – some say *the* finest. The Irish inside-forward was one of the legends of the game and a master tactician on the pitch. Doherty excelled at dribbling, tackling, passing and heading, and delighted the City fans with his endless energy. He signed in 1936 for £10,000 – a club record – and was the star of the Championship-winning side the following season, scoring 32 goals in 45 matches.

Doherty was part of the team that followed up the League title with relegation – despite having scored more goals than anybody else had achieved! Only City could do such a thing. The Second World War stole seven years from Doherty, as it did all footballers throughout the world, though he still played 89 times, scoring 60 goals during wartime for the club. If those were added to his official total, he would have scored 141 goals in just 222 games. Peter died in April 1990 and a commemorative plaque was recently unveiled in his native Ireland.

DONACHIE, WILLIE – 1968 TO 1980
Appearances: 421 + 5 as a substitute
Goals: 2
Position: Full-back
Born: Glasgow

One of City's longest-serving players and, until last season, assistant to Kevin Keegan, Willie Donachie won 35 caps for Scotland during his 12 years with the Blues. A member of his country's 1978 World Cup squad, Willie was an excellent defender for the club and was one of the most respected players of his generation. Classy on the ball and very comfortable in possession, he played his part in a solid City side for over a decade, but it could have been very different.

He'd joined City as a junior in 1968, not as a defender, but as a midfielder. It was only when Glyn Pardoe broke his leg that Donachie was converted to a left-back. From then, he never looked back. He joined Portland Timbers in 1980 for £200,000 and later finished his playing career at Oldham. He returned as Joe Royle's assistant but left for Sheffield Wednesday in 2001 to form a managerial team with Terry Yorath.

DORSETT, GEORGE – 1904 TO 1912
Appearances: 211
Goals: 65
Position: Winger
Born: Brownhills

The £450 paid for West Bromwich Albion's George Dorsett in 1904 was a record fee for a winger at the time. The skilful outside-left arrived at Hyde Road and was soon converted to wing-half in the best interests of the team. He averaged around eight goals a season during his time with City and, in 1910, City returned to West Brom to sign his brother Joe. The pair played for a short time together in the City side before George retired through injury in 1912. His brother Joe stayed with the Blues until he left for Southend United in 1920.

DOWD, HARRY – 1958 TO 1970
Appearances: 219
Goals: 1
Position: Goalkeeper
Born: Manchester

Harry Dowd spent 12 successful years at Maine Road, appearing 219 times and was deputy to Bert Trautmann for several years before he eventually shared first-team duties with the big German, earning rave reviews for his impressive performances. With an almost legendary indifference to football – Joe Mercer once had to tell him the colours of the opposition! – Dowd also holds one of City's most unique records. During a match against Bury, he suffered an injury to his shoulder making it impossible for him to continue. With no substitutes allowed at that time, Harry swapped shirts with Matt Gray and played the last 36 minutes as a striker. In one of those aforementioned 'this only could happen to City' moments, Dowd equalised seven minutes from time and earned the Blues a 1–1 draw! Harry lost his place due to injury during the 1968 Division One Championship season, but won an FA Cup-Winners' medal in 1969. He later joined Oldham and played 111 times for the Latics as they climbed the Football League, but, alas, scored no more goals

DOYLE, MIKE – 1962 TO 1976
Appearances: 551 + 7 as a substitute
Goals: 40
Position: Defender
Born: Manchester

Famed for hating all things red, Mike Doyle's City career spanned an incredible 16 years, by which time he had become a legendary figure at the club having worked his way up from the ground staff. He played for most of his time at Maine Road in defence, but could play effectively in midfield or, in his early days, as an attacker. Determined and as a tough as they come, Doyle was idolised by the City fans and played a major role in the Blues' most successful period ever.

First Division Champions, FA Cup, League Cup (twice), European Cup-Winners' Cup; City won everything in sight with Mike Doyle's steely determination driving the team on. It would be 1975 before he was appointed captain, such was the strength of the City team at the time, but it was perhaps fitting that Tony Book, Doyle's skipper for so many years, should appoint him to lead his team when he himself became manager. Doyle proudly lifted the League Cup trophy in 1976 and in June 1978 he joined Stoke City for £50,000.

DRAWS
There has been one season in particular where City have been the darlings of the pools coupons. In 1993–94, the Blues drew 18 matches – 11 scoring and 7 no-score draws. With City failing to score in another nine League games, it was hardly surprising that the top scorer, Mike Sheron, had only six goals. The fewest drawn games in a season was exactly a hundred years earlier when only two of 28 League games ended with honours being even. Three ties from 42 games played in 1959–60 is an even more impressive figure. The highest-scoring draws were against Everton in 1925–26 and Chelsea 1936–37 when both games ended 4–4. There was a 6–6 draw during the war, against Stockport County (1939), but the record does not stand officially.

DUNNE, RICHARD — 2000 TO PRESENT
Appearances: 74 + 3 as substitute*
Goals: 1*
Position: Defence
Born: Dublin

Joe Royle never lost faith in Richard Dunne's ability after the big Irish defender signed for City from Everton for £3 million and endured a disappointing first few games with the Blues. Dunne is deceptively quick and very skilful for a defender and he quickly won over the City supporters with a series of top-class defensive displays, particularly during the 2001–02 campaign when he was outstanding for several months. The football equivalent of 'the immovable object', Dunne's strength and calmness on the ball earned him a place in the Republic of Ireland World Cup squad for Japan and Korea, but he surprisingly never played a game. A talented lad, it's only his timekeeping for training that has been a problem.

E

EDDIE THE EAGLE

'Eddie the Eagle', the plastic suspended bird that dangles from the new Kippax Stand roof, also known as 'Hudson Hawk' and no doubt a few more monikers, was placed there to prevent pigeons nesting and subsequently pooping on the punters below. It has been associated, by some, with a return to fortune at Maine Road since its introduction several years ago. It remains to be seen whether the club takes the unofficial mascot to the City of Manchester Stadium for the 2002–03 season. There could be riots . . .

EDGHILL, RICHARD — 1993 TO 2002

Appearances: 206 + 4 as a substitute
Goals: 1
Position: Right-back
Born: Oldham

The curtain finally came down on Richard Edghill's long career at City when he became a free agent in the summer of 2002. The former team skipper decided to take his chances elsewhere after a 14-year association with the Blues, the club he signed for as a schoolboy. He had battled back before from injury after damaging his cruciate ligament in 1995 and didn't play again until 1997. Though he scored only one goal during his time with the Blues, his confident penalty in the shoot-out with Gillingham helped City win promotion back to the First Division. It was ironic, perhaps, that after battling back so many times from serious injuries and finally winning over his numerous critics, 'Edgy' should decide to leave. He was playing some of his best football at the club when he bravely tackled a Sheffield Wednesday player and had to be carried off with yet another painful knock. It was a cruel blow and he found it hard to re-establish himself in the side.

ENGLAND

For England caps won while playing for City, Colin Bell is way ahead of anybody else with 48. Bell would have no doubt added many more but for injury, and both club and country suffered as a result. Strapping centre-back Dave Watson earned 30 caps between 1975 and 1979 while Franny Lee won 27, also over a four-year period. Legendary goalkeeper Frank Swift won 19 caps and record City goal-scorer Eric Brook won just one less. Peter Barnes (14), Trevor Francis (10), Joe Corrigan (9), Mike Summerbee, Rodney Marsh and Ivor Broadis (8) all served their country proudly.

Other cap-winners were: Bray, Tueart, Revie (6), Doyle and Barkas (5). Tilson, Burgess, Roberts and Royle each won four. Thirteen other City stars won three caps or less and the last to appear for the national team was Keith Curle, who cruelly won all three of his caps while being played out of position at full-back.

EUROPEAN CUP

City have ventured into the competition of European Champions – when it was strictly for winners of the respective Leagues of Europe and not like today, when every man and his dog can qualify. The Blues went out at the first hurdle and naivety and inexperience no doubt played a large part of the Blues' swift exit but Malcolm Allison's statement that his team would 'terrify Europe' didn't seem to help much, either. Fresh from being crowned League Champions, City began the 1968–69 season full of hope and expectations were high. Little was known about Turkish Champions Fenerbahce when they ran out at Maine Road for the opening round's first leg. The visitors proved to be master defensive tacticians and held the Blues to a frustrating 0–0 draw. The second leg, played in front of a 45,000-strong hostile Turkish crowd, looked to be tilting City's way when Tony Coleman scored the opening goal but the home side bided their time, continually applied pressure and eventually won 2–1. A tough lesson had been learned, but City would put it to good use just 12 months later . . .

EUROPEAN CUP-WINNERS' CUP

A tournament that Manchester City certainly mastered and almost successfully defended. The FA Cup final victory over Leicester City had given Joe Mercer's side a fast-track back into Europe following the European Cup disappointment 12 months earlier. In what would prove to be an exciting adventure on the continent, the Blues put on a terrific display of gutsy, attacking football to hold Atletico Bilbao to a 3–3 draw in Spain and then dispatched them confidently 3–0 at Maine Road. Belgian side SK Lierse were soundly beaten 3–0 on their own soil and then 5–0 in Manchester.

Next up were Portuguese outfit Academica Coimbra. They proved a much tougher nut to crack but it was the Blues' turn to play spoilers with a 0–0 draw in Portugal followed by a hard-fought 1–0 home win, with Tony Towers scoring the vital winner – the lessons of European Cup failure being put to good use. City moved into the semi-finals to face German side Shalke 04, losing the away leg in Shalke by 1–0. In one of the best performances by a Joe Mercer side, City ran riot at Maine Road winning 5–1 in front of more than 46,000 fans. At last, Allison's prediction that City would be the *enfant terrible* of Euopean football became reality.

Around 6,000 City fans then made the trek to Vienna to see a wonderful 2–1 win over Gornik Zabrze, with the goals coming from a Lee penalty conversion and Young. The conditions were atrocious and in weather more typical of Manchester than Vienna, rain lashed down on the uncovered crowd throughout the game. City had their first – and to date only – European trophy. Many clubs are still waiting for such an honour.

The Blues began the defence of their trophy in 1970 with a narrow win over Northern Irish side Linfield. A 1–0 home win was nearly not enough as the plucky minnows beat City 2–1 in Belfast. Only Franny Lee's strike enabled the defending champions to limp through embarrassingly on the away-goals rule. A more professional display against Honved resulted in a 3–0 aggregate win after victories at home and away, setting up a re-match against the Poles Gornik Zabrze.

An awesome crowd of 100,000 buoyed the Polish side to a 2–0 win and the home players were rightly pleased at their efforts when the final whistle went. In an exercise in reverse psychology, several City players began hugging each other as if they'd won the trophy itself (see *Celebrations – Players*). City won the return 2–0 and won the right to a replay. There were no winners when the neutral venue was announced – Copenhagen! A crowd of 12,100 saw the Blues win 3–1 and move into the semi-finals for the second successive year.

The draw pitted the Blues with the only other English team left, Chelsea, and the familiarity of the two clubs did no favours for either side. With a crippling injury list including Alan Oakes, Colin Bell, Mike Doyle, Glyn Pardoe and Mike Summerbee, City lost the first leg 1–0. Tommy Booth and Joe Corrigan were also absent from the second leg and a 1–0 defeat at Maine Road was hardly surprising. With a fit and full squad, Mercer's side may well have gone on to win the Cup-Winners' Cup again, but, alas, we'll never know.

EVER-PRESENTS

The player who holds the record for appearing in every League game in a season the most times is winger Eric Brook (1928–40), who on five occasions played in all the matches in a season – hardly surprising that he also holds the record of consecutive appearances as well. Joe Corrigan (1967–83), Billy

Meredith (1894–1905) and Frank Swift (1932–49) – these three legendary figures each have had a total four seasons of never having missed a game. Steve Redmond (1984–92), with three full seasons of playing is the most recent in the list. It seems, with the phrase 'squad rotation' becoming more and more a by-word in the modern game – especially among the bigger clubs – that being an ever-present these days is quite an achievement.

EWING, DAVE – 1949 TO 1962
Appearances: 302
Goals: 1
Position: Half-back
Born: Perth, Scotland

Dave Ewing was a tough, uncompromising half-back who adopted a no-nonsense approach that earned him a reputation as one of the country's meanest and toughest defenders. He had been at City for four years before he finally made his first-team debut, but once he'd finally claimed his place, he made it his own. Alongside two other defensive giants, Roy Paul and Ken Barnes, Ewing was one of the main reasons City reached the FA Cup final in successive years during the mid-1950s, winning the trophy in 1956. Renowned for his 'vocal encouragement', the tough Scot eventually joined Crewe in 1962. He later returned to the coaching staff and managed City reserves, winning the League for the first time ever in 1977–78.

F

FA CUP – GLORY

Winners on four occasions and finalists on another four visits to Wembley,
City have done fairly well in the FA Cup over the past 112 years. The first time
the Blues lifted the trophy was in 1904 when a narrow 1–0 win over Bolton at
the Crystal Palace softened the blow of finishing runners-up in Division One
and thus missing a historic double. Bolton, unfortunately, would have their
revenge in 1926, winning the cup by scoring the game's only goal in City's
first-ever Wembley appearance. Seven years after that, City were again on the
losing side, this time to Everton. Determined to get it right, Wilf Wild's side
returned the following year to lift the cup for the second time after beating
Portsmouth 2–1, with captain Sam Cowan's inspirational leadership.

History repeated itself in 1955 when City went down 3–1 to Newcastle
United only to go all the way the next year and win the competition 3–1 over
Birmingham City. It would be 1969 before City returned to the Twin Towers
– a Neil Young thunderbolt giving Joe Mercer's side a 1–0 victory over
Leicester. The last appearance in the final by a Manchester City team was in
1981 when Tottenham triumphed 3–2 in a replayed match after the first game
ended 1–1. There were memorable goals by Tommy Hutchison, Steve
Mackenzie and Ricky Villa over the two matches, watched by a combined
attendance of 192,500.

FA CUP – NIGHTMARES

City have had their share of disastrous FA Cup ties down the years and the club
became synonymous with giant-killing acts against them, until recently. Top of
the pile would have to be the 1980 third-round defeat at Fourth Division
Halifax Town. The Blues, managed by Malcolm Allison, must have thought
The Shay was hell on earth as they ran out into a dilapidated stadium and a
glue-pot of a pitch. With record-signing Steve Daley probably worth more
than the entire Halifax team – and ground – failing to inspire City, the game
looked to be heading for a 0–0 draw.

Then, with ten minutes to go, Halifax striker Paul Hendrie – father of
Aston Villa's Lee – tucked away a low drive that proved to be the gut-

wrenching winner. Malcolm Allison later claimed the stain of the result would never be forgotten. He was right and the game is replayed on third-round day year after year – the public loves watching a good flogging. The year before, City had gone to Third Division Shrewsbury Town and gone down 2–0 on a rock-solid frosty pitch at Gay Meadow. Further embarrassments included a 2–1 defeat at Blackpool in 1984, a 3–1 loss to Brentford in 1989 and a 1–0 reverse at Cardiff City in 1994.

FAGAN, FIONAN — 1953 TO 1960
Appearances: 164
Goals: 35
Position: Winger
Born: Dublin

Fionan, or 'Paddy', Fagan was one in a fairly long list of Irish wingers that City have had down the years. The skilful forward was comfortable on either flank and was hugely popular with the City fans who have always held wingers in the highest esteem. He was a vital supplier to the likes of Bobby Johnstone and Joe Hayes and he also had the rare treat of playing for seven years for the Blues under one manager, Les McDowall, so his time with the club was fairly settled. He won two caps for Ireland while with City and he left in 1960 to join Derby County for £8,000, winning more caps for his country while at the Baseball Ground.

FAGAN, JOE — 1938 TO 1951
Appearances: 158
Goals: 2
Position: Centre-half
Born: Liverpool

Former Liverpool legend Joe Fagan became a City player aged only 17 in 1938. However, it was some nine years before he finally made his debut due to the outbreak of war. On New Year's Day 1947, Joe Fagan pulled on the No. 4 shirt and played his part in a 4–0 victory over Fulham. It would be the first of 121 consecutive League games for the club. The solid, dependable defender clocked up 153 appearances for City and one can only imagine how many it might have been had he not been forced to miss nine years of action. He left for non-league Nelson in 1951 and he later became part of the famous Liverpool boot-room staff, working alongside the great Bob Paisley for many years before being rewarded with the manager's job when Paisley stepped down. The Anfield Reds won three major trophies in his first season and he announced his retirement in 1985 shortly before the tragic European Cup final in Brussels.

FANZINES

The fanzines produced by Manchester City fans are among the best in the country. Well written, self-effacing and full of the gallows humour that epitomises what it really means to be a Blue. The first and longest-surviving is Dave Wallace's *King of the Kippax* – the broadsheet of the City 'zines. Noel Bayley's *Bert Trautmann's Helmet* is well produced and a little more vociferous with its opinions, while *City 'til I Cry* and *Chips and Gravy* have appeared over the past few seasons and have been well received in a surprisingly competitive market.

Among the all-time best, the now defunct *Blue Print* played a huge part in the late 1980s plastic banana invasion and its editor Bill Borrows is now a high-flier on the editorial team of *Loaded*. Also gone, but not forgotten, are *Main Stand View*, *This Charming Fan* and *Blue Murder*. The writer of the present book was once a fanzine editor, though the subject matter was not football. Credit is due to the fanzine editors for the hard work and efforts they put in for little reward. Standing on corners on match days in the pouring rain is no fun but it goes with the territory. There is no shortage of talent, either, and long may they continue.

FASHANU, JUSTIN – 1989

Appearances: 0 + 2 as a substitute
Goals: 0
Position: Striker
Born: Hackney

Justin Fashanu, brother of former Wimbledon striker John, found his way to Maine Road towards the end of a controversial career. He began life with Norwich City and scored a memorable goal against Liverpool that arguably made his fortune. He then joined Brian Clough at Nottingham Forest, and it is hard to imagine two more different individuals. In October 1989, Mel Machin gave Fashanu an opportunity to prove himself again at the highest level after a spell at Edmonton in Canada. He managed just two appearances, both as substitute in a 2–0 defeat to Aston Villa and a 6–0 defeat at Derby County, the latter being Mel Machin's last game in charge. A week later and Fashanu was off to West Ham, his time with the Blues being unimpressive. He was, sadly, found dead in the mid-1990s in a London garage.

FATHER AND SON

Ken Barnes and his son Peter were the first father and son to represent City – both came through the ranks into the first team to serve the club well. Former manager John Bond signed his son Kevin from Seattle Sounders in 1981 to become the second family double to achieve the feat (though John never appeared for the Blues as a player). Mike Summerbee and his son Nicky both joined the Blues from Swindon Town and both played as wingers for the club. Colin Schindler's book *Fathers and Sons* is dedicated to the above subject matter.

FLITCROFT, GARRY – 1992 TO 1996

Appearances: 134 + 8 as a substitute
Goals: 15
Position: Midfielder
Born: Bolton

Bolton-born Garry Flitcroft progressed through the youth team to the first team with an ease that suggested a glowing future for the powerful midfielder. He played his full part as City battled to remain a Premiership club, forging an impressive partnership with another of City's youth products, Steve Lomas. Beset by niggling injuries, Flitcroft often missed a dozen or so games a season but he was still earmarked for full England honours at some point in his career.

After winning several England Under-21 caps and earning the Player of the Year award for his performances during the 1992–93 season, Flitcroft reluctantly made a big-money move to Blackburn Rovers as the Blues slipped out of the Division One. The move, valued at £3.5 million, raised vital funds for the club. Once again, however, his Ewood Park career was hampered by injuries, some serious, some minor, and though he is playing as well as he ever has for Rovers of late, a sparkling career has undoubtedly been held back by frequent visits to the treatment table.

FLOODLIGHTS

The four floodlight pylons that used to tower out of Maine Road and the surrounding area for decades have long since gone and been replaced by sophisticated lighting from the top of the Kippax and Main Stand. The four iron constructions had been in place since 1953 and caused City fans who ever stood close to them to think the same thought as they gazed up at the never-ending ladder that sometimes seemed to disappear into the low-lying cloud base: 'Thank God *I* don't have to change the lightbulbs!'

The floodlights were first turned on for a friendly against Hearts on 14 October 1953. The Blues wore special 'shiny shirts' for the evening and won an entertaining game 6–3 in front of a healthy 23,979 crowd. With good comes bad and the innovative lighting brought Manchester United back to Maine Road to play various friendlies and cup games until Old Trafford had their own installed in 1957. Not, however, before Maine Road became the first English ground to play host to a European Cup match in 1956 – and the Blues weren't even involved! United beat RSC Anderlecht 10–0 in a close-fought game.

FOOTBALL LEAGUE CUP

There was a time when City threatened to dominate this competition, which has been given a series of oddly sponsored titles over the past 20 years or so, including the Milk Cup, Rumbelows Cup, Littlewoods Cup, Coca-Cola Cup and of late, the Worthington Cup. The trophy came into existence in 1960 and City's first-ever game was a 3–0 win over Stockport County. Four years later and Stoke City defeated the Blues over two legs in the semi-final by an aggregate of 2–1.

In 1969–70, the Cup finally found its way into the Maine Road trophy room. Victories over Southport, Liverpool, Everton and QPR set up a semi-final with United over two legs. City won 2–1 at Maine Road but trailed by the same score in the return leg with minutes left on the clock. The referee awarded City an indirect free kick on the edge of the United box and Franny Lee took a crack at goal. Alex Stepney could have stepped aside and the goal wouldn't have counted but instinct got the better of him and he parried the thunderous drive to Mike Summerbee, who tucked away the equaliser. In the Final, a tired City side (they had recently played a gruelling European Cup match) slogged it out against West Bromwich Albion on a glue-pot of a pitch and it took an extra-time winner from Glyn Pardoe to settle affairs.

City returned in 1974 under Ron Saunders but lost 2–1 to Wolves with Colin Bell the scorer. Two years later and City dispatched Norwich City, Nottingham Forest, Manchester United, Mansfield Town and Middlesbrough to earn the right to play Newcastle United at Wembley. Peter Barnes opened the scoring before Alan Gowling levelled for the Magpies. The best was yet to come and Dennis Tueart's overhead goal spectacularly won the game 2–1 for the Blues.

The last time City made a real impression on the League Cup was in 1980–81 when John Bond's side met Liverpool in the last four. What seemed a perfectly good Kevin Reeves header was controversially ruled out and the Reds won 1–0 at Maine Road. City gave a stirring display in the second leg, drawing 1–1 and hitting the bar but ultimately losing 2–1 overall. An overdue success in this competition is highly likely in the near future.

FOOTBALLER OF THE YEAR

The prestigious 'Football Writers' Footballer of the Year' award has been won on three occasions by City players. In 1955 the press recognised the intelligent role Don Revie had adopted in the City team where he played as a deep-lying forward for the team. Bert Trautmann won the award the following year after his courageous display in the 1956 FA Cup final where he played on despite having a broken neck to help his side beat Birmingham City 3–1. In 1969 it was Tony Book who was bestowed the honour (sharing with Derby County's Dave Mackay) – this despite having a serious knee injury that had kept him out of most of the season.

FOREIGN PLAYERS

There are so many overseas players in the modern game that it would be mere folly to even try and list them all. There are several that undoubtedly paved the way for others and the first foreign player on City's books is believed to have been Canadian Walter Bowman, who toured with his national side in 1891 and subsequently decided he liked the area so much that he signed for Ardwick FC. He made 49 starts and scored three goals in eight years.

City's links with Holland stretch back before the First World War with Dutch international Nico Bouvy playing two reserve games before returning home. Former prisoner-of-war Bert Trautmann became one of the Blues' best goalkeepers ever, with the big German giving the Blues 15 years of superb service. Gerry Baker was born in New York and signed in 1960 from St Mirren. He scored a total of 14 goals in 39 games before returning to Scotland with Hibs a year later.

Colin Viljoen remains the only South African to have played for the Blues and Kaziu Deyna is still the only Polish star to have graced the light-blue shirt. Since Deyna, there have been many nationalities play for City and Kevin Keegan's 2002–03 Premiership side is positively packed with them. Overseas players are here to stay and if there are others like Kinkladze, Benarbia or Berkovic destined for the club, long may they continue.

FRANCIS, TREVOR – 1981 TO 1982

Appearances: 29
Goals: 14
Position: Striker
Born: Plymouth

When the on–off transfer saga of Trevor Francis finally ended with the coveted striker signing for the Blues from Nottingham Forest for £1.2 million, over 10,000 City fans travelled to Stoke to watch him make his debut. He didn't disappoint the Blue Army and bagged two goals in a 3–1 win. Francis was a classy footballer oozing with grace and class. His performances, though blighted by injury, were a treat to watch and he helped guide City to the top of the League with a 3–1 Boxing Day victory over Liverpool and a 2–1 win against Wolves, two days later.

Though he only managed 29 appearances for the Blues, he still scored 14 goals – one from just inside the halfway line against Brighton and Hove Albion – in the process. An intelligent forward, he would bring others into the game and inspired those around him, especially the younger forwards, to greater heights. Had he been injury-free all season, City may well have finished far higher than tenth place, but it wasn't to be. He joined Italian Serie A club Sampdoria for around £1 million having played for just one season at Maine Road but the impression he'd left was huge. A class act.

FRIZZELL, JIMMY
Manager from 1986 to 1987
League Record: Games: 35 W: 7 D: 11 L: 17 F: 31 A: 52

One of football's great 'shoestring managers', Jimmy Frizzell took Oldham Athletic from the Fourth Division doldrums and moulded them into a respected Second Division side over a period of eleven years. He was sacked by the Boundary Park club in 1982 and after a year out of the game he was invited to become Billy McNeill's right-hand man. The hasty departure of McNeill in September 1986 pitched Frizzell into the hot seat without much of a warning, and with no money to spend he was forced to use the motivational skills he'd learned at Oldham, plus a certain amount of intelligent wheeler-dealing in the transfer market. However, an odd mixture of seasoned pro's and raw talent proved impossible to knit together and relegation was not a matter of if, but when. Frizzell was moved sideways to become general manager as young Norwich City boss Mel Machin took over the reins and he became a valued adviser to the new manager.

FULL MEMBERS' CUP
Okay, not the most glamorously named trophy in the world and please don't ask what exactly a full member is – we're trying to keep this book decent, after all. Though the club entered this much-maligned competition on several occasions, it was in 1985–86 – the first time City had been involved – which remains in the memory. Considered as little more than a joke by most of the football world, both the Blues and Chelsea plugged away through the rounds in front of sparse crowds to the final at Wembley.

The press had a field day poking fun at the competition's poor image, but when 68,000 fans turned out on the day the only people laughing were the chairmen of both clubs. The final itself was a terrific advert for the game. City led 1–0 through Mark Lillis but the Pensioners roared back with vengeance to lead 5–1. With minutes left, City pulled three goals back through Lillis, Kinsey and an own goal to narrowly lose 5–4. The Blues never again reached such heights in the competition and their last appearance was in 1991–92 when two Colin Hendry goals weren't enough to beat Sheffield Wednesday, who won 3–2.

FURNISS, LAWRENCE
Manager from 1889 to 1893
League Record: Games: 22 W: 9 D: 3 L: 10 F: 45 A: 40

City's, or West Gorton's first manager, Lawrence Furniss was a former player who suffered a serious knee injury and then moved into the administrative side of the game. A master of all trades, he was, by chance, refereeing a match involving Northwich Victoria when he spotted a young winger by the name of Billy Meredith. Furniss saw at close quarters the potential Meredith had and promptly snapped him up for his own club, after he'd blown for full-time, of course. Meredith's legend still lives on and had that been Furniss' only legacy to the club, it would have been enough. He also, however, helped to establish City as one of the biggest clubs in England and was instrumental in forming Ardwick FC, soon to be known as Manchester City. When he handed over the reigns to Joshua Parlby in 1893, he still remained with the club for 46 years as director, chairman and club president.

G

GAUDINO, MAURIZIO – 1994 TO 1995
Appearances: 21 + 4 as a substitute
Goals: 4
Position: Midfielder
Born: Brule, Germany

Few loan players have managed to make the lasting impression German star Maurizio Gaudino did during his six-month spell with the Blues. A firm favourite with the supporters, he was an archetypal Manchester City midfield maverick and the only question most fans had when his loan spell ended was why he hadn't been signed on a permanent basis. Gaudino was initially loaned to add creativity in the midfield engine room that included the industrious talents of Garry Flitcroft and Steve Lomas. The technical side of his game was excellent and he was fierce in the tackle – a perfect combination.

Born of Italian parents with the Latin looks to prove it, the German international had left behind a colourful reputation in his homeland. It included everything from a playboy lifestyle, complete with mandatory Ferrari to a suspension from his club Eintracht Frankfurt for refusal to play after his friend and teammate Uli Stein was sacked by the club. After an impressive season with the Blues, Gaudino's chance of becoming a City player disappeared with Brian Horton's exit and he moved on to Mexico, leaving behind thousands of disappointed City fans. At 35, he still plays with Turkish side Antalyaspor.

GENE KELLY STAND
The two temporary stands erected at either side of the new Kippax Stand – once popular corner terrace sections – have now been in existence for several years and were introduced to try and satisfy the thousands of fans wishing to watch the Blues during the 1990s and beyond. The stand next to the North Stand has no roof and is known by City fans as the 'Gene Kelly Stand' because, invariably, during a downpour the City fans housed in their free plastic coveralls have nothing to do but sing in the rain. The temporary stand

between the Kippax and the Platt Lane is known as 'Windy Corner' and is more to do with weather conditions than being sponsored by Heinz Beans.

GEORGIA

Once home of the now defunct Tbilisi City Supporters Branch, Georgia proved a happy hunting ground for the scouts of Manchester City during the mid-1990s. Gio Kinkladze became the first player from there to play in England and also became the darling of the City fans almost from his first touch of the ball in 1995. He was signed by Francis Lee for £2 million and stayed with the Blues for three memorable years. Fellow countryman Mikhail Kavelashvili arrived in the latter half of the 1995–96 campaign and made an instant impact by scoring against Manchester United on his home debut. That was about as good as it got for the international striker who made nine full starts and 19 substitute appearances, bagging only three goals.

Kakhaber Tskhadadze was the third Georgian player to join City in 1998 and the player nicknamed 'Peepo' and known in his homeland as 'The King of the Air', looked set for a long and successful stay at Maine Road. After finally establishing himself in his favourite central defensive role, he landed awkwardly in a Division Two clash with Fulham and tore his knee ligaments. He never played for the Blues again. Murtaz Shelia was the final acquisition from Georgia. His most impressive displays were as centre-back but he was forced to play full-back for much of his time with the Blues. His departure in 1999 brought an end to a four-year spell of transfer activity with the Georgians.

GERMANY

The links between City and Germany are possibly stronger than at any other club in Britain. The ties stretch back to 1949, when, shortly after the Second World War, former German paratrooper Bert Trautmann was signed, somewhat controversially, by manager Jock Thomson. Trautmann was understudy to the great Frank Swift but eventually took over and soon won the respect of the fans with his courageous displays.

Few people are likely to be aware that midfielder David Phillips (1984–86) was born in Wegberg, Germany – though he represented Wales at international level – and Northern Irish international Steve Lomas was born in the British Army stronghold of Hanover. In March 1994 Brian Horton signed Uwe Rosler and then brought in Stefan Karl on loan until the end of the season. Rosler was an instant hit with the fans and led the forward line for four highly productive years.

South American-looking Maurizio Gaudino became the sixth German-born player to represent City and became another firm crowd favourite during his six-month loan spell from Eintracht Frankfurt. Eike Immel became only City's second-ever German goalkeeper when he arrived at Maine Road in 1995. He was an ever-present during his first full season but lost his place the following year and returned to his homeland.

Full-back Michael Frontzeck failed to settle – or impress – and he proved the least successful of all the club's German recruits. Finally, City manager Kevin Keegan played for SV Hamburg and helped them win the European Cup during his stay. He is still considered something of an icon by the SV fans some 20-plus years on, and a crowd of 30,000 turned up to welcome him back for a friendly in August 2002.

GIBSON, STAN – 1925 TO 2001

Stan Gibson, head groundsman at Maine Road since August 1960, passed away at his home close to Maine Road on Christmas Eve, 2001. He was 76 years old. Stan was a legendary figure at Maine Road and was quite simply, one of the finest groundsmen that this country has ever produced. Coveted by a whole host of clubs including Manchester United and indeed by England, Stan had blue blood running through his veins and was totally committed to making Maine Road into the best playing surface in the country – a feat he managed comfortably, year after year. The pitch always looked like velvet for the first home game of the season – a perfect playing surface that, one would imagine, must have been a joy to play on. Club secretary Bernard Halford said: 'Stan could grow grass on concrete,' and that just about summed up his magical abilities with the Maine Road pitch. His friendly face and generous personality are greatly missed.

GILLESPIE, BILLY – 1897 TO 1905

Appearances: 231
Goals: 132
Position: Striker
Born: Strathclyde

One of the club's first 'bad boys', a reputation earned for certain actions displayed on the pitch, Billy Gillespie had eight great years with City, winning two Division Two Championships and an FA Cup final. A great player in his own right, he was fortunate to have the legendary Billy Meredith supplying him pinpoint crosses on a regular basis. For the first game of the 1898–99 season, both Meredith and Gillespie scored hat-tricks in a 7–2 win over Grimsby Town – still City's best opening result to date. He also hit all four in a 4–1 win over Blackburn Rovers in April 1902.

Gillespie had joined the club from Lincoln City in 1897. Good-humoured and skilful on the ball, it was no wonder he was popular with supporters. His best season for City was in 1902–03 when he notched 30 goals in 33 games, including a run of 27 in 22 matches. He added 21 in 30 games the following season and in 1905 he quit football and emigrated to South Africa.

GLASGOW CELTIC

City have played the Glasgow giants on ten occasions – all friendly matches. The teams first met as far back as 1891, with Celtic leaving Manchester with a 1–0 win. By 1903, the sides had played each other seven times and that year the Blues visited Parkhead for the first time, drawing 0–0. A large crowd witnessed another no-scoring draw at Parkhead in 1970 and the last meeting between the sides was in 1992, with Celtic winning 3–1 on neutral soil.

City's record against Celtic is:
Pld: 10 W: 3 D: 4 L: 3 F: 8 A: 13

GLASGOW RANGERS

Out of the two Glasgow clubs, the links between City and Rangers are stronger but City have actually played the Gers fewer times than they have Celtic. The first meeting was in 1900 and Rangers won 3–0 at Hyde Road. The last meeting at Ibrox saw City lose 2–0 in 1981. A Rangers and Celtic combined team – imagine that ever happening today – drew 2–2 at Maine Road in 1925.

City's record against Rangers is:
Pld: 8 W: 3 D: 1 L: 4 F: 12 A: 13

GLEGHORN, NIGEL – 1988 TO 1989

Appearances: 30 + 9 as a substitute
Goals: 11
Position: Midfielder
Born: Seaham

Nigel Gleghorn was a most unlikely hero for City, but on several occasions during his time at Maine Road, he just stopped short of putting on a blue suit and red cape. He played pretty much in every position for the Blues, midfield, attack and, best of all, in goal! The £45,000 signing from Ipswich was soon a regular in the side after a string of brave performances and a keen eye for goal. In fact, his first eight goals for City were all scored away from home.

Gleghorn wrote his name into the history books when he took over between the posts from Andy Dibble away to Walsall and played his part in a 3–3 draw. Dibble's groin injury gave way again two months later and again Gleghorn kept a potent Palace attack at bay and helped City to a vital 1–1 draw meaning he had only conceded two goals during his time in the nets. With 11 goals in 30 full appearances, he averaged a goal every three games and proved a bargain for the fee paid. He moved to Birmingham City after only 14 months of sterling service.

GOALKEEPERS

City's tradition of great goalkeepers is well documented throughout this book with reference to the very best shot-stoppers liberally sprinkled alphabetically. Frank Swift, Bert Trautmann, Harry Dowd, Joe Corrigan, Tony Coton and Alex Williams were among the best but there were times when the 'only City' factor raised its head when least expected. Harry Dowd, City's keeper during the late 1960s once injured his arm and couldn't continue in goal and ended up scoring a goal (see *Dowd, Harry*). Joe Corrigan once kicked a ball downfield during a match at home to West Ham and turned his back after doing so. Though the crowd tried to warn him, the ball had been volleyed back first-time and sailed over his head and into the back of the net. West Ham won 5–1 and Joe became the target of the boo-boys. He buckled down, lost weight and eventually became one of the best goalkeepers the club has ever had.

Andy Dibble will never forget the day City visited Nottingham Forest in a crucial relegation match in March 1990. With the scores locked at 0–0, Dibble held the ball in one hand ready to kick downfield. From behind crept Gary Crosby, who nodded the ball out of his hands and rolled it into the net. The referee allowed the goal, which caused uproar among the players, Howard Kendall and the travelling army of City fans. Forest won 1–0 and the goal was the subject of heated debate in the media. Unfortunately for Dibble, a picture appeared afterwards showing him staring at the empty palm of his hand, which has dogged him for the remainder of his career.

Reserve goalie Martyn Margetson once came on as an outfield player during a 4–0 League Cup win over Wycombe Wanderers and nearly scored a late goal. Tony Coton's sending off against Derby County at Maine Road in 1991 allowed Niall Quinn the chance to face Dean Saunders from the penalty spot. The former Gaelic footballer guessed right and saved the kick and City went on to win 2–1 and relegate the Rams in the process! Nicky Weaver's amazing display in the 1999 play-off final with Gillingham when he saved two of the Gills' four spot-kicks is also worthy of a golden goalkeeping moment, as was his victory run afterwards.

GOALS SCORED

The top ten goal-scorers, taking into account League goals only, are as follows:

1. Eric Brook (1928–40)	159
2. Tom Johnson (1919–30)	158

3. Billy Meredith (1894–1906 and 1921–24)   145
4. Joe Hayes (1953–65)   142
5. Billy Gillespie (1897–1905)   126
6. Tommy Browell (1913–26)   122
7. Horace Barnes (1914–24)   120
8. Colin Bell (1966–79)   117
9. Frank Roberts (1922–29)   116
10. Francis Lee (1967–74)   112

GOATER, SHAUN – 1998 TO PRESENT
Appearances: 173 + 10 as a substitute*
Goals: 97*
Position: Striker
Born: Bermuda

Shaun Goater, or 'The Goat' as he is affectionately known at Maine Road, has become something of a phenomenon during his four years with the Blues. Signed by Joe Royle for a bargain £400,000 from Bristol City, it was a while before fans realised that for the first time in many, many years, the Blues had an instinctive striker who could bang in 20 to 30 goals each season. Shaun's goals steered City out of Division Two in 1999 and his 29 goals the following campaign ensured a second successive promotion for the Blues. Injury beset the Bermudian international during the doomed 2000–01 Premiership campaign, but he still finished the season in red-hot form with seven in his last nine games. In Division One, he captained the side for the first time at Grimsby Town – a deserved honour for the man City fans adore – and once again he ended top scorer for the fourth consecutive term with 32 goals. His anthem, 'Feed the Goat and he will score', is a firm favourite at Maine Road.

GOLDEN GOAL
Long before certain cup competitions were settled by the Golden Goal rule (or 'next goal wins!' as every schoolkid used to shout as the playtime bell rang), City used to have their own version of the Golden Goal. A stamped four-figure number would be inside the match-day programme and when the first goal was scored, the number of seconds was calculated and that was the Golden Goal. It was easy to identify the winner after a 0–0 draw because there was always one time printed as '0000'. The winner won something like £100 or lunch with Peter Swales. I never won it and I don't know anybody who did.

GORTON AFC

At the joining of West Gorton and Gorton Athletic in 1883–84, a decision on the club's new name was taken and it became Gorton Association Football Club, the forerunner of Ardwick FC and eventually Manchester City FC. Gorton AFC played the majority of their home games at Pink Bank Lane but later moved to Reddish Lane.

GOW, GERRY – 1980 TO 1982

Appearances: 36
Goals: 7
Position: Midfielder
Born: Glasgow

Gerry Gow joined City on 23 October 1980, costing £175,000 from Bristol City. He was a gritty, highly respected midfielder, famed for his crunching tackles, total commitment and endeavour. It was hardly surprising that the lightly built Glaswegian had become a terrace hero after only a handful of appearances. In fact, City would go on to lose only two of the next 17 games in all competitions with Gow inspirational in the middle of the park. There was more than one player who turned pale at the sight of Gerry sliding towards them and his record of winning 50–50 balls, time after time, soon convinced City fans of one thing – you wouldn't want to meet Gerry down a dark alley!

Injury began to take its toll on him the following season, and after City played Spurs at Maine Road in September 1981, he was sidelined for several months with a knee injury. Sadly, he would never play for City again. He was sold to Rotherham United in January 1982, having played a total of 36 times for the Blues, yet he had more than paid back the original fee several times over.

GRAY, MATT – 1963 TO 1967

Appearances: 97 + 4 as a substitute
Goals: 23
Position: Forward
Born: Renfrew

Canny City boss Les McDowall returned to Scottish outfit Third Lanark for the services of Matt Gray in 1963. As the inside-forward had built an impressive reputation and with the Blues signing Alex Harley just six months earlier while playing in Scotland, it seemed only right to deprive Lanark of the rest of their talented forward line! Harley and Gray joined forces up front for the first time in March 1963 and helped beat Birmingham City 2–1, with both players scoring the goals. The pair added a total of 12 goals between them in the final 17 games but it couldn't prevent the club slipping out of Division One. Harley decided to stay in the top flight and joined Birmingham City.

Gray proved an excellent foil for Derek Kevan the next season. Gray, never a prolific scorer, managed just eight League goals in 37 starts, while Kevan ended with 30 strikes from 40 matches. His role in the first team began to lessen and over the next three years he became a squad player rather than a regular and in 1967 Joe Mercer sold him to South African side Port Elizabeth.

GREENACRE, CHRIS – 1996 TO 1999
Appearances: 3 + 6 as a substitute
Goals: 1
Position: Striker
Born: Wakefield

Chris Greenacre was never really given the opportunity to show what he could do for City, the club he'd played for since signing as a 14-year-old schoolboy along with Lee Crooks. An instinctive striker, he was restricted to a handful of chances, mostly from the substitutes' bench, and he eventually moved to Mansfield Town. Given the confidence of first-team football, he flourished into one of the most coveted striker in the lower leagues, twice hitting 20-plus goals for his new club. He moved to Stoke City under the Bosman Ruling and is hoping to continue his progress on a bigger stage.

GROENENDIJK, ALFONS – 1993 TO 1994
Appearances: 12
Goals: 0
Position: Midfielder
Born: Leiden, Holland

Alfons Groenendijk arrived at Maine Road with the pedigree of a player who demanded respect. The former Ajax star had won a UEFA Cup winner's medal with the Dutch giants and, at £500,000, he seemed an excellent investment. As one reporter put it, 'He could shell a can of peas with his left foot'. Unfortunately, it was never found out whether this party trick was true or not because Alfons played a mere dozen games for the Blues. The highlight of his stay was a 30-yard pile driver that crashed against the bar but, in truth, that was about it. Fairly popular considering the brevity of his stay, the Dutchman returned to Holland and joined Sparta Rotterdam for £100,000, just over a year after arriving in Manchester.

GROUNDS

Encompassing all the names City have played under, the following is a list of the grounds the club has, at some point or other, called home:

1880–81	Clowes Street
1881–82	Kirkmanshulme Lane Cricket Club
1882–84	Queens Road
1884–85	Pink Bank Lane
1885–87	The Bull's Head Hotel, Reddish Lane
1887–1923	Hyde Road
1923–2003	Maine Road
2003–	City of Manchester Stadium

H

HAIR

Footballers weren't always the fashionable, hip and trendy young men that today are seen on the covers of magazines and appear in multi-million pound television commercials. Far from it. In fact, you don't have to go back too far to discover that there was a time when many footballers were anything but hip and trendy. There is, after all, no hiding the hair on your head.

With the World Cup 2002 still fresh in the mind and some individuals still sporting a 'Beckham', it is prudent to look back at some of the haircuts of City stars of yesteryear. It's not fair to go too far back so we'll begin at a time when hair became more than something you either had or you hadn't – the 1970s.

Rodney Marsh has always had a 'footballer's haircut', but, back in 1974, it was actually a trendy one. Short and spiky on top and long at the back with obligatory sideburns, Marsh was up there with the best of them. Francis Lee's hair began to get confusing around the time he left Maine Road for Derby County. He went from semi-cool to the worrying beginnings of a 'wrap-around' within a few short months. One sharp gust of wind and look out!

Moving on, Asa Hartford had a 'Rod Stewart' in his early days at City before conservatism caught up with him and he sported a short, neat cut that he still has today. There was, however, an abomination of a perm that appeared in the 1980s but he wasn't the only one, was he, Kevin? Garry Flitcroft launched a fair few junior City-fan cuts with his one-length style from the early 1990s, while German loan player Stefan Karl resembled an extra from *Staying Alive*. Fellow countryman Uwe Rosler soon learned that mullet cuts can be offensive in England and slowly phased his out. Ian Bishop's cut wavered from cool to uncool at the start of his City career before settling into an acceptable style.

Both Barry Silkman and Maurizio Gaudino favoured the Romany gypsy look that suited their stylish way of playing. Peter Beardsley reminded us all that a pair of safety scissors and a hand-held mirror are not the way forward. The leading cuts from today's City stars belong to Darren Huckerby's spiky barnet and Eyal Berkovic's stylish locks.

HANNAH, GEORGE – 1958 TO 1964
Appearances: 131
Goals: 16
Position: Midfielder
Born: Liverpool

George Hannah caught the eye of the City scouts when he scored one of the goals that helped defeat the Blues in the 1955 FA Cup final for Newcastle United. He left the Magpies for Lincoln City before arriving at Maine Road for £20,000. A busy, skilful midfield schemer, Hannah was never a guaranteed first-team player and 37 was the most games he managed in one season during 1960–61. He played for City during a fairly miserable era and the club steadily sunk until they were relegated in 1963. Hannah's role was also diminishing and he left in 1964 for the bright lights of Nottingham, signing for Notts County in a deal worth £2,000.

HARLEY, ALEX – 1962 TO 1963
Appearances: 49
Goals: 32
Position: Striker
Born: Glasgow

Alex Harley had achieved hero status for his club Third Lanark after cracking 71 goals in two seasons for the Scottish team. City picked him up for a bargain £19,500 just in time for the 1962–63 season and he scored his first goal for the club in his third match, with City losing 4–2 at Tottenham. His second home appearance endeared him even more to the fans as he scored both goals in a 2–1 win over Ipswich Town. Ten days later and he was all but immortalised for scoring a last-minute winner at Old Trafford. However, the Blues were on their way to Division Two despite Harley's heroics. Even when his former strike partner at Third Lanark, Matt Gray, arrived, City still couldn't pull their season around. There were a few thrashings along the way, too, and by the last match, a 6–1 loss to West Ham, the Blues had conceded 102 League goals. Of the 58 League goals scored, Alex Harley had impressively hit 23 of them, with a further nine coming in cup competitions. Relegation proved too bitter a pill to swallow and he decided he'd seen enough and joined Birmingham City for £42,000 after almost exactly a year at Maine Road.

HART, JOHNNY – 1944 TO 1963 AND MANAGER IN 1973

Appearances: 178
Goals: 73
Position: Forward
Born: Golborne
League Record: Games: 22 W: 9 D: 6 L: 7 F: 27 A: 24

Good luck never featured too highly in Johnny Hart's career as first a player and then as manager. As a young striker he battled hard to establish himself and his first four seasons totalled just 23 starts and three goals. He was given a longer run for the 1950–51 season and was impressive in scoring 14 goals in 27 games. He hit double figures for the next four campaigns and was about to take a deserved place in the 1955 FA Cup final side but broke his leg a month before. Having played in 31 of the previous 33, he had, at last, become a regular. It was an awful blow for club and player who endured six operations before he was pronounced fit enough to play again.

He returned for the final game of the following season and had to watch his team-mates play at Wembley again, once more from the sidelines. After just four games of the 1956–57 season, Hart's luck deserted him once again when he broke four ribs and punctured a lung during a collision with Tottenham's Ted Ditchburn. So bad were his injuries that Hart later admitted he thought he was dying. Such events would knock the stuffing out of most players and Johnny Hart – not for the want of trying – failed to ever regain the first-team place that his hard work had merited and in 1963 he retired as a player.

He then spent ten years on the coaching staff at Maine Road before being rewarded with the vacant manager's job in 1973. Malcolm Allison had quit, saying he could no longer motivate his players, and for Hart to be pitched in at the deep end surprised many. If Allison couldn't motivate the team, how could he be expected to? How could anyone, for that matter? Hart suffered ill-heath barely six months into his new role but not before he'd tempted Denis Law back to Maine Road and signed Keith MacRae for £100,000 – then a record for a goalkeeper. A wonderful servant for Manchester City, Hart's son, Paul, is now following in his father's footsteps as manager at Nottingham Forest.

HARTFORD, ASA – 1974 TO 1979 AND 1981 TO 1984

Appearances: 317 + 1 as a substitute
Goals: 36
Position: Midfielder
Born: Clydebank

Hugely popular Scottish International Asa Hartford was the lynchpin of a great City side during the mid-to-late 1970s. A busy, all-action midfielder, Hartford was signed from West Bromwich Albion in 1974. He was due to sign for Leeds United but a medical revealed he had a hole in his heart. It didn't stop City moving in for the player and it proved to be the Blues' gain and Leeds United's loss. Asa went on to won 36 caps for his country while at Maine Road – a record number of Scottish caps for a City player – and formed an excellent partnership with Gary Owen.

He was the driving force behind the Blues' bid to lift the League title in 1976–77 when they agonisingly missed out by a point to Liverpool. He was sold by Malcolm Allison in 1979 to Nottingham Forest for £500,000 but returned two years later, making another 88 appearances for City before setting off once more in 1984, this time for the North American Soccer League. He returned to the club for a third spell in 1995 to assist Alan Ball after management spells at Shrewsbury and Stockport. He is currently in charge of the reserve team.

HAT-TRICKS

Billy Meredith, Fred Tilson and Tommy Browell have all scored six hat-tricks for City in the League and Irvine Thornley has scored five. There was only one occasion when three players scored a hat-trick for City in the same game and that was when Huddersfield Town lost 10–1 at Maine Road in 1987. Tony Adcock, Paul Stewart and David White all scored three times that afternoon – only the fifth time in Football League history that such a feat has been achieved.

Dennis Tueart was something of a hat-trick specialist. In 1977–78 he scored three in a 4–1 win at Villa Park, another three in a 6–2 win over Chelsea in November of the same year and he made it three hat-tricks in five months with another in a 4–0 win over Newcastle United on Boxing Day 1977. Ken Barnes scored three penalties in a 6–2 win over Everton in 1957.

HAYES, JOE – 1953 TO 1965
Appearances: 363
Goals: 152
Position: Forward
Born: Kearsley

Had it not been for a serious knee injury, Joe Hayes would probably have been City's all-time top goal-scorer. Just 26 short of Eric Brook's record of 178, Hayes was a poacher supreme and scored one of the goals in the 1956 FA Cup final victory over Birmingham City. A pocket dynamo, Hayes arrived for a trial game at Maine Road with his boots in a brown-paper parcel and duly scored four goals. Two months later, he made his debut against Tottenham Hotspur aged only 17. He played alongside the likes of Dave Ewing, Bobby Johnstone, Johnny Hart, Don Revie and Joe Fagan – the latter three becoming managers at City, Leeds and Liverpool respectively. It was a magnificent era for the club. His only international honours were two England Under-23 caps – scant reward for such a prolific striker. Joe had worked in a cotton mill and a colliery before signing for the Blues so it wasn't difficult for him to keep his feet on the ground at a huge club like City. At 5 ft 8 in. high, he wasn't the tallest of forwards and he also had poor eyesight, too, but Joe Hayes made the very best of his abilities and still sits proudly among the top all-time scorers for the Blues 38 years on.

HENDRY, COLIN – 1989 TO 1991
Appearances: 70 + 7 as a substitute
Goals: 10
Position: Centre-half
Born: Keith

Colin Hendry was one of the more popular players to wear a City shirt in recent years. The rugged Scot became a favourite at Maine Road with a series of energetic, whole-hearted displays along the back four with an eye for a goal or two, if the opportunity arose. Originally from Blackburn Rovers, Hendry was Mel Machin's final signing, barely a month before he was sacked as manager in November 1990. Hendry's arrival soon steadied things and under new boss Howard Kendall, City ended the season as a difficult team to score against with the gritty Scot outstanding. His well-taken goal against Manchester United in the October 1990 derby at Maine Road is still fondly remembered.

Yet barely a year after signing, Hendry was playing under his third manager at Maine Road after Peter Reid took over from Kendall. Though Hendry kept his place for much of Reid's first year, he started the following term by being dropped following the £2.5 million purchase of Keith Curle and despite the player's popularity among City supporters, he was sold back to Blackburn a few months later. What should have been a long, successful career at Maine Road was mystifyingly over. He won one Scotland 'B' cap while a City player.

HENRY, TONY – 1974 TO 1981
Appearances: 79 + 12 as a substitute
Goals: 12
Position: Midfielder
Born: Houghton-le-Spring

Tony Henry is yet another player who filled a multitude of roles at Maine Road and never quite made the shirt his own. Predominantly a midfielder, he had to wait until 1976 to make his League debut and then only played twice, both times coming on as substitute. It was 1979 when he finally was given a sustained first team run, playing in the last 13 games of the campaign. Almost established, Henry played 33 times the following season, scoring his first League goal in a 2–0 win over Manchester United. The adaptable Henry had also scored two goals in the last two minutes of a game with City trailing 1–0 to Sheffield Wednesday in a League Cup match. He was in and out of the side during the season 1980–81 with 25 starts, and made two more as substitute before joining Bolton Wanderers and later Oldham Athletic.

HERD, ALEX – 1933 TO 1948
Appearances: 290
Goals: 124
Position: Forward
Born: Bowhill

Scottish striker Alex Herd played his full part in one of City's greatest-ever teams. Herd, who arrived at Maine Road from Hamilton Academicals, was an inside-right who played from deep-lying positions and made probably as many goals as he scored – an impressive 124. Despite the fact that he had been at City for barely 15 months, he'd already played in two FA Cup finals in 1933 and 1934 and, three years after that, the Blues were crowned League Champions. One of a handful of players to continue his career with City during the wartime period with 60 goals in 90 appearances, he eventually joined Stockport County on a free transfer in March 1948, some 15 years after becoming a City player. He uniquely played alongside his son up front for County against Hartlepool in 1951.

HESLOP, GEORGE – 1965 TO 1972
Appearances: 195 + 6 as a substitute
Goals: 1
Position: Half-back
Born: Wallsend

Versatile defender George Heslop was signed from Everton in 1965 for £20,000 by Joe Mercer after failing to establish himself at either Goodison Park or his previous club Newcastle United. Under the Mercer–Allison influence, however, Heslop finally gained the first-team spot that had eluded him elsewhere. His contribution during City's historic trophy-winning period should not be underestimated and, in his first four years at Maine Road, Heslop had collected four medals for winning the Second Division, First Division, League Cup and European Cup-Winners' Cup.

His remaining years at City were spent between the first team and the reserves, and in 1971 Heslop joined Cape Town City on loan for a year before eventually joining Bury for £3,000. He later went on to become licensee at the Hyde Road Hotel – the original headquarters of Manchester City Football club.

HINCE, PAUL – 1966 TO 1968
Appearances: 11
Goals: 4
Position: Forward
Born: Manchester

Though Hince may not possess the most impressive record for City, he is worthy of note for the few games he did play and his career path later on. He made his debut as a gangling teenager in March 1967 against West Brom. In something of a dream debut, he scored both goals in a 2–2 draw, but in typical Mercer style (Stan Bowles would start with a double on his debut and was dropped), he didn't play again that season.

His big chance came – and went – during City's Championship season of 1967–68. Hince played well enough, and City won all five of the games he played in at the start of the season, losing to Arsenal in the sixth. He played a further three times in the League Cup and never played for the Blues again.

He left for Charlton Athletic and later turned to journalism, eventually becoming reporter of City's fortunes for the *Manchester Evening News*. He is still Chief Sports Writer for the paper and a constant source of self-effacing amusing stories and anecdotes from his days as a player for the Blues.

HINCHCLIFFE, ANDY – 1985 TO 1990
Appearances: 134 + 5 as a substitute
Goals: 11
Position: Full-back
Born: Manchester

Andy Hinchcliffe joined City straight from school and looked set for a long and illustrious career at Maine Road. He was an important part of the FA Youth Cup-winning side of 1986 and, just as many others did from that team, he soon progressed to first-team action.

He was given the opportunity of establishing himself by Mel Machin, who gave the 18-year-old his debut for the opening game of the 1987–88 season. He played all but two of the 44 League games and at last solved City's troublesome left-back problem. Beset by back injuries, he had to play in a specially designed corset that gave him the support he required to be able to continue playing. He missed nine games of his second full season as a first-teamer scoring five goals and creating havoc with his right-sided in-swinging corners and once scored direct from the flag against Shrewsbury Town in December 1988.

City won promotion and were back in the top division for the 1989–90 campaign and it was Andy Hinchcliffe who crowned an unbelievable 5–1 derby victory over United with a powerful header, the fifth of the afternoon. Howard Kendall's arrival, a few months later, was the beginning of the end of Hinchcliffe's career at Maine Road. He only made the subs' bench for three of the last four games and in July 1990 he joined Everton, aged 22, with Neil Pointon moving to Maine Road in part-exchange. The young star would go on to play for England, and is currently with Sheffield Wednesday.

HMS MANCHESTER

A particularly strong City Youth side beat naval HMS *Manchester* in August 1985 by 13–0. The prolific Paul Moulden demonstrated his predatory instincts by scoring five goals in 20 minutes.

HODGE, PETER
Manager from 1926 to 1932
League Record: Games: 252 W: 115 D: 59 L: 78 F: 552 A: 430

Peter Hodge arrived at Maine Road with a reputation as one of the best managers in Britain. He cut his teeth as a boss in his native Scotland with Dunfermline, where he was secretary, and then at Raith Rovers. He arrived in England as Stoke City's saviour, taking them from the Southern League to the Football League before going north of the border during the war. In 1919 he returned to the Midlands to take charge of Leicester City and took his new club to promotion – his third such triumph as a manager.

He then accepted the offer from City to take over from David Ashworth, who had resigned in November 1926. His arrival was timed badly as the Blues lost an FA Cup final and were then relegated by a point on the final day of the season. This all happened within a week, though for City it was a somewhat typical seven days!

Hodge soon stamped his ideals on his new side and City just missed promotion in his first full season but won the Division Two Championship the next term. Exciting forwards such as Eric Brook and Ernie Toseland became household names under Hodge and his decision to switch Tommy Johnson from inside-left to centre-forward proved inspired with the player scoring 38 goals in 1928–29 and creating a club record that still holds today.

City finished third the season after Johnson's heroics but Hodge had taken the club as far as he could. When his former employers, Leicester City, offered him a long contract and more money, he departed for Filbert Street, safe in the knowledge that he had left the Blues in better shape than he had found them.

HOLDEN, RICK – 1992 TO 1994

Appearances: 57 + 1 as a substitute
Goals: 5
Position: Winger
Born: Shipton

When Peter Reid became boss at Maine Road, he identified the lack of an out-and-out winger as a problem that needed to be rectified. He didn't have to look too far for the player who he felt could solve the problem and in August 1992 the Blues paid neighbours Oldham Athletic in cash and player exchanges for the services of Rick Holden.

Steve Redmond and Neil Pointon moved to Boundary Park as part of the transfer and many City fans felt the Latics had the better half of the deal. Holden had a somewhat lumbering run and had a physique that suggested a lack of fitness. In short, when the chips were down he became an easy target and never really won over the City supporters during his two-year stay.

Though Holden's place in the Blues' history may not be as distinguished as many other players', most who saw him would agree that it is doubtful that City have ever had a better crosser of the ball. Holden would get to the goal line and somehow swing an inch-perfect cross that swerved out and away from goalkeepers at the ideal height for strikers. Yet, Niall Quinn would only score eight times in 45 League games alongside Holden – the dream combination had failed to work.

HOME RECORDS

City's record home win was 11–3 against Lincoln City in March 1895 in Division Two. A 12–0 win over Liverpool Stanley had been recorded in October 1890 for an FA Cup qualifying round and in February 1926 the Blues thrashed Crystal Palace 11–4. Three more occasions resulted in City reaching double figures. In 1898–99, Darwen returned home after a 10–0 drubbing in a Division Two fixture and City hit Swindon Town for ten in the FA Cup with the visitors replying once. The most recent double-figures win was during a Division Two game in November 1987 when City hammered Huddersfield Town 10–1.

There have also been three 9–0 wins: Burton Swifts in 1897–98, Gainsborough Trinity in 1902–03 and Gateshead in 1932–33. On the flip side, West Bromwich Albion's 7–2 win at Maine Road on New Year's Day 1934 remains the Blues' heaviest-ever home loss. The Blues have completed four unbeaten seasons at home and only one of them has been at Maine Road. The seasons are: 1895–96 (Division Two), 1904–05 (Division Two), 1920–21 (Division One) and 1965–66 (Division Two).

HORLOCK, KEVIN – 1997 TO PRESENT
Appearances: 187 + 12 as a substitute*
Goals: 41*
Position: Midfielder
Born: Bexley

Signed for £1.5 million in January 1997, Northern Irish midfielder Kevin Horlock has proved to be an excellent buy for the club and ended the 2001–02 season just one game short of 200 appearances including a dozen as substitute. With a healthy return of goals during his time with the club, Horlock has established himself as a hard-working defensive midfielder who can pick a 50-yard pass with deadly accuracy and is also a threat from any dead-ball situation.

He's played at left-back, central midfield and, of late, an anchoring role behind Eyal Berkovic and Ali Benarbia. His performances in 2001–02 earned him runners-up spot in the Player of the Year award behind Benarbia when in any other year he would have walked away with the trophy himself.

One of many highlights Horlock has provided for the Blues was his 89th-minute goal against Gillingham – often forgotten – that enabled Dickov's last-gasp equaliser and effectively changed the course of the club's path. He also successfully dispatched the first penalty in the resulting shoot-out. Deceptively good in the air and as a ball-winner, the popular Horlock, or 'Super Kev' as the fans call him, has repaid the original fee many times over and is an integral part of City's present and the future.

HORNE, STAN – 1965 TO 1969
Appearances: 63 + 3 as a substitute
Goals: 0
Position: Half-back
Born: Clanfield

Half-back Stan Horne played for City from 1965 to 1969. He was part of the team that won the Division Two and Division One titles within three years but injury robbed Stan of a greater career at Maine Road. He was perhaps unfortunate to have had so many top-quality players around him that made it all but impossible to win back his place by the time he'd returned to full fitness. Stan followed manager Joe Mercer from Aston Villa after a misdiagnosed blood pressure condition. He looked all set to retire but decided to write to his former boss Mercer at City and ask for the chance of proving himself fit. Joe granted him a trial, was impressed by what he saw and gave him a contract.

Stan joined City while they were in the old Division Two – probably the club's lowest ebb ever. He soon broke into the first team and played as a regular the following season. City won the championship and promotion to Division One. The following season, Stan suffered a crippling snapped Achilles' tendon and was out for the rest of the year, with City finishing in 15th place. By this time, the Blues were assembling a side that would take on – and invariably beat – the best teams in the country. Stan recovered from injury but found it difficult to break into a side that had the likes of Mike Doyle, Alan Oakes and George Heslop in his position. It was time to move on.

Stan Horne may not be the record appearance holder for City – he made 63 starts plus 3 more as substitute – but he has a unique place in the history of Manchester City FC. He was the very first black player to sign and play for the Blues.

HORTON, BRIAN
Manager from 1993 to 1995
League Record: Games: 79 W: 21 D: 29 L: 29 F: 89 A: 106

The media enjoyed the fact that Brian Horton had replaced Peter Reid because he was clearly a shock choice to City fans who had been expecting a higher-profile boss to take over at Maine Road. He was the selection of new general manager John Maddock, who had swept into his new position and promptly sacked Reid and assistant Sam Ellis, boldly telling anyone who would listen: 'I'm in charge.' Few were fooled that he was anything but Peter Swales' hatchet man, but it could be safely assumed that the City chairman had needed to deflect any more criticism aimed in his direction by employing Maddock.

The upshot was that Oxford United boss Horton was installed and forced to face questions about his ability and experience with a club as huge as City and, in truth, there was little he could say. Blues' fans were in no doubt as to who they blamed for the way things had been handled (Reid had been sacked just four games into the new season) and that was the chairman himself.

Horton endured newspaper headlines such as 'Brian Who?' and buckled down for the task in hand. In truth, Reid's reign as City boss had become stale and despite never having finished outside the top ten in the Premier League under his control, the side looked likely to struggle during the 1993–94 season. Horton's first two games in charge saw the Blues beat Swindon Town 3–1 away, and QPR 3–0 at home. It was a start they could not maintain and the remainder of the season was spent battling against relegation.

Horton brought in forwards Paul Walsh, Uwe Rosler and Peter Beagrie before the March transfer deadline, having also signed David Rocastle in a swap deal involving David White moving to Leeds United. The new players gave City a much-needed impetus at a vital time and the team lost only one of the ten games left.

Horton's only full season in charge in 1994–95 brought a feast of attacking football back to Maine Road with two wingers, Nicky Summerbee and Beagrie supplying Walsh, Rosler and Quinn. Up until December, City were flying, having scored 28 in 17 games and collected 28 points from 51. Memorable wins over Tottenham (5–2) and Everton (4–0) plus two 3–3 draws at home to Southampton and Nottingham Forest delighted the home fans who had seen 23 goals and 18 points from the opening eight home games.

Strangely, the season began to fall flat and City won only 4 of the last 25 matches and, even worse, had suffered two crushing defeats by Manchester United during the campaign. Only two wins in April against Liverpool and Blackburn Rovers, both of whom were loftily placed at the time, saved the club from relegation. Horton was sacked following Francis Lee's successful take-over but City supporters recognised his efforts amidst bitter boardroom fighting as a more than honourable effort.

HOWEY, STEVE – 2000 TO PRESENT
Appearances: 77*
Goals: 9*
Position: Centre-half
Born: Sunderland

England international Steve Howey ended a long association with Newcastle United when he signed for the Blues for £2 million in the summer of 2000. The strapping defender had enjoyed life at St James' Park but had been plagued by injuries for many years. However, a successful operation has seen him miss few City games in the first two seasons at Maine Road, where he's been one of the most consistent performers.

HUCKERBY, DARREN – 2000 TO PRESENT
Appearances: 46 + 16 as a substitute*
Goals: 28*
Position: Striker
Born: Nottingham

Joe Royle rescued Darren Huckerby from Leeds United at the end of 2000 and he made his debut against Charlton Athletic on 30 December, scoring City's only goal from the penalty spot in a 4–1 defeat. His full home debut saw him score after a trademark dribble and shot from distance against Birmingham City in the FA Cup. He was played out wide for the rest of the season but the Blues were already sliding out of the Premiership. Under Kevin Keegan, Huckerby has flourished into a leaner, fast, direct attacker that scored 25 goals for the club as they ran away with the First Division title. A match-winner on his day and an exciting player to watch, Huckerby will be keen to re-establish himself at the highest level.

HUGHES, MICHAEL – 1988 TO 1992
Appearances: 32 + 1 as a substitute
Goals: 1
Position: Midfielder
Born: Larne, Northern Ireland

There were rumblings around Manchester that the young Irish kid City had on their books was showing signs of being the next, gulp, George Best. Michael Hughes was indeed an exciting prospect and his ability and technique suggested he was heading for a bright future at Maine Road. He joined City from Carrick Rangers in May 1988 and his performances for the reserves soon brought him to the attention of the management and the local media. However, it wasn't until April 1991 that Peter Reid gave him his debut, coming off the bench in a 3–1 win over Nottingham Forest.

He'd made enough of an impression to be given an opportunity to oust left-sided midfielder Mark Brennan and he had a run of 21 consecutive first-team games and soon established himself as a firm favourite with supporters. City fans were slightly bemused when, a month before the 1992–93 season was to begin, the Blues accepted a bid of £250,000 from French club Strasbourg.

Hughes' departure was not at all popular – here was a talented youngster who had more than contributed to City finishing higher than United the previous season for the first time in many years and the paltry fee was a fraction of his market price. Hughes, now a full international for Northern Ireland, adapted well to French football and returned a couple of years later on loan to West Ham, for whom he signed permanently, and enjoyed several successful seasons alongside another popular former City star, Ian Bishop. He later left Upton Park for Wimbledon and became skipper of the Dons.

HUTCHISON, TOMMY – 1980 TO 1982
Appearances: 57 + 3 as a substitute
Goals: 5
Position: Winger
Born: Cardenden

Tommy Hutchison may have made only 57 starts for City but the stylish Scottish winger left a long-lasting impression on those Blues' fans that were fortunate enough to see him play. He joined City from Coventry for just £47,000 and formed part of the tartan trio including Gerry Gow and Bobby McDonald that transformed an ailing City side into the 1981 FA Cup finalists. Hutchison oozed class – excellent control and vision and a will to play football the purist's way. Strangely overlooked by his country for international honours, Tommy has the rare privilege of appearing on a Trivial Pursuit question card. The question is: who is the only player to score for both sides in an FA Cup final? Of course, we all know the answer is Tommy Hutchison, who scored with a flying header for City in the first half and then deflected home a Spurs' free kick after eavesdropping on Glenn Hoddle's plans. D'oh!

HYDE ROAD
Now the site of a Manchester bus company, Hyde Road was City's first enclosed ground and was home to Ardwick FC from 1887 to 1894 and then Manchester City FC from 1894 until 1923. The ground was hemmed in by a railway track to the west and sidings north – train drivers would often slow down to catch a glimpse of City in action! Crowds were only estimated at the time and ranged from 500 to 40,000 and the Blues were Division One runners-up on two occasions while at the ground, but with the team's popularity growing rapidly it became clear that a new home was desperately needed. Even more so after the Main Stand burned down in 1920. Belle Vue, a few miles up the road, was sited as a possible home but the eight-acre plot was not nearly enough to house the club.

A space was found in Moss Side, several miles away, and the foundations of a new stadium were soon visible to curious supporters. In the summer of 1923, Maine Road was completed and City closed the gates at Hyde Road for the last time. The Main Stand roof was sold to Halifax Town for the princely sum of

£1,000 and was still standing when the Blues lost 1–0 at The Shay in 1980. Today, the area the pitch once occupied is now a skid pan for training bus drivers in Bennett Street – no jokes, please!

I

IMMEL, EIKE – 1995 TO 1997
Appearances: 50
Goals: 0
Position: Goalkeeper
Born: Marburg, Germany

Tony Coton's departure to Sunderland led former German international goalkeeper Eike Immel arriving at Maine Road for £250,000. He became the second German to play in goal for City following in the footsteps of the legendary Bert Trautmann. Immel made his debut against Spurs on the opening day of the 1995–96 season but the magnitude of keeping goal for the Blues soon became apparent as they drew two and lost nine in a horrific start to the season, scoring 3 and conceding 21!

November was better with the unpredictable Blues winning three and drawing once with Immel keping four clean sheets out of the next five. A couple more in the League Cup meant that the popular keeper had made seven stop-outs by the turn of the New Year. City were, however, heading for the drop and Immel was powerless to stop the steady flow of goals past him. Though the Blues only lost six of their remaining 17, it was too little too late. He played four games of the following season but those were his last in a City shirt. He had made exactly 50 appearances.

INGEBRIGTSEN, KARE – 1992 TO 1993
Appearances: 6 + 10 as a substitute
Goals: 3
Position: Midfielder
Born: Trondheim, Norway

Peter Reid signed Norwegian international Kare Ingebrigtsen for £500,000 in January 1992, after a month's trial, to add experience and depth to his squad. With Reid's own legs unable to complete more than the odd substitute appearance every now and then and Steve McMahon and Paul Lake out injured, Ingebrigtsen seemed like a wise move to make by the player-boss.

His pedigree with Rosenborg was unquestioned but he struggled to make an impact in the remaining games of the 1992–93 season. After a disagreement with Reid, the Norwegian returned to Rosenborg on loan. Several months later Brian Horton took over as manager and soon recalled Ingebrigtsen. He was used as a sub on six occasions before being given a start in the FA Cup third-round tie at home to Leicester City. His response was a hat-trick against the Division One outfit as City romped home 4–1.

He also scored one of the goals that put City 2–0 ahead against Ipswich Town but the game was abandoned due to torrential rain and the goal scrubbed from the records. Ingebrigtsen started two more League games but they were to be his last. In May 1994 he returned to Norway and played on loan for several clubs. He never returned to Maine Road.

INJURIES

Three players stand out more than most in this unfortunate list of injuries to City players. The first is Bert Trautmann – it is hard to imagine the pain he must have been in after breaking his neck in the 1956 FA Cup final and then courageously staying on the pitch until the final whistle; there were no substitutes to call on back then. The second is Colin Bell, who lay in agony after a tackle from United's Martin Buchan during a League Cup quarter-final at Maine Road. Bell, aged 29, was at the very peak of his game but the knee injury was so bad it would be over two years before he returned to the first team. He was never the same player and looked restricted in his movement. His bravery and determination drove him on where others would have retired far sooner.

The last of this exceptional trio is Paul Lake. The tragedy of Lake's career is that the best was yet to come and his injury struck when he was on the verge of full England honours. Without doubt destined to become one of City's and England's greatest players, Lake jumped for a header with Aston Villa's Tony Cascarino and landed awkwardly in September 1990. His knee injury took two years to mend but after just a couple of games of the 1992–93 season, Lake once more collapsed in agony at Middlesbrough. Though none of the City fans present that evening knew it, Lake had played his last game for the Blues. His fight for fitness included trips to America and all kinds of revolutionary new treatments, which were doomed to fail. He was forced to retire in 1996.

INTERNATIONAL MATCHES PLAYED AT MAINE ROAD

There have only been a couple of international matches at Maine Road since the Second World War and England have a 100 per cent record for their appearances in Moss Side. The first time the national squad played at City's home ground was on 13 November 1946, when they beat Wales 3–0. Just over three years later on 16 November 1949, England crushed Northern Ireland 9–2 in a World Cup qualifier. There have been numerous England Under-21 games played at the ground, many during the late 1970s when the side was sprinkled with talented City youngsters such as Barnes and Owen. If Wembley Stadium continues to lie in a state of disrepair, one might assume that England will grace the City of Manchester Stadium before too long.

INTERNATIONALS – MOST CAPS

The record number of international caps won by a City player is 48 and is held by Colin Bell while representing England. Scotland midfielder Asa Hartford is the second most-capped player, with 36, and fellow Scot Willie Donachie is one behind on 35. Centre-half Dave Watson earned 30 caps for England while at Maine Road and Niall Quinn won the same number playing for Eire. Franny Lee was another City striker to play for his country, and the 27 he won for England puts him sixth in the list. Three Welsh legends are next – Roy Paul with 24 caps and Billy Meredith and Roy Clarke are level with 22 each. Mick McCarthy won 20 for Eire while at City and later went on to manage the side.

J

JEFFRIES, DEREK – 1966 TO 1973

Appearances: 83 + 10 as a substitute
Goals: 0
Position: Defender
Born: Manchester

Derek Jeffries spent seven years at Maine Road but made less than 100 appearances for the club, before joining Crystal Palace in 1973. Jeffries, who was born in Longsight, not too far from the city centre, was similar to another utility player from the same era, Dave Connor, given the tasks he was asked to do for the club. He was once assigned to mark Kevin Keegan in an FA Cup fourth-round tie against Liverpool at Anfield. He did his job to perfection helping City to grind out a 0–0 draw and the Blues won the replay 2–0. The 1972–73 season was far and away Jeffries' best campaign for City after seven years of being a fringe player. Despite playing in the Nos 2, 4, 5, 6, 10, 11 and 12 shirts and clocking up 33 starts, he was allowed to join his old boss Malcolm Allison at Selhurst Park for £100,000 by manager Johnny Hart after finally proving his worth.

JOHNSON, TOMMY – 1919 TO 1930

Appearances: 354
Goals: 166 goals
Position: Striker
Born: Dalton-in-Furness

Tommy Johnson holds the record for League goals scored for City in one season with a grand total of 38 and is second only to winger Eric Brook in the list of all-time goal-scorers for the club. He may never have had the chance of such glories but for City defender Eli Fletcher, who insisted the club sign the promising youngster from Dalton Casuals. Fletcher threatened to leave the Blues unless they made Johnson a City player – Fletcher might unknowingly have been one of the first football agents of his day!

Fortunately, the club heeded his advice (or threats) and Johnson marked his debut in 1919 with a goal but would take three more years to establish himself fully in the Blues' starting line-up, forming an impressive partnership with Horace Barnes. He also won two international caps for England while at City. The popular striker finally moved on to Everton in 1930 for £6,000, much to the supporters chagrin and ironically played a large part in the 1933 FA Cup final win over the Blues for Everton.

JOHNSTONE, BOBBY – 1955 TO 1959
Appearances: 138
Goals: 50
Position: Forward
Born: Selkirk

Bobby Johnstone was an exceptional inside forward, whose skill on the ball earned him the nickname 'Bobby Dazzler'. The Scottish international, who was born in Selkirk, arrived at Maine Road in March 1955 from Hibernian for a fee of £20,700. He made a sensational start to his Scotland career when he scored against England at Wembley, establishing him as one of the hottest properties of that generation. He quickly became a popular figure on the terraces, his lively performances in attack striking the right chords with the Blues' supporters. Bobby made his debut against Bolton Wanderers and quickly made his way into the history books, when he became the first player ever to score in consecutive FA Cup finals.

In all, Bobby played 138 times for City, winning four of his 17 Scotland caps while at Maine Road, and rifled in 50 goals before he was transferred back to Hibs for £7,000 in 1959. Bobby was also selected to represent the Great Britain side that locked horns with the Rest of Europe in August 1955. He was also a keen cricketer and crown green bowler. He finished his career playing for Oldham Athletic. Sadly, Bobby died in 2001, aged 71.

JUNIOR BLUES
City were the first club to set up a junior supporters' club, the Junior Blues, and it proved to be the role model that other clubs aspired to over the following years. Based loosely around an idea by Malcolm Allison, the project came to light under the chairmanship of Peter Swales in 1973. The Junior Blues are stronger today than ever before, and players and management regularly attend their monthly meetings, as do the club mascots, Moonchester and Moonbeam.

The aims are simple – discipline and good behaviour towards each other and other youngsters, particularly from other clubs, and to have as much fun as possible. The success of the Junior Blues has led to other clubs – believed to be as many as 70 – contacting the Blues for advice and guidance to enhance their own junior schemes.

K

KANCHELSKIS, ANDREI – 2000 TO 2001
Appearances: 8 + 3 as a substitute
Goals: 1
Position: Winger
Born: Kirovograd, Ukraine

Joe Royle took the football world by surprise when he signed Ukrainian winger Andrei Kanchelskis, on loan from Glasgow Rangers, during City's ill-fated 2000–01 Premiership campaign. The former Manchester United and Everton star had been languishing in the Scottish giants' reserve team for months after an alleged falling-out with boss Dick Advocaat and the move back to Manchester seemed the ideal opportunity for the speedy wide player to relaunch his career.

Largely accepted by the Maine Road faithful, Kanchelskis only occasionally displayed the awesome pace and skills that had once made him one of the most feared forwards in the Premier League. His confidence, no doubt drained from playing the likes of Partick Thistle and Motherwell reserves on a weekly basis, was understandably running low. He managed to net one goal for City – a wickedly deflected drive in an FA Cup tie at Anfield – but there was little else of any note to recall during his stay, which ended with the Blues being relegated. He returned to Ibrox and towards the end of last season won a surprise return to the first team under new manager Alex McLeish and recently signed for Southampton

KARL, STEFAN – 1993 TO 1994
Appearances: 4 + 2 as a substitute
Goals: 1
Position: Midfielder
Born: Germany

German midfielder Stefan Karl may have played only six times in a blue shirt but the solitary goal he scored inspired City to gather just enough points to survive relegation from the Premiership. Karl was an unknown quantity to the City supporters when Brian Horton signed him on a short-term loan not long after signing fellow countryman Uwe Rosler, who no doubt played a part in the deal. His first two games ended with City failing to score in either match and he was dropped for the next three games. The Blues were in dire need of points as they travelled to one of their traditional graveyards – The Dell – against fellow strugglers Southampton.

Defeat for City could have been disastrous and the tension was unbearable as the game entered the final few minutes. Then came Stefan Karl's moment of glory. Playing as a substitute, the ball fell to him and he drilled a powerful drive into the back of net to give the Blues a crucial 1–0 win – and a first away win for almost seven months. Promoted to the starting line-up for the next three matches, Karl struggled to impress, his City career was over before it had begun and he returned to Germany. In the grand scheme of things, however, he had played his part.

KEEGAN, GED — 1971 TO 1979
Appearances: 39 + 9 as a substitute
Goals: 3
Position: Midfielder
Born: Bradford

Kevin was not the first Keegan to be associated with Manchester City – that honour went to Ged Keegan, who played for the club from 1971 to 1979 and played less than 50 times for the Blues. The flame-haired midfielder was amazingly loyal while with City and was almost a permanent fixture in the reserve team, of which he was captain. He waited patiently until March 1975 for his debut – stepping off the bench as sub in a 2–1 home defeat to Carlisle. Tony Book then played him for the next three matches. For the 1975–76 campaign Keegan won his chance to shine when he was granted a first-team run, missing only one of the Blues' 19 games from 27 December onwards. The team lost ten of those games and finished eighth, with Colin Bell's absence proving costly.

Possibly the highlight of Keegan's career came during the second leg of a UEFA Cup first-round tie away to Juventus. City lost 2–0 but the experience must have made up for the many years spent in the reserves. Keegan added another eight games to his career total during the season City missed out on the First Division Championship by one point – 1976–77 – ironically to Kevin Keegan's Liverpool! At least the team he regularly captained won the Central League title for the first time in the club's history the same season.

He was never destined to become a first-team regular at Maine Road and had to settle for another 12 starts and two more sub appearances in his last three years at the club before moving to Oldham Athletic – and regular football – in February 1979, after serving City with both patience and loyalty.

KEEGAN, KEVIN
Manager from 2001 to present
League Record as manager: Games: 46 W: 31 D: 6 L: 9 F: 108 A: 52

Kevin Keegan returned to club management in June 2001 after spending several months out of football, relaxing and catching up with odd jobs at his Northumberland home. When the call came from Dennis Tueart and City chairman David Bernstein, he invited them over to talk about the position. Convinced Manchester City was the right club for him, he felt his batteries were once again fully charged and ready for one of the few jobs he felt would still represent a challenge to him.

The manager's role at Maine Road requires a big personality and they don't come any bigger than Kevin Keegan. He fought tooth and nail to attain his status as one of Britain's best club managers and he is living proof of what hard work and dedication can achieve. Born in Doncaster in 1951, Keegan cut his teeth at Scunthorpe United, playing 120 games for them before the great Bill Shankly signed him, on recommendation from a friend, for Liverpool. 'I felt I had to sign Kevin', Shankly commented in his autobiography, because one of his coaches 'wouldn't stop going on about him'.

Keegan arrived at Anfield in the spring of 1971 and set about making a name for himself and quickly made an impression on Shankly, who had probably envisaged Keegan as a player for the future. However, so great was Keegan's impact that he was named in the team for the opening fixture of the 1971–72 season against Nottingham Forest. In what was to become typical of the man, he scored after just 12 minutes of his Anfield debut. With the season only five games in, Keegan had scored three goals and was already a firm favourite on the Kop.

Keegan would go on to win most domestic honours with Liverpool and form an almost telepathic partnership with John Toshack. In the 1973–74 season, Keegan played in all 61 of Liverpool's League and cup fixtures, scoring 19 goals.

The start of the 1974–75 season was probably Kevin's lowest ebb as a professional. He was sent off in a friendly in Germany, then he and Billy Bremner received their marching orders for a fight during the Charity Shield at Wembley, just four days later. Keegan was probably more angry with himself than Bremner as he tore off his Liverpool shirt and stormed off to the dressing-room. This was the general public's first indication that Keegan wears his heart on his sleeve and is an incredibly passionate individual.

Normal service was resumed for the start of the 1975–76 season, with

Liverpool completing a League and cup double, but Keegan was already thinking ahead. At the start of the 1976–77 season, Keegan announced that it would be his last at Anfield. Liverpool fans were stunned that their hero was planning so far ahead and many resented the fact that anybody would want to play for any club other than Liverpool FC.

Many made their feelings known, but nobody could doubt that Keegan, honest to a fault, gave anything less than 100 per cent each time he pulled on the red jersey. After yet another League title, the Keegan-inspired Liverpool added the European Cup to their trophy cabinet – a fitting epitaph to King Kev's reign on Merseyside.

Keegan joined SV Hamburg for three successful years, winning the coveted European Player of the Year twice, before returning to England with Southampton. He then headed north, sparking a Newcastle United revival and near hysteria, as what could only be described as 'Keeganmania' gripped Tyneside. He retired in 1983, and spent several years in Spain. However, when an ailing Newcastle United once more offered him the opportunity of saving them from what was then Division Three, the temptation proved too great and Keegan returned to St James' Park for his first managerial role.

His effect was nothing short of miraculous and, within three years, Newcastle were challenging for the Premier League title, eventually finishing runners-up to Manchester United after famously giving up a 12-point lead. He would later take charge of Fulham before landing the England job – with the backing of a whole nation – and though things didn't work out, Keegan proved the one constant that has followed him throughout his glittering career: what you see is what you get.

Many people have commented that Keegan and City are made for each other and it took just one season for his Midas touch to guide the Blues to the First Division Championship with a style and swagger not seen at Maine Road for over 30 years. Long live the king.

KENDALL, HOWARD
Manager from 1989 to 1990
League Record: Games: 32 W: 11 D: 16 L: 5 F: 39 A: 31

City's capture of Howard Kendall in December 1989 was something of a coup for Peter Swales and his board. Maine Road possessed the hottest of hot seats under Swales' reign and even the bravest of souls must have shuddered at the thought of attempting to lift City on to bigger and better things. The joke was that there was no manager's seat at Maine Road, just an ejector seat with a wire linked to Peter Swales' office.

Many City fans were shocked, in the nicest possible way, that Kendall had agreed to become manager of their club. Here was a man with one of the highest profiles around and a proven winner at the very highest level of club football. His time with Everton is still legendary on Merseyside and with the two League titles, FA Cup and European Cup-Winners' Cup triumphs, plus three as losing finalists in domestic competitions, Kendall was up among the very best.

He left Goodison Park in 1987 for the challenges of European management with Spanish club Atletico Bilbao before being lured to Maine Road and the task of saving the Blues from the drop. He replaced Mel Machin halfway through the 1989–90 season and was forced to act quickly to avert the club from relegation. He wasn't afraid to sacrifice crowd favourites Ian Bishop and Trevor Morley for the likes of Alan Harper, Adrian Heath and Wayne Clarke. His immediate signing of Peter Reid from QPR as player-coach was inspirational.

He tightened up a leaky defence in his very first game – away to Everton – and secured a 0–0 draw to steady a rocking ship, and, in an incredible about-turn in form, were beaten just four times in the 21 games under Kendall that season. It wasn't pretty to watch but it was effective and saved the Blues from relegation. Kendall had signed Niall Quinn to spearhead the attack and Tony Coton was brought in from Watford to provide a daunting last line of defence for opposition attackers. It looked like, at long last, City were once again set to challenge the very best for honours. One defeat in the opening 11 fixtures had City fans wondering just how far Kendall's magic could take the club.

Despite his short-term success, the football world was left in shock when Kendall sensationally quit to return to Everton, leaving behind a club on the verge of great things and bemusing thousands of City fans and officials. How far he might have taken City will never be known but his own career went steadily downhill after leaving Maine Road and it's hard to believe that Kendall does not regret his decision, even today.

KENNEDY, BOBBY – 1961 TO 1969
Appearances: 251 + 3 as a substitute
Goals: 9
Position: Wing-half/Full-back
Born: Motherwell

Signed from Kilmarnock for £45,000 – a record at the time for a wing-half – the popular Scot played for City during a difficult time for the club. For the first five years of his career at Maine Road the Blues spent two seasons in the First Division and a further three in the Second Division.

Kennedy, who had overcome a serious illness which kept him out of football for eight months, helped Kilmarnock to two Scottish Cup finals and the runners-up spot in the League Championship before he moved to Manchester. He converted to a full-back and enjoyed three more years under Joe Mercer before leaving in 1969 to become player-manager of Grimsby Town. He was never capped by Scotland and played 251 times for City, scoring on nine occasions.

KENNEDY, MARK — 1999 TO 2001
Appearances: 63 + 14 as a substitute
Goals: 11
Position: Winger
Born: Dublin

There was no doubting the quality Mark Kennedy possessed and his £2 million move to City from Wimbledon gave him the chance to prove the many doubters wrong. His stay prior to that with the Merseyside Reds had been particularly unproductive and, considering the start he had at Millwall, his progress came to an abrupt halt.

Joe Royle soon had the Irishman back to his best and, with his ability pitted against the defences of the other sides in Division One, he inspired City to their second successive promotion. Shaun Goater probably benefited most from Kennedy's crossing ability and scored 29 goals in his first season alongside the mercurial wide-player.

Kennedy scored goals as well as making them for the Blues and one of the abiding memories of the promotion-clinching victory at Blackburn in May 2000 was his clinical finish and then the run to Joe Royle to celebrate with a bearhug.

The classy winger failed to continue his progress in the Premiership, only occasionally showing glimpses of his undoubted talents. There was a belief that if Kennedy didn't perform, neither did City, and the club were eventually relegated back to Division One. Question marks were once more being put alongside his name while playing at the highest level.

In 2001, shortly before the new season was due to begin, Kennedy was sold to Wolves for £2 million by Kevin Keegan. He told the winger that City wouldn't be playing with wide-men and his first-team chances would be limited. A move seemed best for everybody. Ironically, the transfer of Kennedy almost inspired Wolves to promotion in his first season at Molineux. For long periods they were City's main rivals for the title but their alarming drop in form on the run-in had coincided with Kennedy's absence through injury.

KEVAN, DEREK – 1963 TO 1965
Appearances: 77
Goals: 56
Position: Inside-forward
Born: Ripon

George Poyser's decision to bring Derek Kevan from Chelsea for just £35,000 was one of his most inspired actions during his two-year reign as manager. Kevan was one of the most prolific strikers of his day and had netted 157 goals in 262 games for West Bromwich Albion before his move to the Pensioners.

Poyser hoped his new charge could help fire the Blues back into the top flight at the first time of asking and Kevan almost single-handedly inspired City to do just that. He scored an amazing 36 goals in 46 League and cup games but the Blues finished in sixth position, despite bagging 95 goals in all competitions.

Kevan was a great player in a mediocre City side. The following season he scored 20 times from 30 games before sustaining a knee injury in a 2–0 defeat at Derby County in January 1965. He was out for the season and would never play for City again. Crystal Palace took him back to London in July 1965, ending his prolific and explosive exploits for the Blues.

KIDD, BRIAN – 1976 TO 1979
Appearances: 127 + 1 as a substitute
Goals: 57
Position: Striker
Born: Manchester

A £110,000 buy from Arsenal in 1976, Brian Kidd soon erased the memory of his heroics for United by playing a large part in City's successful mid-1970s team. He took ten games in the League to find the net for his new club and by the end of November he'd managed just one strike in 13 games. If there were any doubters, they were silenced well and truly as Kidd suddenly hit form – and how. He scored ten goals in his next seven outings, managing four in a 5–0 win over Leicester City. He finished the season with 21 goals from 39 games and had almost helped bring home the Championship in his first season.

City finished fourth the next season and Kidd impressed again with 16 from 39 League games. He also won the goal of the month on BBC 1's *Match of the Day* for the superb diving header he scored against Aston Villa, New Year's Eve 1977. The 1978–79 season started with Kidd scoring in all the first three games but it was downhill after such a bright start. He scored just four more goals in his next 16 starts for the Blues and in March 1979 he joined Everton for £150,000.

KINKLADZE, GIO – 1995 TO 1998

Appearances: 120 +1 as a substitute
Goals: 22
Position: Midfielder
Born: Tbilisi, Georgia

Francis Lee undoubtedly masterminded Georgian international Gio Kinkladze's £2 million move from Dynamo Tbilisi. City were without a manager for several months during the summer of 1995 yet the deal moved along at a pace with neither former boss Brian Horton or soon-to-be boss Alan Ball involved in negotiations. Little was known of the 21-year-old midfielder but Lee was convinced he was going to be an exciting addition to the side. Shortly after Ball was installed as City's new manager, he announced that Kinkladze would have the City fans 'hanging from the rafters' to watch him play. Many City fans waited to make their own judgements but Ball would ultimately be proved correct.

Not long into his debut against Spurs on a hot, sunny August afternoon, it was clear to all in attendance that Kinkladze had the kind of individual skill never seen at Maine Road before. Within a few months he was idolised by the fans and heralded by the pundits and the national media. Here was a player that got people out of their seats with his incredible dribbles and incisive precision passing. He made goals, scored them and invariably there would be at least two or three moments in a game when he could take your breath away.

Each goal he scored for the club was memorable and the solo effort against Southampton when he beat five players before chipping the ball impudently past Dave Beasant is regarded by most as the best ever goal by a Manchester City player. 'Kinky', however, couldn't stop the Blues escaping relegation and left the pitch in tears when a 2–2 draw with Liverpool was not enough to prevent City returning to the murky waters of Division One.

The vultures hovered over Maine Road waiting to pick the bones clean. Kinkladze was the jewel in City's slightly off-kilter crown and Celtic, Liverpool and Barcelona were all continually linked with £10 million swoops for him. Sir Alex Ferguson, off record, is alleged to have said that the only player at that time he would have signed was Kinky but he knew City would never sell to their deadly rivals.

Gio stayed to try and help the Blues bounce back at the first attempt. He still sparkled and scored a dozen League goals but was now the target for the division's hatchet men and received little protection from the officials after some outrageous tackles. City finished a disastrous 14th, and City fans, aware that Kinky would probably leave during the summer, staged an amazing show of support for the Georgian in the final game of the season at home to Reading. The injured star had his name chanted throughout the game and fans waved Georgian flags. His walk around the pitch at the end was stirringly emotional as supporters pleaded with him not to go. It was almost cruel. Incredibly, he stayed for another season.

His final year was not a happy one. He looked frustrated and disappointed as City headed towards Division Two. Frank Clark had taken over from Ball and Joe Royle took over from Clark as the managerial merry-go-round continued at the club. Royle was bemused by what he felt was an unhealthy obsession with Kinky at the club and so the writing was pretty much on the wall. A deal was agreed with Ajax and, at the end of the season, the love affair between the City fans and Kinky was over. The memories of this most gifted player, at his very best, will last for many years.

KINSEY, STEVE — 1979 TO 1986
Appearances: 97 + 17 as a substitute
Goals: 17
Position: Winger
Born: Gorton, Manchester

Steve Kinsey shares a unique record with Shaun Wright-Phillips in that they are the only City players to have been voted Young Player of the Year for three successive years. A former England youth international, the lightly built forward made his debut aged 18 against Wolves in April 1981. He then broke into the first team under John Bond the following season, playing 13 times plus another 3 as sub and played one less full start the season after, breaking his scoring duck in a 2–1 win over West Brom in December 1982. Billy McNeill played him slightly more often and his 16 starts and 7 more from the bench yielded a creditable return of 7 goals for the 21-year-old.

He had done enough to impress the new boss that he would be worth a regular place for the 1984–85 campaign and Kinsey impressed as the Blues won promotion to Division One. His contribution of 7 goals in 33 starts had played a part in the team's success. Life at the top level began well for the Gorton-born youngster, now 23, with 8 starts in the No. 9 shirt, but a mixture of injury and form loss meant he would only feature in five more games all season with no futher goals. Jimmy Frizzell took over from McNeill in 1986 and a few months of reserve-team football convinced the player to look elsewhere for an opportunity to play in the first team. He joined Minnesota Kicks in October 1986, while his former colleagues were relegated six months later.

KIPPAX STAND
Home to thousands upon thousands of City fans since 1923, this famous, much-loved old terrace was often the extra man for the Blues as the supporters

roared them on to success. It could also mean the end of a player if the poor soul wasn't performing well over a period of time. Many an opposing winger has turned a pasty shade of white at the sight of a packed Kippax terrace.

It was over 35 years before a roof was erected to keep the regular Mancunian drizzle off the supporters' heads and, with a smart new covering, the side of the ground known as the 'popular side' was officially named the Kippax Stand. It was home to 32,000 loyal Blues, though this was reduced to 26,155 when the North Stand was completed in 1971. Further reductions meant that only 18,300 City fans stood in the cavernous old stand near its lamentable demise.

It would be impossible to say how many times City fans have actually stood on the terrace but a safe estimate would be several million. The Taylor Report, a government-backed investigation into the safety of standing areas at football grounds, recommended that all terracing become seated areas, effectively signalling the end for the Kippax as a terraced stand. City supporters paid their final respects to their favourite part of the ground on 30 April 1994 when City took on Chelsea. Fancy dress, flags and balloons festooned the Kippax and celebrated its 71-year life. Many shed a tear after the final whistle and attempted to chip bits of concrete off steps as a souvenir.

A couple of days later, the demolition teams moved in and pictures appeared in the local media of rubble and steel girders where the Kippax had once stood proudly. From the dust arose the new Kippax, three tiers high and visible for miles around. The new stand was opened to City fans for the first home game of the 1995–96 season. Many fans groaned as they took their seats in the second and the top tier on first inspection – nothing to do with the perfect view of the pitch, but because Old Trafford was now visible in the distance!

L

LAKE, PAUL — 1986 TO 1996
Appearances: 130 + 4 as a substitute
Goals: 11
Position: Midfielder
Born: Manchester

The description 'Rolls-Royce' was often applied to Paul Lake, such was his abundance in quality and ability – none of which was diminished by a change of position. Full-back, centre-half or central midfield – Lake could play anywhere and make it look like his natural role. Coveted by many other clubs and possibly a future England skipper, Lake was beset by injury and suffered more than any footballer should have to in his career. His attempts to overcome devastating knee ligament damage were both brave and, ultimately, doomed.

A harmless-looking clash with Aston Villa striker Tony Cascarino saw Lake out of action for two years. His comeback in the 1992–93 season lasted two matches as his old injury resurfaced for what would tragically be the last game of his career. Despite several 'revolutionary' new operations, Lake retired from the game and moved into physiotherapy. Such was the respect for the player, more than 25,000 turned up for his testimonial against United on the same day his wife gave birth to their first child.

LARGEST CROWD
There was nothing spectacular about Eric Brook scoring the only goal of a hard-fought FA Cup sixth-round tie against Stoke City in March 1934. The crowd of 84,569 was special, however, and remains a record English attendance. It was 26,000 higher than any League game that season and the Blues went all the way to Wembley, beating Portsmouth 2–1 to lift the trophy.

LAW, DENIS – 1960 TO 1961 AND 1973 TO 1974
Appearances: 77 + 2 as a substitute
Goals: 37
Position: Forward
Born: Aberdeen

Though Law spent much of his career at Manchester United, he had enough memorable games in a City shirt to be forgiven for his efforts elsewhere. That rarest of beasts, a natural finisher, he once famously scored a double hat-trick against Luton, only for the game to be abandoned due to severe weather. Typically, City lost the re-match 3–1!

Law had scored 23 times in his first season (29 times if you throw in the abandoned match) when Italian giants Torino made a British record offer of £125,000 and City simply could not refuse the lucrative bid. As time went on, the talented Scot finally found his way back to Maine Road and, even in the twilight of his career, Law scored important goals for the Blues and featured in a dream forward line of Marsh, Summerbee and Lee. His final kick in League football was an impish back-heel that confirmed his former club United's relegation to Division Two.

LEE, FRANCIS – 1967 TO 1974
Appearances: 320 + 1 as a substitute
Goals: 143
Position: Striker
Born: Westhoughton

Francis Lee signed for City as a 23-year-old in 1967 and became one of the club's finest servants in doing so, with the club paying Bolton Wanderers £60,000 for the pint-sized striker. Lee was part of the glorious era that won trophy upon trophy under the genius of Joe Mercer and Malcolm Allison. A lethal finisher, with a cannonball shot, Franny was the all-time penalty king of Maine Road, notching a record 15 in one season, and winning many of them himself with – some believe – outrageous dives. He even earned the nickname 'Lee One Pen'. He averaged just under a goal every other game for City but was sold to Derby County in 1974. Still angry at City's decision to sell him – or even to consider selling him – after all he had achieved for the club, he inspired Derby to the First Division Championship and scored a blistering goal on his return to Maine Road.

He eventually did return to City but this time as chairman. He promised much and had been the saviour of fans eager to see Peter Swales step down after many trophy-less years. The take over battle was bitter and drawn out, but fan-power won the day and Lee was installed in his new role. The millions of pounds that were promised to buy new players never really materialised and his first appointment as manager was Alan Ball – a move that left many supporters disappointed. Unfortunately, it was a pointer to Lee's reign as chairman and he never really delivered the goods for the fans that had helped him into power. In 1998, barely four years into his tenure, Lee was – ironically – forced to step down by fan-pressure. Considering his history as a player, it is, with hindsight, a pity things turned out the way they did.

LEIVERS, BILL – 1953 TO 1964
Appearances: 281
Goals: 4
Position: Defender
Born: Bolsover

Strapping defender Bill Leivers gave 11 years of dependable and solid service to City, the club that he joined from Chesterfield for £10,500. A centre-back by nature, he established himself as right-back in the side and played in the 1956 FA Cup final victory over Birmingham City. Totally committed and fearless, Leivers went back to his original position in the middle of defence later in his City career and suffered an incredible five broken noses during his time with the Blues. It was surprising that he was never given international recognition but the club was on the slide at the time and shipping goals aplenty. In 1964, having played 250 League games for City, Leivers became player-manager of Doncaster Rovers. He won promotion with them and also later as boss of Cambridge United.

LOMAS, STEVE – 1993 TO 1997
Appearances: 127 + 10 as a substitute
Goals: 11
Position: Midfielder
Born: Hanover, Germany

Popular midfield terrier Steve Lomas was a young player that City fans had the pleasure of watching grow in stature during his time at Maine Road. He made his debut for the Blues under Brian Horton in September 1993 – a 1–0 win at Sheffield United. Energetic and hard-tackling, Lomas impressed sufficiently to play 22 times and a further 7 from the bench in his first season at senior level in all competitions. Inspired by midfield warhorses Steve McMahon and, before that, Peter Reid, the youngster continued to press for a regular place and Horton obliged on 18 occasions through the 1994–95 season, scoring 2 goals for good measure – one being an excellent header in a 5–2 victory over

Tottenham. A double injury at Crystal Palace in January ended his promising season four months early.

By the season 1995–96, Lomas had firmly established himself as a regular in City's starting line-up. Along with Garry Flitcroft, he provided a hard-working engine room to complement the delightful skills of new signing Gio Kinkladze and yet things still went badly awry for the Blues. Lomas scored a crucial winner against Aston Villa in April 1996, leaving the Blues needing a win to guarantee the club's Premiership status. After clawing back to 2–2 against Liverpool on the final day, Lomas memorably took the ball to the corner flag and tried to waste time after being given the message that a point all that was now enough. Astonishingly, the fans knew differently and as precious seconds melted away, the final whistle blew and the club was relegated.

With Flitcroft gone, Lomas became the senior midfielder but he couldn't inspire his colleagues to promotion and reluctantly signed for West Ham in 1997. He very nearly rejoined the Blues under Joe Royle's reign as City boss but elected to remain at Upton Park, where he is still captain.

M

MCADAMS, BILLY — 1953 TO 1960
Appearances: 134
Goals: 65
Position: Inside-forward
Born: Belfast

Billy McAdams' career at Maine Road was steady if not spectacular, but he was to make the headlines again in 2001 when Jermaine Defoe hit consecutive goals for Bournemouth while on loan from West Ham. Defoe had scored in ten consecutive matches and the national media was heralding his feat as a record. Phil Noble, City's curator at the time, thumbed through the history books and alerted the media that Defoe would have created a record only if he'd made it 11 (which he didn't) successive scoring appearances. The fact is that Northern Irish forward Billy McAdams had held the record of ten since 1957 – and still does.

McAdams, who won five caps for his country while at Maine Road, ended with 19 goals in 28 games and helped form a lethal front-line with Bobby Johnstone, Joe Hayes and Colin Barlow. It was an amazing season for City, who scored 104 and conceded 100 in the League! A tighter defence would have surely seen the Championship return to Maine Road but fifth place was the final standing. McAdams scored 21 in his final year at City (1959–60) before moving to Bolton Wanderers for £15,000.

MCCARTHY, MICK — 1983 TO 1987
Appearances: 163
Goals: 3
Position: Centre-half
Born: Barnsley

Mick McCarthy joined City from his hometown club Barnsley in 1983 and became a rock of City's defence for four seasons. Signed by Billy McNeill halfway through the 1983–84 campaign to replace the Arsenal-bound Tommy

Caton, McCarthy joined too late in the day to help City win promotion from the Second Division, with the club eventually finishing fourth. The City fans were sufficiently impressed to vote McCarthy the Player of the Year at the end of the season, and, with only 24 League games since his arrival, he holds the record of being the winner with the fewest appearances.

The following year saw McCarthy form a formidable partnership with Nicky Reid and the Blues won promotion, though he was forced to miss the dramatic final match with Charlton that City won 5–1. McCarthy found he had yet another defensive partner the next season with Kenny Clements rejoining the club from Oldham. The Blues began McCarthy's final year at Maine Road with an awful run of one win in the opening 13 and were relegated at the end of a miserable season. McCarthy joined Celtic soon after and is currently one of Ireland's most successful national managers.

MCDONALD, BOBBY – 1980 TO 1983
Appearances: 111 + 1 as a substitute
Goals: 16
Position: Full-back
Born: Aberdeen

Part of the Scottish trio that turned City's fortunes around, Bobby McDonald enjoyed his best playing days at Maine Road. He arrived in October 1980 with Tommy Hutchison from Coventry City and cost the Blues a fee of £247,000. Gerry Gow signed the day after and the three respected Scots had an unbelievably positive effect on an ailing side. The former Aston Villa and Sky Blues defender slotted in at left-back and soon became a cult hero on the terraces. 'Bobby Mac' was a serious threat at set-pieces and at least half of the goals he scored for City were from corners flicked on at the near post that he bravely forced home. The club set off on an FA Cup run that would see them beaten only at the final hurdle by Spurs.

McDonald easily outlasted his fellow musketeers and added 36 appearances for the 1981–82 season, adding 4 more League goals. The 1982–83 campaign began with three wins in a row and McDonald was rightly hailed a hero. Joe Corrigan had to leave the pitch shortly after the kick-off with an injured shoulder and, without a substitute goalie, McDonald pulled on the green jersey. With City leading 1–0 through a third-minute strike from Dennis Tueart, they then defended heroically and Bobby Mac played superbly well, keeping the Hornets at bay for 87 minutes. The Blues won 1–0 and topped the division with 100 per cent record. In typical City style, it was downhill from there and the club were relegated on the final day of the season.

With Billy McNeill the newly installed manager at Maine Road, McDonald was summoned by the boss over a disciplinary problem. The pair fell out and McDonald left for Oxford, his exciting adventure with the Blues over.

MCDOWALL, LES – 1938 TO 1949 AND MANAGER FROM 1950 TO 1963
Appearances: 129
Goals: 8
Position: Half-back
Born: Gunga Pur, India
League Record as manager: Games: 546 W: 199 D: 118 L: 229 F: 978 A: 1064

A player and then a manager for the club, India-born Les McDowall's association with Manchester City stretched an incredible 25 years, save for one year at Wrexham. It was the 1930s depression that first brought Les McDowall into the spotlight. An aircraft draughtsman, he was laid off due to lack of work and was playing a match with other unemployed men when a scout from Sunderland spotted him. He signed for Sunderland and played 13 games for the Roker Park outfit until City came in with a bid of around £7,500 in 1938.

Within a year McDowall was skipper at Maine Road until war broke out, ironically putting his football career on hold while he returned to his former trade. Times changed and following the war he handed over the captaincy to Sam Barkas and not long after he was appointed manager of Wrexham. A little over a year later and City returned for their former captain – this time with the offer of being manager with an immediate challenge of hauling the club out of Division Two. It would be a historic appointment in many ways as his tenure was never short of excitement and drama. In charge for some 13 years, he was also, behind Wilf Wild, just one year short of leading the club for a record length of time.

His first three years in Division One were more about survival and the Blues never finished above 15th in that time. The completion of the 1954–55 and 1955–56 seasons saw City finish in seventh and fourth respectively. There would be one more campaign with a top-ten finish – 1957–58 – and the rest were all 12th or below. Never afraid to adopt innovative ideas, he was in charge when the famous 'Revie Plan' (see *Revie, Don*) was instigated and he began his reign with instant promotion. He also tried the little publicised 'Marsden Plan', which involved Keith Marsden acting as a sweeper. City lost 6–1 to Preston and 9–2 to West Brom and the plan was indefinitely shelved! More positively, the club went on to successive FA Cup finals in 1955 and 1956; the latter was, of course, a victorious journey to the Twin Towers.

Players such as Denis Law were signed and in 1960 his £55,000 transfer fee was a British record. City eventually were relegated under McDowall and in 1963 he left for Oldham Athletic, where he stayed for two years. He died in 1991, aged 78.

MACKENZIE, STEVE — 1979 TO 1981
Appearances: 74 + 2 as a substitute
Goals: 10
Position: Midfielder
Born: Romford

Malcolm Allison made Steve Mackenzie the most expensive teenager in British history when he bought the 17-year-old to Maine Road from Crystal Palace for £250,000. He had no first-team experience but Allison's contacts at Palace were good and three weeks later the youngster was pitched straight into City's first team to make his debut – against Crystal Palace. He scored 2 goals in his first 7 games and made a total of 17 starts in the League with two more from the bench. Allison lasted a dozen games of the 1980–81 season and Mackenzie, wearing the No. 9 shirt, must have wondered about his future with his mentor departed. He needn't have worried – at least, for the time being. John Bond played him in every game during his first season in charge.

In an amazing turnaround, City powered towards two major cup finals. Mackenzie played in 14 of the 15 matches played in cup competitions and while the Blues narrowly lost to Liverpool in the League Cup semi-final, they went all the way to face Spurs in the FA Cup final. A 1–1 draw led to a replay and Mackenzie's finest moment in a City shirt. Trailing 1–0, Hutchison cushioned a header to Mackenzie on the edge of the Spurs box. He let fly a 25-yard volley that flew into the top corner for one of the best goals Wembley had ever seen. The shine was taken off by a 3–2 defeat but the 18-year-old had written his name into the history books forever.

His total of 53 games plus 8 goals was a fantastic return for a teenager and few could understand the thinking of John Bond when, in the summer of 1981, he allowed the talented midfielder to move to West Bromwich Albion. His debut for the Baggies was against City at Maine Road, just 16 days later!

MCMAHON, STEVE — 1991 TO 1995
Appearances: 94 + 4 as a substitute
Goals: 1
Position: Midfielder
Born: Liverpool

Signed from Liverpool for £900,000 on Christmas Eve 1991, Steve McMahon arrived at Maine Road towards the end of an impressive career. The former Everton and Aston Villa midfielder had built up a fair reputation for mixing it in the middle of the park and when Peter Reid's legs began to go, it was McMahon he turned to, to lead the troops in a similar vein. McMahon soon won over the City faithful with his blood-and-thunder displays, though his tough reputation sometimes worked against him and a reasonable challenge often ended with a yellow card, or worse, and suspensions were not uncommon. He was also a skilful player with a powerful shot yet scored only one goal during his time with the Blues. He now manages Blackpool and is showing signs of being a promising young manager.

MCNAB, NEIL – 1983 TO 1990
Appearances: 261
Goals: 19
Position: Midfielder
Born: Greenock

Neil McNab was probably one of the most underrated footballers to play for City for many years. The skilful hard-working Scot joined the Blues from Brighton in 1983 for a bargain £35,000 and soon became a firm favourite with the Blues faithful for his consistency, invention and endeavour, though some fans thought he was a bit of a crab (likes to move sideways). Busy and workmanlike, with no shortage of skill and tenacity, McNab slotted perfectly into the cavernous role that Asa Hartford had left and made the central midfield his own, eventually becoming Player of the Year at the end of the 1988–89 season following City's promotion back to the top division. He finally left the Blues during the 1989–90 season, signing for Tranmere Rovers and subsequently helping them to promotion two years later. His twin sons were once on City's books and he was last in employment as part of the Portsmouth backroom staff.

MCNEILL, BILLY
Manager from 1983 to 1986
League Record: Games: 133 W: 53 D: 37 L: 43 F: 180 A: 150

In Scotland, Billy McNeill, MBE, was a hero. The former Celtic star had collected 23 winning medals from major competitions, including the famous European Cup triumph in 1967. With 9 championships, 6 League Cup victories and a further 7 Scottish Cup successes and 29 full caps for the national side, it is understandable why he was considered as an icon to the supporters at Parkhead. He was awarded an MBE in 1974 after playing a quite incredible 831 games for Celtic and then moved into management, first with Clyde and then Aberdeen. In May 1978 he returned to Celtic to win more trophies until City enticed him south of the border for the first time to become manager of the Blues in 1983.

His pedigree could hardly have been higher. Astute in the transfer market –

he had to be – Jim Tolmie and Derek Parlane were signed for peanuts and started like a house on fire in McNeill's first season. It wasn't to last and City finished a disappointing fourth, well behind the promoted top three. David Phillips, Mick McCarthy, Neil McNab and Jim Melrose were signed and in 1984–85 the Blues regained their top-flight status on the final day of the season. City's return was far from impressive and they ended in 16th place after struggling for much of the season. A chronic run of form almost saw them relegated – four draws and nine defeats were a sign of even worse to come.

McNeill quit Maine Road for Aston Villa in September 1986 and left Jimmy Frizzell to try and keep the club afloat, but it was to prove too great a task and the Blues were relegated, ironically along with McNeill's new club Aston Villa. He was sacked and returned to Celtic for five more successful years.

MACRAE, KEITH – 1973 TO 1981
Appearances: 70
Goals: 0
Position: Goalkeeper
Born: Glasgow

Keith MacRae spent much of his City career in the shadow of Joe Corrigan and he may have even been the catalyst that inspired Big Joe to become a full England international. MacRae was signed from Motherwell for £100,000 – then a record fee paid by City for a goalkeeper – to challenge for the keeper's jersey, and became first choice for the 1973–74 season, following some erratic performances from Corrigan. Indeed, of his 56 League appearances for City, 52 came in the first two years.

MacRae's arrival was the wake-up call Corrigan needed and when he got the chance to play for the first team again he made sure he wasn't going to lose it and went on to miss only one game from 1975 to 1980. MacRae, amazingly loyal, was also watching a promising career ebb away. He joined Portland Timbers in 1981 having played only four League games in over six years. For loyalty and patience alone, Keith deserves to be remembered.

MACHIN, MEL
Manager from 1987 to 1989
League Record: Games: 103 W: 46 D: 23 L: 34 F: 174 A: 137

Even though Mel Machin resembled an insurance salesman rather than a football manager, he quietly turned an ailing giant into an attacking, vibrant side that was easy on the eye and full of potential. Machin arrived from Norwich City, where he'd established himself as a promising coach. He signed players such as Ian Bishop, Clive Allen and Trevor Morley during his tenure and brought in wily old heads such as John Gidman, Paul Cooper and Brian Gayle.

Whilst he was not shy of bringing in new talent, he was keen to nurture the exciting crop of youngsters that had won the FA Youth Cup in 1986. Lake, Hinchcliffe, White and Brightwell would all become first-team regulars under Machin, and the mix of old and new, on this occasion, worked extremely well. His first full season saw City scoring goals by the bag full and in the space of four days they beat Huddersfield Town 10–1 and Plymouth 6–2. The momentum trailed off in the middle of the season and seven defeats in nine League games effectively ended hopes of an instant return to Division One. Quarter finalists in both the FA and League Cups proved Machin's side was capable of bigger and better things.

The progress continued and the following season the Blues won promotion – albeit on the final day – but it was no more than they deserved. Machin had stated on his arrival that he had a three-year plan in mind to take City back to Division One and, in truth, the promotion achieved may have a come a year too early. Machin will always have the glory of a 5-1 victory over the Reds to recall to his grandchildren, but a 6–0 defeat at Derby County saw Peter Swales' razor-sharp axe fall once again and Machin was sacked.

Swales said that Machin had failed to connect with the supporters – a slight case of the pot calling the kettle, perhaps? There was a feeling that the board wanted a higher profile boss to lead the club and the quietly spoken Machin was never going to be a Malcolm Allison or John Bond-type figure. He later became manager of Barnsley and Bournemouth but has never risen to the heights his early promise once threatened.

MAINE ROAD

Home to Manchester City since 1923, the club finally ends its tenure at the famous old ground for the last time against Southampton on 11 May 2003. Many a tear will be shed when City leave Maine Road but the promise of the state-of-the-art City of Manchester Stadium will no doubt cushion the blow, somewhat. City first played at their new home in 1923, just four months after Wembley Stadium was completed, after leaving Hyde Road and its limited capacity. Designed by local architect Charles Swain, the original plan was for the ground to match Wembley and hold 90,000 spectators – 'a stadium fit for Manchester's premier club' as stated by officials at the time.

The opening game in August 1923 introduced the fans to this huge arena and many were in awe of its size. With only the Main Stand's 10,000 seats covered, the rest of the ground was open terracing. Buoyed on by a record crowd of 56,993, the Blues beat Sheffield United 2–1 with goals from Tom Johnson and Horace Barnes. The next home game proved that the new ground was sadly not impregnable and City lost 2–1 to Aston Villa but the club would lose just twice more at home that season.

The 'popular side', later known as the Kippax, had a flagpole positioned roughly level with the halfway line at the very back of the terracing. Before each home game, a member of staff would proudly raise the club flag with 'City FC' on and then lower it after the match had ended.

Surprisingly, City have only once gone an entire League season at Maine Road without defeat when the club went up as Second Division Champions in the 1965–66 campaign. For 17 months the Blues were undefeated at home in the League. Maine Road has seen various changes over the years but was famed for its terrace, the Kippax, where most City fans gathered to frighten the life out of opponents – and the occasional home player! The various stands – the North Stand (formerly the Scoreboard End), Platt Lane and the Main Stand and the new Kippax Stand – have all been developed at different stages over a number of years, giving the stadium an unusual and unique look.

None of the four roofs match and the four sides are all of different designs and heights. Maine Road's eccentricity has matched the team's eccentric ways over the 80 years and just when the side is looking settled and full of promise, the club packs up lock, stock and barrel and moves across town to Eastlands. Despite the emotional attachment of the City faithful who have bared their souls to the concrete and steel that makes up Maine Road, they were fully behind the change of grounds. When all is said and done, City have only won the Division One Championship twice while in Moss Side and for all the happy memories the ground holds there are equal measures of disappointment, despair and heartbreak. After 80 years, the time is right to move on, but Maine Road will remain in each fan's heart for many years to come.

MALEY, TOM
Manager from 1902 to 1906
League Record: Games: 140 W: 83 D: 21 L: 36 F: 305 A: 165

Tom Maley was City's first successful manager, and even today his record stands proudly among the best and he was also one of the first managers to achieve success with style. Very much his own man, Maley could call on the advice of his older brother Willie, who was manager at Glasgow Celtic, if needed. He wanted his side to play with a penchant for style as opposed to kick and rush, and he targeted players specifically who would fit into his ideals. In his first season he steered City to the Second Division title and the following year the club very nearly pulled off a historic double, winning the FA Cup but cruelly finishing second in the First Division.

His management techniques were second to none and he subtly changed several players' roles in the team to great effect. He was also not overawed by the legendary Billy Meredith, as perhaps his predecessor had been. He turned average footballers into great footballers by intelligently playing them in positions they were more suited to. Sandy Turnbull, Sammy Frost and Jimmy Bannister all found a new lease of life under Maley, but his reign ended in 1906 during a scandal that saw the chairman and manager suspended for life from the club and several officials and players being fined. So ended the career of a fine manager and also a successful period in City's history.

MANAGERS — GENERAL

Up to and including Kevin Keegan, manager of City for the start of the 2002–03 campaign, the Blues had 32 managers in 113 years – not as many as the media might indicate each time a new team boss is appointed at Maine Road. This doesn't take into account caretaker managers, such as Asa Hartford and several others during the club's more recent history. Each full-time boss has obviously had varied lengths of time either through choice or otherwise. The longest to survive in the hot seat is Wilf Wild, who managed the club from 1932 to 1946. Les McDowall was in charge for 13 years and Ernest Mangnall was at the helm for 12 years.

The shortest period of time was Steve Coppell's month-long reign in 1996. The club's reputation for something of a merry-go-round of managerial appointments stems from the time John Bond quit in 1983. Twelve bosses in 18 years equate to an average of 18 months for each boss. The overall average is three years and six months. Prior to 1983, it was an average of almost five years in the manager's chair.

MANGNALL, ERNEST
Manager from 1912 to 1924
League Record: Games: 324 W: 139 D: 76 L: 109 F: 463 A: 431

The one and only manager to move from one Manchester club to another, Ernest Mangnall had steered United to the League Championship in 1907–08 and again in 1910–11. Sandwiched between was an FA Cup triumph. Irony upon irony . . . the success of United owed much to the fact that following an illegal payments scandal in 1906 at City, the United manager signed up Billy Meredith, Jimmy Bannister and Sandy Turnbull for peanuts and watched his side flourish while the Blues almost went out of business.

Mangnall arrived at Hyde Road looking for a fresh challenge and was appointed secretary/manager in 1912. Financially, the Blues hadn't two pennies to rub together but Mangnall kept the club afloat and somehow kept City alive during the First World War. He never had the resources to repeat his successes at United but, in a difficult time, he worked wonders for the club. His eye for talent hadn't deserted him and he brought Horace Barnes and Tommy Browell to Hyde Road. The founder of the Central League and the Football Managers' Association, Mangnall's contract was not renewed in 1924 after 12 loyal years of service to the club.

MARADONA, DIEGO

Unbelievable as it seems, City were once – allegedly – on the trail of Argentine superstar Diego Maradona at a time when he was a young, slim and supremely gifted athlete. The stories floated around the newspapers for a couple of weeks in the early 1980s and the source is, predictably, impossible to trace but it is almost too bizarre not to be true. Other 'nearly men' are Luis Figo, the Portuguese star who Peter Reid tried to bring to Maine Road in the early 1990s and Arthur Numan, who now plays for Glasgow Rangers. Gio Kinkladze's best mate Shota Arveladze was also said to be close to joining City at one point. The former Ajax star is, like Numan, also now with Glasgow Rangers.

MARSH, RODNEY – 1972 TO 1976

Appearances: 142 + 2 as a substitute
Goals: 46
Position: Forward
Born: Hatfield

The ultimate entertainer and clown prince of Maine Road, Marsh had the City fans eating out of his hand for much of his time at the club with his mercurial talents and trickery. Signed from QPR to boost City's 1972 title run-in, he was blamed by many for City's limp finish to the season. In a recent autobiography, Marsh himself claimed he cost City the title. In a period packed with personalities and stars, his sublime skills and invention still shone brightly and he went on to play 142 times for the Blues, scoring on 46 occasions.

A falling-out with boss Tony Book led to him being dropped from the first team and he was transfer-listed for being accused of not giving 100 per cent – something he vehemently denied. He almost moved to Anderlecht during November 1975 after the two clubs agreed a fee but he decided the language could be a problem and stayed at Maine Road. He finally ended his City career by moving to Tampa Bay Rowdies several months later, in 1976. He continued to sparkle throughout his career and, in his brief time at Fulham with George Best, the football was exhibitionism and showmanship of the highest calibre. Today, Rodney sits on a panel for Sky Television's *Soccer Saturday* and is as outspoken and controversial as ever, and for those who remember his days in a sky-blue jersey, they probably wouldn't want him to be any other way.

MASCOTS

It was once tradition for a tracksuited youngster to run out before the Blues came on at Maine Road and run around the perimeter of the pitch. There have always been kids that walk on the pitch with the City players and have a kick-around with one of the players but, as for official club mascots, 'Moonchester' was the first real mascot City had. The blue alien is popular with the Junior Blues and in December 2001 the club introduced 'Moonbeam', Moonchester's female companion.

Most clubs have a mascot; the most memorable for many City fans was 'Mr Posh', the mascot of Peterborough United. Thousands of Blues had made the journey for an FA Cup fifth-round tie at London Road and poor old Mr Posh came in for the royal treatment as he passed the packed City enclosure complete with monocle and top hat. Talk about sitting ducks! It was all good fun, of course.

The banana craze of the late 1980s could also be considered an unofficial kind of mascot – the City players ran out at Stoke City with giant bananas on Boxing Day 1988 as a tribute to the fans but it didn't help the team too much as they went down 3–1. Another unofficial mascot was 'Big Helen', who used to sit on the front row of the North Stand and ring a bell during times when the Blues needed a lift – she was kept very busy most of the time.

MAY, ANDY – 1980 TO 1987

Appearances: 164 + 10 as a substitute
Goals: 8
Position: Midfielder
Born: Bury

Andy May spent over seven years at Maine Road and has possibly never had the kind of recognition he deserved. A versatile player who was happy in midfield or defence, he filled a number of roles when asked during his time with the club. It was John Bond who gave him his debut as a sub in April 1981 against Ipswich Town – the Blues lost 1–0 barely a fortnight after beating the same side by the same score in an epic FA Cup semi-final at Villa Park. May only made three starts during 1981–82 and four the following season as City lost their First Division status.

Playing under his third manager in three years, May found himself in favour with new boss Billy McNeill, who immediately installed the youngster as left-back. May was an ever-present and also chipped in with five goals. For the 1984–85 season, he missed the first three games and then played the following 39 and it was his header that began the promotion-clinching 5–1 rout of Charlton Athletic on the final day of the season. He was moved into midfield for most of the Division One campaign but failed to register on the score sheet in 36 starts. Jimmy Frizzell took over and as the Blues slipped back into the second tier, May played only 17 times in several different positions. Huddersfield Town made an acceptable bid in the summer of 1987 and May left for Leeds Road.

In a cruel twist of fate, his return to Maine Road just four months later ended in a humiliating 10–1 defeat for May and his new club. He scored their only goal and was saluted by the Kippax – a gesture that was duly acknowledged by the player.

MEGSON, GARY – 1989 TO 1992
Appearances: 92 + 5 as a substitute
Goals: 2
Position: Midfielder
Born: Manchester

Now a highly promising young manager, Gary Megson arrived in 1989 from Sheffield Wednesday to add vital experience to Mel Machin's young squad and his arrival in January led to the Blues winning six games in succession. Megson started with a debut goal – the winner – in a 1–0 win at Oldham and went on to lose only 4 of the 22 games he played in, culminating in promotion. Injury prevented him starting the 1989–90 campaign but he returned in time to play a part in new manager Howard Kendall's defensive plan to save City from the drop.

City would lose only three of the 19 matches Megson featured in. Now part of a tough, gritty midfield with Peter Reid and Mark Ward, City would eventually finish fifth in Division One and Megson played 19 times and another 18 starts the season after with City again finishing fifth. He left for Norwich in the summer of 1992 and has since managed several clubs, most notably Stockport County and his current club, West Bromwich Albion. Tough, uncompromising and definitely no-frills, Megson gave good service to the Blues during his stay.

MERCER, JOE
Manager from 1965 to 1972
League Record: Games: 294 W: 126 D: 85 L: 83 F: 448 A: 329

Joe Mercer, OBE, was simply the best manager Manchester City have ever had. His record was so good that it will take someone extra special to emulate it and, much as Blues' fans may wish, his record may never be bettered. Only time will tell. Yet, before he ever became a manager, he was respected throughout football as one of the game's true stars. Regarded by many as not just a great wing-half in his days at Everton, but possibly the best ever, Joe remained with the Toffees from 1932 until 1947, collecting a League Championship medal in 1939. The war stole many years from him and when the League resumed, things had changed at Goodison Park and he moved to Highbury.

With Arsenal he went on to even greater glory, including two more League Championships plus another winner's medal for clinching the FA Cup. A broken leg forced retirement and robbed him of yet more playing years. His first move into management was with Sheffield United and he impressed sufficiently to be later installed as Aston Villa boss. He took them to promotion from Division Two, won the League Cup and led them to two FA Cup semi-finals. The pressures and stress of management took their toll on him and he suffered a stroke. He recovered and when the doctors gave him a clean bill of health, the Villa board sacked him. He decided to retire and many thought they had seen the last of 'Genial Joe'. But Mercer's love of the game pulled him back and in 1965, when Manchester City offered him the opportunity of waking a sleeping giant, he grabbed the chance with both hands.

His first move was to bring young coach Malcolm Allison to City as his assistant and though the pair were as alike as chalk and cheese, they would prove the perfect managerial team and as good as any in the history of English football. Within a year, Mercer's new-look City side had won the Division Two title, and two years later the Blues were crowned Champions of England for only the second time, winning the First Division with style and panache.

The trophies just kept on coming. The FA Cup in 1969, the League Cup in 1970 and later that same season, the first and only European trophy City have won – the Cup-Winners' Cup – was brought proudly back to Manchester by Mercer and his talented troops. Five trophies in five years – the City fans were in their own blue heaven. Malcolm Allison was involved in some bitter arguments with the City board and in 1970 he very nearly was sacked, but, with Joe Mercer's backing, Allison remained at the club. After seven years as number two, Allison manipulated events that led to Mercer leaving his position and eventually joining Coventry City in 1972. Allison believed he deserved a chance to call the shots himself and though nobody would have denied him the chance, many were upset by the events leading to Mercer's departure.

A general manager at Coventry, he became England boss on a temporary basis in 1974 in order to, as he put it himself, 'try and restore some laughter' following the national side's omission from the World Cup qualifiers. He deservedly was awarded the OBE in 1976 for services to football and he remained as a director at Highfield Road until his resignation in 1981. He retired to his beloved Merseyside and died in August 1990. A legendary and much-loved figure to all Manchester City fans and a lovely, caring man who tried to put a smile back on the face of the game. The world of football lost one of its greatest sons when Genial Joe passed away.

MEREDITH, BILLY – 1894 TO 1905 AND 1921 TO 1924

Appearances: 394
Goals: 151
Position: Winger
Born: Chirk

Billy Meredith may have played for City for the first time over a hundred years ago but his legend lives on to this day. Meredith – a somewhat controversial character – is ranked by many alongside the great Sir Stanley Matthews in stature and was a magnet for football fans and the media in his day. Bandy-legged and invariably chewing a toothpick, Meredith was a fantastic player and the scourge of many an Edwardian defender. The immensely talented right winger could pinpoint a cross for a forward or cut inside and lash the ball home himself if the mood took him.

With 151 goals for the club, he is among the all-time top scorers for City. He was involved in a bribe and illegal payment scandal that rocked the club to its foundations and he eventually joined Manchester United before finally returning to City in 1921. He also won 22 Welsh caps as a City player and holds the record for being the oldest footballer to turn out for the Blues. He was aged just a 120 days short of his 50th birthday in his last game for the club – a 2–0 defeat to Newcastle United in an FA Cup semi-final.

MILLWALL FC

For some reason that is unclear, City and Millwall are not the best of friends. Crowd trouble flared during City's visit to the New Den in 1998 when Lee Bradbury equalised for the Blues in the last minute to earn a 1–1 draw from a bad-tempered affair. Chaos ensued outside the ground as the home fans laid siege to the travelling army in disgraceful scenes that are all too common with certain factions of the Lions' support. The return game saw around 2,500 Millwall fans tearing seats up in the North Stand as their team was roundly beaten 3–0. Trouble flared outside the ground before and after the match with many innocents caught in the middle. With Millwall and City once again in the same division for the 2001–02 season, the clubs wisely agreed that there could be no repeat of the violence and took the unusual step of banning the away fans from each fixture. City won 3–2 at Millwall and Darren Huckerby applauded the empty stand that should have housed the City fans after his goal to the delight of the thousands watching on a huge screen back at Maine Road. The Blues reciprocated the ban and won the return 2–0.

MORLEY, TREVOR – 1988 TO 1989
Appearances: 79 + 3 as a substitute
Goals: 21
Position: Striker
Born: Nottingham

When Trevor Morley signed for City in January 1988 for £200,000, little was known of the player. He had scored quite a few goals for Northampton Town, but he was unproven at a higher level. He made his debut in a 2–0 home defeat to Aston Villa, making little impression on the then leaders of the former Second Division. He fought hard to win over City supporters but it wasn't until March 1989 – a full 14 months after his arrival – that Trevor Morley finally heard his name chanted on the Kippax. The moment, however, was all but lost as City favourite Paul Lake sickeningly clashed heads with a Leicester City player and swallowed his tongue.

Fortunately, Lake made a full recovery, but the incident cast a black cloud over the match leaving an odd, flat feeling among supporters. Typical, then, that the much-maligned Morley should score a first-class hat-trick as City ran out 4–2 winners. From then on, Morley led the line with confidence and he etched his name into the history books with a goal four minutes from time at Bradford City to earn the Blues the point they needed for promotion to Division One.

It was also Morley's goal, a minute or so after David Oldfield had put City ahead in the 1989 Manchester derby, that set the scene for the eventual 5–1 victory. A few months later and manager Mel Machin had been sacked. Howard Kendall's arrival signalled the end for Morley and his appearance in the 1–0 Boxing Day victory over Norwich was his last for City. Two days later, he and another crowd favourite, Ian Bishop, were transferred to West Ham, with Mark Ward making his way to Maine Road in exchange.

MORRISON, ANDY – 1998 TO 2002
Appearances: 47 + 1 as a substitute
Goals: 5
Position: Centre-half
Born: Inverness

The impact Andy Morrison had on an ailing City side during the dark days of Division Two is immeasurable. A natural leader, Morrison was the missing link in City's armour at a time when the younger players desperately needed guidance and somebody to encourage them while being prepared to tear a strip off them if they needed it, too. Costing £80,000 from Huddersfield Town, manager Joe Royle initially brought Morrison to City on loan but the impact he had was so great that he'd signed the strapping Scot before the loan period had barely started. He was soon made captain and started with three goals in his first four games, including a spectacular volley in a 3–0 win at Oldham.

Morrison was soon a big crowd favourite as fans related to the passion he showed playing for their club every time he pulled on a blue jersey. Morrison, or 'Mozzer' as everyone knew him, was rarely beaten in the air, was an excellent passer of the ball and was quite fearsome in the tackle. His inspirational qualities as captain guided City into the Division Two play-offs and after a tense semi-final victory over Wigan Athletic, Andy Morrison lead the Blues out for what was to be one of the most dramatic matches Wembley had ever seen. Injury blighted his remaining years at Maine Road and in 2002 he and City parted company amicably.

MOULDEN, PAUL – 1984 TO 1989
Appearances: 58 + 21 as a substitute
Goals: 26
Position: Striker
Born: Bolton

Arguably one of the finest prospects ever to play at any level for Manchester City, Paul Moulden, many believe, should have become a striker regarded in the same bracket as Robbie Fowler or Michael Owen. City have had many fine, instinctive forwards on their books throughout their history but Moulden had the promise to eclipse them all. Signed from Bolton Boys, the Blues fought off a whole host of clubs eager to take the young forward on. His scoring exploits at schoolboy level are the stuff of legends and he is officially entered in the *Guinness Book of Records* after netting an unbelievable 289 times in 40 matches – an average of just over seven per game!

He scored 12 goals in 13 FA Youth Cup games for City and picked up a winners' medal along the way and finished top scorer in the reserves for three out of four seasons. He forced his way into the first team on New Year's Day 1986 and played his part in a 1–0 away win at Aston Villa. A couple more games here and there in 1986–87 and then Jimmy Frizzell gave him a longer run and he scored four in four games at one point in a side destined for relegation. A broken leg – one of four leg breaks in his City career – kept his progress on hold under Mel Machin's reign but for the 1988–89 campaign he ended top scorer making 29 starts and scoring 13 goals as City gained promotion.

Yet in June 1989 he was part-exchanged to Bournemouth in a deal that brought Ian Bishop to City. He stayed with the Cherries for less than a year, returning to his native north-west with Oldham Athletic. The glittering career that had once beckoned was all but ruined by injury.

MOVIES

Though some of City's escapades would have lent themselves well to a Hollywood disaster movie adaptation, there have been a couple of moments of real movie stardom for City stars in the past. Mike Summerbee was in *Escape to Victory* and can therefore truthfully claim he has played alongside Pelé and Sylvester Stallone! Polish star Kaziu Deyna was also featured in the movie. Colin Bell wasn't in the classic *Italian Job* but a flag draped out of a white van with his name on was featured in the movie. It's doubtful he received any royalties.

The film *There's Only One Jimmy Grimble* starring Robert Carlyle and Ray Winstone was based around a young boy and his dream to one day play for Manchester City. Many scenes were filmed in and around Maine Road and the final portion featured Jimmy Grimble finally realising his dream and playing on the hallowed turf. It's not been made to date, but *Bend it Like Benarbia* would go down a storm with the blue half of Manchester.

MULHEARN, KEN – 1967 TO 1971

Appearances: 61
Goals: 0
Position: Goalkeeper
Born: Liverpool

Liverpudlian Ken Mulhearn joined City in September 1967 from neighbours Stockport County. He was signed by Joe Mercer, who had stated that he wanted two top-class keepers in his squad – Harry Dowd being the other – and soon made the No. 1 jersey his own during the 1967–68 Championship season. His contribution to the team at this historic time was enormous though he made only 61 appearances for City in total.

He began as first choice for the 1968–69 season but the Dowd–Mulhearn battle would continue as both men shared the green jersey with equal distinction making an easy choice almost impossible for Mercer. Following a 3–1 win over Leeds, Harry Dowd regained the number one spot and Ken never quite managed to reclaim his first-team place again, and there was also the emerging youngster Joe Corrigan pressing for first-team football. He would only play a few more times for the Blues before joining Shrewsbury Town in March 1971.

MURRAY, JIMMY – 1963 TO 1967
Appearances: 78
Goals: 46
Position: Striker
Born: Dover

Wolves benefited greatly from the scoring prowess of Jimmy Murray as he bagged 155 goals in 276 League games for the Molineux side. No wonder, then, that new City manager George Poyser should target the Dover-born forward as the man to steer his club back out of the Second Division at the first attempt. Having already signed the prolific Derek Kevan from Chelsea, Poyser sat back and waited for the goals to flow. He wasn't disappointed. Murray's debut in November 1963 saw him and his new strike-partner Kevan both score in a 4–2 defeat at Southampton. Three weeks later and Murray began a scoring streak that is still among the very best in the club's history. He scored 12 times in just 6 games and banged in successive hat-tricks in doing so. Kevan had notched 9 in the same period, which meant that the pair had managed 21 goals in just 8 games – quite a start!

Injury kept Murray out of the next seven matches and City failed to win a single one and scored only five times. He returned and the goals, once again, began to flow. In fact, in his 19 games played for the Blues in his first season, City lost only four times and failed to score just once, scoring a total of 53 goals. Murray finished with figures of 21 in 19 starts. He managed a further 13 in 30 the following season but with Derek Kevan gone, goals had become harder to come by. Joe Mercer took over the next season and though he still managed 7 from 11 games, Murray's time at Maine Road was coming to an end. He was still at the club throughout the 1966–67 season but played only ten times, scoring twice. He left for Walsall in May 1967, still the holder of a tremendous record for the Blues.

N

NASH, CARLO – 2000 TO PRESENT
Appearances: 30 + 1 as a substitute*
Goals: 0*
Position: Goalkeeper
Born: Burnley

Carlo Nash signed for the Blues towards the end of the 2000–01 Premiership campaign. He was spotted playing non-league football by a scout from Crystal Palace who came in with the offer of a contract and his stay at Selhurst Park was only ended when Stockport County gave him the chance of regular first-team football and a return to his native north-west. The big keeper became a firm favourite among the Edgeley Park support and spent several impressive seasons in goal. Linked with a big-money move to Wolves, Nash seemed set for pastures new but the deal, for one reason or another, never happened and he stayed with County. With his contract due to expire in the summer, Joe Royle moved in with a bid of £100,000 – a fraction of his true worth. Stockport were in no position to bargain and rather than have to watch Nash leave on a free transfer they accepted the bid.

Nash was signed as cover for Nicky Weaver, whose form had been somewhat indifferent, but after a succession of errors from City's number one, he was given an opportunity to claim the place for himself. Within 35 minutes of his debut, he had seen four goals go past as a rampant Arsenal raced into an unassailable lead. Nash was not to blame for any of the goals and made several impressive saves to keep the Gunners down to just four. When Kevin Keegan became City's new manager, he began with Weaver then played Nash and by the end of his first season in charge both men had shared the duties on an almost equal basis. Yet both players look likely to be forced to wait for a year in the shadows following the capture of Peter Schmeichel, who seems set for a last season at the top.

NEAL, PHIL
Manager from November 1996 to December 1996
League Record: Games: 10 W:2 D:1 L:7 F:10 A:19

Phil Neal's track record in management had been poor to say the least before he was given the job of filling in for Steve Coppell in 1996. He lasted just a few games before tendering his resignation. His appointment, while only on a trial basis, lacked imagination and foresight. Sometimes good ex-footballers don't necessarily make good managers and Neal is a case in point.

NEUTRAL GROUND
Maine Road has played host to a number of games that didn't involve the Blues. Manchester United played many times in Moss Side after Old Trafford was bombed during the Second World War and there have been several FA Cup semi-finals held at the ground prior to the Kippax becoming an all-seater stand. A memorable game from the late 1970s involved non-league Altrincham FC, who took on Tottenham in an FA Cup replay. Having held the north Londoners to a 1–1 draw at White Hart Lane, a large crowd containing thousands of City fans saw Spurs win the game 3–0. Several Rugby League games of varying importance have also been held at Maine Road.

NEWBOULD, HARRY
Manager from 1906 to 1912
League Record: Games: 228 W: 86 D: 57 L: 85 F: 362 A: 356

Harry Newbould was left to pick up the pieces of the previous administration and it was a minor miracle that he succeeded at all. Though successful, Tom Maley, the chairman and several players were involved in a scandal that led to wholesale changes at Hyde Road. Newbould had acquitted himself well at Derby County, where he'd been both secretary and manager. The former sprinter and outside-right was also a qualified accountant and seemed the ideal man to restore City's reputation.

He effectively built a new team and though they lost his first two games by 4–1 and 9–1, the side soon bonded and became a more than useful outfit. His second season was even better and the Blues finished in third position in Division One but, in typical style, were relegated the next. Newbould guided the club to its third second-tier title in 1909–10 but in 1911–12 it was only a tremendous 17 points from a possible 20 that saved the club from yet another demotion. Newbould left City in 1912 and was a leading light in the formation of what is today known as the PFA

NICKNAMES

Club nicknames entered in football books not specific to a particular team invariably list names that the supporters either never call their heroes or have never even heard of. That City are known as 'The Citizens' in several books will no doubt produce a smile on the faces of many City fans. The only true nickname for City is the 'Blues'. As for players, there have been several that have survived the passage of time. 'Buzzer' applied to Mike Summerbee and, for a time, to his son Nicky during his spell at Maine Road. 'Nijinsky' was Colin Bell's nickname after a thoroughbred champion racehorse. Joe Corrigan was known simply as 'Big Joe' and another great City keeper was Tony Coton, who was better known by his initials, 'TC'. Of late, there has been 'Mozzer' for Andy Morrison, 'The Goat' for Shaun Goater, 'Kinky' for Gio Kinkladze and 'Psycho' for Stuart Pearce. New signing Nicolas Anelka is also known as 'Nico'.

NIXON, ERIC – 1983 TO 1988
Appearances: 84
Goals: 0
Position: Goalkeeper
Born: Manchester

To begin with, confidence was never a problem for local lad Eric Nixon and his belief in his own abilities eventually led to a contract with the Blues. He arrived at Maine Road and asked for a trial, which he was granted, and after several reserve games he signed professional forms and became the stand-by for Alex Williams. Nixon's early days at City were spent in the shadow of Williams who was ever present from March 1983 to September 1985. Injury to Williams allowed Nixon the chance to establish himself under Billy McNeill, and the acrobatic goalkeeper did enough to earn a run of 27 League games as the club's number one and kept eight clean sheets during this sustained spell.

It soon became clear that Williams was not going to return as first choice and Nixon must have been devastated when McNeill splashed out on Perry Suckling and then made him first choice. Nixon waited patiently and with five games remaining was reinstated in nets. He kept three clean sheets out of five but City were still relegated.

Though Nixon began the 1987–88 season as first choice it was clear that new boss Mel Machin had other plans for him. A disastrous fumble in a League Cup tie at home to Wolves was too much for Machin and the City fans also seemed to now lack confidence in their goalkeeper. Nixon was dropped and Bobby Mimms and later Mike Stowell were both brought in on loan and Suckling played a handful of matches.

During a vital clash with promotion rivals Crystal Palace, Ian Wright faced up to Nixon as he was about to kick it out. Whatever Wright said worked and Nixon pushed him away. Wright collapsed in a heap and the referee awarded a penalty and sent Nixon off. From 1–0 up and looking comfortable, City lost 3–1. Things then went from bad to worse for him and his confidence drained away visibly. When Tranmere Rovers came in with a bid, he left for Prenton Park and became something of a legend over there a period of time.

NON-LEAGUE

Given the history and tradition of Manchester City, nobody should be surprised that the Blues have, when the rare occasion has arisen, struggled to beat non-league opposition. All five games have, of course, been in the FA Cup. The early fixtures are harder to gauge, as non-league in the late 1890s didn't necessarily mean 'duff' opponents. Hence Fleetwood Rangers drawing 1–1 and then winning the replay 2–0 in 1892. A year later West Manchester won 3–0 to send the club crashing out. Wigan County became the first minnows to succumb to the Blues by 1–0 and it would be 73 years before City would face non-leaguers again when in 1971 they scraped past Wigan Athletic 1–0, with Colin Bell scoring the only goal in front of 46,212 fans at Maine Road.

NORTH STAND

Formerly the Scoreboard End, the North Stand was completed for the 1972–73 season and reduced the Maine Road capacity by some 12,000. Seats replaced terracing and, with a smart new roof, the North Stand looked slightly out of place with the ageing Main Stand, Platt Lane and Kippax terrace. It boasted a new electronic scoreboard in tradition with the stand it replaced but the stand lacked atmosphere.

While the New Kippax was being built, many of the more vociferous supporters were temporarily housed in the North Stand and, with no space for away fans, it took on a new, vibrant life. Many remained in the stand when the Kippax was completed and as the Blues go into their final season at Maine Road, the North Stand, which also houses around 2,500 visiting supporters, is largely recognised as the liveliest and loudest of the four stands.

O

OAKES, ALAN — 1958 TO 1976

Appearances: 665 + 4 as a substitute
Goals: 34
Position: Half-back
Born: Winsford

City's Mr Dependable, Alan Oakes gave solid, reliable service to the club for over 18 years. He is the record appearance holder and is unlikely ever to be surpassed with 676 competitive starts under his belt. He was a quiet unassuming player who was criminally overlooked at all international levels for England, due almost entirely to the fact that he played a similar role to Bobby Moore. His cousin was another unsung hero from the same era, Glyn Pardoe. Best known for his surging runs from deep and penetrative passes, Oakes was happy to let others take the limelight yet was vital to the glorious all-conquering Mercer side of the late 1960s and the management showed their faith in Oakes by naming him captain for the 1968–69 season.

He was also named in the original squad of 40 for the 1970 World Cup but missed out on a trip to Mexico when the final squad was named. Consistent right up until the end of his days at Maine Road, he was named Player of the Year in 1975, just a year before he left City for Chester in 1976, where he eventually became player-manager of the club after adding another 211 appearances to his career total. He had made over 900 appearances for the Blues at all levels. His son, Michael Oakes, is Wolves' first-choice goalkeeper.

OASIS

Burnage-born brothers Noel and Liam Gallagher, the driving forces behind rock band Oasis, are famously also lifelong City supporters. During the mid-1990s, the band and the club seemed to merge into one with the same style of branding, followers and fashion. City ran out to 'Roll with It' for a while and it was rare for an Oasis record not to be playing during the half-time break at Maine Road. The Gallaghers were happy to promote the Blues by wearing the new shirts or mentioning their allegiances whenever they could during interviews. On at least two occasions the lads have walked out on to the pitch to the acclaim of the City faithful. Noel even has 'MCFC' on one of his guitars.

In 1995 the City support turned their classic 'Wonderwall' into a swooning tribute to Kinkladze and, wait for it, Alan Ball, though Noel commented that he wasn't too happy about the Alan Ball verse. The culmination of mutual admiration between band and club reached epidemic proportions when Oasis played several sold-out gigs at Maine Road. Once touted as potential owners, Noel recently agreed during the Division One Championship celebrations to record a version of 'Blue Moon' at Kevin Keegan's request but later said that he'd been drunk and would probably have agreed to anything!

OMEROD, SAM
Manager from 1895 to 1902
League Record: Games: 226 W: 108 D: 47 L: 71 F: 419 A: 315

Even Kevin Keegan would have been proud of Sam Omerod's attacking style during his reign as City manager and there were 3.25 goals scored on average in every match while he was in charge. His first season saw the Blues qualify for the Test matches – a very early version of the play-offs – but City failed to win promotion. Three years later and Omerod celebrated taking the club into the First Division for the very first time. His side had an imposing, physical defence while having a quite breathtaking, lethal attack, which included Meredith and Gillespie.

In the club's first season in the top flight, City finished seventh – higher than any other Lancashire team – and Omerod was given the dubious moniker of 'The Wizard of Longsight'! Things were about to get worse for Omerod and the following season saw City relegated. Angry shareholders voiced concern over a £1,000 debt and the manager and board were replaced. Omerod had still played an important part of the next stage of City's development and laid the foundations for future success.

ONE-MATCH WONDERS
There have been 53 'one-match wonders' for City since the club first formed. The majority of these were First World War when things were slightly different regarding who played where and how often. The list is composed of players who started a League or cup match for the Blues on one occasion only. Substitutes are under another section. The most notable of these singular stars is probably former Northern Irish international Neil Lennon. The flame-haired midfielder played his one and only game for City's first team on 30 April 1988 as a promising, inexperienced teenager. City won the game away to Birmingham

City 3–0. Lennon moved to Leicester City and later to Celtic for £5 million.

Five of the 53 managed to find the net on their only appearance. B. Campbell scored two goals in a 12–0 FA Cup qualifier in 1890 and never played for the club again. A. Spittle was the second to achieve the feat in 1894 as City lost 2–1 at home to Crewe Alexandra. J. Dennison bagged two goals during a 5–2 win over Blackburn Rovers in 1904. S. Eyres scored a goal in the final game of the 1906–07 season in a 3–2 home defeat by Sunderland and never played again and F. Gorringe scored twice in a 7–3 home win over Barnsley on 2 January 1928.

O'NEILL, MARTIN – 1981 TO 1982
Appearances: 15 + 1 as a substitute
Goals: 0
Position: Midfielder
Born: Kilrea, Northern Ireland

Few of the club's younger fans will be aware that Celtic boss Martin O'Neill was once a City player. Even those who were aware could be forgiven for forgetting that he ever was – so brief was his stay at Maine Road. John Bond signed the Northern Ireland player from Norwich City for a fee of £275,000, but it was with Nottingham Forest that O'Neill really made his name. Signed to add much-needed experience to a youthful midfield, he played only a dozen games for City before returning to Carrow Road after just a few months. The Blues had won five, drawn five and lost six with O'Neill in the side and he later went on to manage Wycombe Wanderers, Leicester City and, of course, Celtic with enormous success.

ONES THAT GOT AWAY
City are quite rightly proud of their youth system, which has brought countless youngsters through to the first team and saved the club millions in the process. But some talented youngsters have slipped through the net. Ryan Giggs is probably one of the most famous – it's difficult to imagine that he could have been starring for the Blues all these years instead of United. Ashley Ward, John Beresford, Gary Bennett, Danny Allsopp, Chris Greenacre, Paul Warhurst, Neil Lennon and maybe Chris Killen are several others who left the club for small fees to carve out successful careers elsewhere.

OWEN, GARY – 1974 TO 1979
Appearances: 122 + 2 as a substitute
Goals: 23
Position: Midfielder
Born: Whiston

Skilful midfielder Gary Owen won ten England Under-21 caps while at Maine Road and formed an excellent partnership with Asa Hartford, Paul Power and Peter Barnes. Together they formed the rock of City's title challenge of 1976–77 and 1977–78 when the club finished second and fourth respectively. Owen was a skilful playmaker, predominantly left-footed, with the ability to create chances out of nothing. He made his League debut against Wolves at Maine Road with City running out 3–2 winners. He kept his place for the next game, a 1–0 defeat at QPR, but only played twice more that season.

With Colin Bell absent due to a long-term injury, Tony Book decided not to buy another player but to give the young Owen a sustained run in the first team. He was recalled for the visit of West Ham and marked his appearance with a goal in a 4–2 victory. It was his only League goal of the season but he went on to miss only four games, clocking up 30 full starts. He cemented his place the following season by making 33 starts and, with his confidence in front of goal growing, scored 7 goals.

His third full season was to be his last and most productive for City. He started 34 games and took over penalty-taking duties and, by the end of the season, he finished with 11 goals and was joint top scorer with Mick Channon – a tremendous feat for a midfielder. Malcolm Allison's Second Coming was to signal Owen's exit and the devastated youngster was sold to West Bromwich Albion in May 1979. He now commentates on the Blues as Century FM's resident City expert.

OWN GOALS
Dave Ewing holds an unenviable record that will probably never be beaten. With ten own goals during his playing career, nobody even comes close to taking away his unwanted crown. John McTavish scored three past his own goalkeeper in just four games in November 1959 – how many black cats must he have run over to earn such rotten luck? Derek Kevan and Steve Mackenzie both scored at either end for the Blues; Kevan's came in a 4–3 defeat at Charlton in 1964 and Mackenzie's dubious double was at Middlesbrough in 1980, with the game ending 2–2.

The most famous own goal of all was also one of the most painful. Tommy Hutchison's flying header had put City 1–0 up in the 1981 FA Cup final but he deflected a Spurs free kick past Joe Corrigan to become the only man to score at both ends in an FA Cup final – a record that still stands. The Blues' history might have been different had Dave Watson not bizarrely slid the ball past his own goalkeeper with two minutes to go of a crucial game against Liverpool. City had been leading 1–0 and the Merseyside Reds ended up winning the title five months later by a point over the Blues. The positions would have been reversed but for the fateful Watson error and City would have been champions for the second time in eight years.

Finally, the most entertaining of all the own goals ever scored came in a non-competitive match for Bert Trautmann's testimonial. A combined City and United team took on an International XI before a crowd of more than 48,000. United's Maurice Setters, playing in sky blue for the first and only time, received the ball and headed towards his own goal, kept by Trautmann. Setters then promptly tucked it past the German legend and ran off celebrating. His explanation was that he'd never managed to score against Trautmann before and this match represented his last opportunity. 'I couldn't resist it!' he added.

P

PALMER, ROGER – 1975 TO 1980

Appearances: 29 + 11 as a substitute
Goals: 11
Position: Striker
Born: Manchester

Roger Palmer proudly walked out with Manchester City for the 1974 League Cup final against Wolves – but only as a ball boy. Three years later and he would be making his full League debut for the club. An instinctive striker with a laid-back approach that was often misinterpreted as laziness, Roger Palmer's strike rate while at Maine Road was impressive enough. A prolific poacher for the youth and reserve sides – he finished top scorer when the Blues lifted the Central League trophy for the first time in 1977 – Palmer finally broke into the first team in December 1977 as cover for the injured Dennis Tueart. Though he started only four times, he scored three goals, including a double at Newcastle United and the winner at home to Ipswich Town.

Perhaps a little unfortunate to have so many quality forwards ahead of him, Palmer took his chances whenever they came and his first three appearances of the 1978–79 season yielded three goals making his record six in seven starts – an excellent return from the youngster. Many felt he'd done enough to win an extended run with the seniors but it was never to be, and in 1980, with 11 goals from 29 games, Palmer was sold cheaply to Oldham Athletic. He became an almost legendary figure to the Latics fans, scoring goals with the frequency his ailing ex-club desperately needed throughout the 1980s. On a cold day, if the wind is blowing in the right direction, you can still hear the Latics fans singing 'Ooh, Roger Palmer, ooh, Roger Palmer!' around Boundary Park.

PARDOE, GLYN – 1961 TO 1976

Appearances: 374 + 2 as a substitute
Goals: 22
Position: Full-back
Born: Winsford

Though Glyn Pardoe played in almost every position for City during his long career at the club, it was left-back that was his preferred role. The cousin of another City great, Alan Oakes, Pardoe was also part of the great City side of the late 1960s and early 1970s. Like Oakes, he'd joined from Mid-Cheshire Boys and was born in Winsford. Pardoe famously scored the winner in the 1970 League Cup final, one of 22 goals during his time at Maine Road.

He was desperately unlucky when he broke his leg in the Manchester derby later that same year and never managed to fully reclaim his left-back berth owing to the form of a young Willie Donachie. The holder of two unique records being the youngest player to ever play for the Blues aged just 15, Pardoe was also the Blues' first ever substitute for the opening game of the 1965–66 season. He later became a hugely successful youth-team coach at Maine Road following his retirement in 1976, serving the Blues with equal loyalty and dedication.

PARLANE, DEREK – 1983 TO 1985

Appearances: 51 + 1 as a substitute
Goals: 23
Position: Striker
Born: Helensburgh

Former Rangers and Scotland striker Derek Parlane was still a Leeds United player when Billy McNeill signed him on a free transfer in 1983. He'd been on loan with Hong Kong club Bulova, and his career seemed to be steadily winding down. McNeill tied up the Parlane deal and five days later paid £30,000 to Belgian club SC Lokeren for another Scottish forward, Jim Tolmie. As sometimes happens in football, the two new forwards clicked and formed a lethal partnership for City during the 1983–84 season. Parlane made a scoring debut in a 2–0 opening-day win over Crystal Palace and by the seventh game of the season he had scored seven goals and his new partner Jim Tolmie had scored five. Parlane hit two trebles within five weeks – one in the League against Blackburn Rovers and another in the League Cup against Torquay United – and by the 12th game of the season, he'd hit a dozen goals.

The Blues' early form began to dip and though they were in the hunt for promotion for most of the season, they hit a bad patch at the wrong time and took just 5 points from the last 18. Parlane had scored 19 goals and finished top scorer. The following season began even more impressively for him as he scored four in the opening three games but that was about as good as it was going to get for him. New signings Tony Cunningham, Gordon Smith and Jim Melrose made competition for places fierce and Parlane would play only four more times before joining Swansea in January 1985.

PARLBY, JOSHUA
Manager from 1893 to 1895
League Record: Games: 58 W: 22 D: 5 L: 31 F: 129 A: 143

Joshua Parlby became the first secretary to be paid by City and received a weekly wage of £2.50 for the privilege. He couldn't have taken the job at a worse time and the club endured a crippling defection of players in 1894 and were then declared bankrupt. Fireside stories would grow about Parlby and his 'ways', and one of them was smuggling players on to trains for away games because they couldn't afford the travel expenses. He would later successfully secure City's place as a League side when he argued for re-election just a few months after being declared insolvent.

He enjoyed a good wrangle, whether it was legal or otherwise, and this energetic, large man who bore a resemblance to Sir James Robertson Justice from the *Carry On* movies played a crucial part in making Manchester City the club it is today. He garnered enough local support to lay to rest Ardwick FC and form the slick, new Manchester City Football Club Limited. He became a pub landlord in 1895 but still served City intermittently as a director or in an advisory capacity.

PARTNERSHIPS
Some of the best striking partnerships City have had are as follows (goals in all competitions):

    58 – Roberts (30) and Browell (28) – 1925–26
    57 – Goater (32) and Huckerby (25) – 2001–02
    57 – Kevan (36) and Murray (21) – 1963–64
    54 – Doherty (32) and Brook (22) – 1936–37
    52 – Meredith (22) and Gillespie (30) – 1902–03
    52 – Johnson (38) and Brook (14) – 1928–29
    52 – Tait (31) and Marshall (21) – 1929–30
    49 – Lee (35) and Bell (14) – 1971–72
    48 – Browell (31) and Barnes (17) – 1920–21
    48 – Stewart (28) and Varadi (20) – 1987–88
    48 – Meredith (30) and Gillespie (18) – 1898–99

47 – Johnson (25) and Hicks (22) – 1926–27
47 – Halliday (32) and Marshall (15) – 1931–32
46 – Browell (26) and Barnes (20) – 1921–22
46 – Westcott (25) and Smith (21) – 1950–51
45 – Barnes (23) and Browell (22) – 1919–20
45 – Hayes (26) and McAdams (19) – 1957–58
44 – Roberts (32) and Johnson (12) – 1924–25

PAUL, ROY – 1950 TO 1957
Appearances: 293
Goals: 8
Position: Half-back
Born: Ton Pentre

Roy Paul was Manchester City's very own Captain Fantastic. An inspirational figure to colleagues and fans alike, he captained the Blues to the 1955 FA Cup final, where they lost to Newcastle United and then vowed to return to win the cup the next year. The former coal miner drove the Blues on to the 1956 FA Cup final and this time City were victorious over Birmingham City.

Paul had arrived from Swansea Town in 1950 and was versatile in that he could play anywhere across the back line. A true 'Roy of the Rovers'-type player, Paul is one of the greatest captains the club has ever had and he was only the second Welshman to skipper the Blues to FA Cup glory – the first being Billy Meredith. Paul left for Worcester City in June 1957 after clocking up nearly 300 matches for City. He died in the spring of 2002.

PENALTIES
Ask most City fans and they will tell you they just don't trust one of their players to score from the spot in open play. By tracing back through history the origins of uncertainty are easier to understand and by passing on the fear, generation after generation have inherited their parents' pessimism.

For instance, in 1912, City managed to miss three penalties in one game! Irvine Thornley and Eli Fletcher (twice) were the guilty parties and the game with Newcastle ended 1–1. It was back to St James' Park for another unfortunate day from the spot, this time for Billy Austin, when in 1926, the Blues, who needed a point to avoid relegation after five successive wins, missed from the spot and lost 3–2 and were subsequently relegated. On a brighter note, Ken Barnes scored a hat-trick of penalties against Everton in December 1957 in a 6–2 victory and scored another in the return fixture at Goodison Park.

Franny Lee is the club's most successful penalty-taker ever with 46 spot-kicks successfully dispatched in his time at Maine Road. Lee won many of the penalties himself and earned the nickname 'Lee One Pen'. Dennis Tueart scored an impressive 24 times from the spot, including several double strikes.

Keith Curle scored nine times from the spot for City and Gio Kinkladze scored on seven occasions. Kevin Bond scored penalties in the 44th and 45th minutes of a home game against Huddersfield Town in April 1984 to bring the scores level at 2–2, but the Blues still lost 3–2. Kevin Reeves scored City's solitary Wembley penalty, awarded during 90 minutes in the 1981 FA Cup final replay with Spurs to put his side 2–1 up in the second half. Shaun Goater and Neil McNab have both missed last-minute kicks that would have turned draws into victories.

There was a controversial incident in March 1960 when Denis Law made his home debut against West Ham. Trailing 1–0, Law was fouled in the box and the Blues were awarded a penalty. Ken Barnes placed the ball on the spot, ran up and tapped it forward for Billy McAdams to run from behind and tuck the ball away. The referee gave the goal but amidst furious protests from the Hammers, he consulted a linesman and ordered the kick to be retaken. Barnes stepped up again and missed! Fortunately, City went on to win 3–1.

The list of the most successful takers is:

	SEASON	LEAGUE	CUP	TOTAL
1. Francis Lee	1967–74	34	12	46
2. Eric Brook	1928–40	29	6	35
3. Dennis Tueart	1974–78 & 1980–83	18	6	24
4. Tom Johnson	1919–30	20	1	21
5. Ken Barnes	1950–61	13	–	13
6. Keith Curle	1991–95	9	1	10
6. Gary Owen	1976–79	9	1	10
6. Neil McNab	1983–87	8	2	10
6. Don Revie	1951–56	8	2	10
9. Mark Ward	1989–91	9	–	9
9. Tom Browell	1913–26	8	1	9

☆

PENALTY SHOOT-OUTS

The dramatic 1999 play-off victory over Gillingham was the most famous penalty shoot-out City have ever featured in. With a place in Division One awaiting the winners, Kevin Horlock put City 1–0 ahead from the spot and after the Gills missed their first effort, Paul Dickov stepped up. His shot hit one post, rolled agonisingly along the line behind Vince Bartram and hit the other post before bouncing to safety. The Gills missed their second and Terry Cooke safely dispatched City's third penalty for a 2–0 lead. The Gills made it 2–1 and Richard Edghill stepped up for the crucial fourth. He confidently

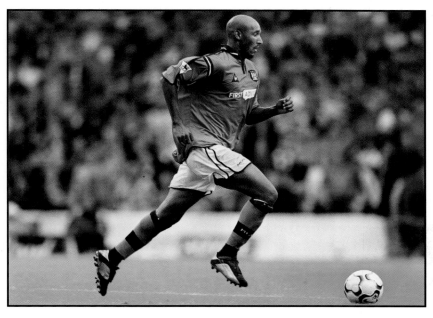

Nicolas Anelka — at £13 million, the most expensive signing ever for City

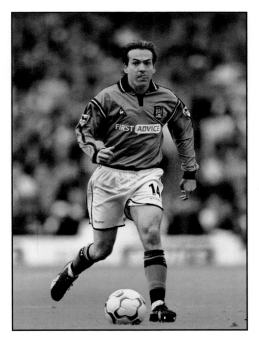

Eyal Berkovic — Israeli midfielder who formed a fantastic partnership with Benarbia

Mike Doyle — 1962–78. Tough-
tackling former City captain

Ali Benarbia — sheer class.
Algerian midfielder who became
captain in 2002/03

Maurizio Gaudino — German loan star
who left a lasting impression

Shaun Goater & Paul Dickov —
two of the most popular players
to ever wear a blue shirt

Tony Book in his playing days

Gerry Gow — tough, uncompromising
Scottish midfielder who became a terrace
hero

Denis Law on the ball shortly before his
retirement

Joe Royle — the striker
who later became manager

Alex Williams — youth team product
who emerged to succeed Joe Corrigan

Gio Kinkladze — Georgian genius. The most skilful player to ever wear a City shirt

Paul Lake — Rolls Royce of a footballer whose career was cruelly cut short by injury

Alan Oakes — 1958–76. Played over a
thousand times for City at all levels

Stuart Pearce — former City,
England and Forest skipper who is
now a coach at Maine Road

Mike Summerbee — legendary former City and England winger.

David White — the free-scoring forward who forged a lethal partnership with Niall Quinn

Johnny Marr — iconic former Smiths and Electronic guitarist and longstanding City fan.
© Karon Malcom

Mark Radcliffe and Marc
Riley — the true saviours
of Radio One and season
ticket holders at Maine
Road.

struck the ball against the underside of the bar for 3–1. Nicky Weaver saved the next penalty and City were promoted.

The only other occasions the Blues have been involved in shoot-outs were in 1997 when Blackpool and City each won their home leg of the Worthington Cup ties by 1–0 and couldn't be separated in extra time, but City eventually lost 4–2 on penalties. An even more dramatic shoot-out occurred in 1981, once again in the League Cup. After beating Stoke City 2–0 at Maine Road, the Blues lost the return by the same score and so began an epic shoot-out for the right to progress into the third round. Both teams were competent from the spot and with scores locked at 8–8, Joe Corrigan saved well to present substitute Aage Hareide the chance of being a hero. The Norwegian stepped up and coolly stroked the ball home for a 9–8 win.

PHELAN, TERRY – 1992 TO 1996
Appearances: 121 + 1 as a substitute
Goals: 3
Position: Full-back
Born: Manchester

The protracted negotiations involving the transfer of Eire defender Terry Phelan caused him to miss the first three games of the 1992–93 season. Peter Reid had returned to Wimbledon and paid £2.5 million for the services of the Manchester-born defender after a year earlier buying Keith Curle in a similar deal. Phelan settled in well at Maine Road and was popular with the City fans that serenaded the defender with their own version of 'You've Lost That Loving Feeling', re-titled 'We've Got That Terry Phelan (and he's fast, fast, fast, whoah-whoa-whoa)'. Quick and lithe, Phelan and Curle were among the fastest defenders in the Premiership. Phelan also played in the Republic of Ireland's 1994 World Cup squad. His goal against Spurs in the 1993 FA Cup quarter-final was one of the best by a City player for many years, yet he ended on the losing side and crowd disturbances rendered it largely forgotten. Dogged by off-pitch problems, Phelan finally left the Blues in 1996 for a fraction of the fee he had cost City.

PHILLIPS, DAVID – 1984 TO 1986
Appearances: 94
Goals 13
Position: Midfielder
Born: Wegberg, Germany

Welsh international David Phillips is said to have asked why his personalised shirt had been spelled wrong – City's sponsors at the time were Dutch giants Philips, so enough said on the matter! Phillips was equally at home at full-back or in midfield and possessed a fantastically accurate shot, which won a couple of Goal of the Month competitions on *Match of the Day*. Born in Germany, Phillips signed for £100,000 from Plymouth Argyle in 1984 and was an ever-present in his first season at Maine Road, finishing joint top League scorer with 12 goals – at one point scoring eight times in a 13-match period, all of which helped City gain promotion. His double strike in the promotion clincher against Charlton will be long remembered. Having won 10 caps for Wales while at Maine Road, the dependable Phillips was disappointingly sold to Coventry after City struggled back in the First Division.

PHILLIPS, MARTIN – 1995 TO 1997
Appearances: 3 + 13 as a substitute
Goals: 0
Position: Winger
Born: Exeter

Alan Ball purchased young Martin Phillips from one of his former clubs, Exeter City, and proudly announced to the football world, willingly, that Phillips would be Britain's first £10 million footballer.

He showed a few flashes of talent on the odd occasion he was used, usually from the bench, but Ball's words of wisdom may have had an adverse affect on the youngster. 'Buster' Phillips was on his way back to Exeter City after less than two years, having failed to break into the senior squad at Maine Road, and the prospects of him being a £10 million player decrease by the day.

PLASTIC PITCHES
Like the majority of footballers, City players were glad to see the demise of the dreaded 'plastic pitch', or Astroturf if you want be all Stars and Stripes about it. Of the four clubs that laid this monstrosity of a playing surface (QPR, Luton Town, Preston North End and Oldham Athletic), City played three out of the 'Plastic Quartet' in League matches. The Blues drew 0–0 at QPR in 1985–86 and lost 1–0 the following season. Four visits to Kenilworth Road, home of Luton Town, produced two draws and two defeats and the curse continued with a 1–1 draw with Oldham Atlhletic in 1987–88. It would take the debutant Gary Megson to lay the plastic bogey with the only goal of the following season's fixture between City and Latics. One win in eight games on the all-weather pitches – thank God, they're confined to history, if only because they no longer give players a valid reason to wear ladies' stockings for the afternoon.

PLAYED FOR CITY AND UNITED

The highest-profile players to have played for both Manchester clubs at one level or another are as follows: Billy Meredith, Eric Westwood, Denis Law, Peter Barnes, Wyn Davies, Brian Kidd, John Gidman, Tony Coton, Andy Hill, Carlos Nash, Shaun Goater, Terry Cooke and Peter Schmeichel.

PLAYER OF THE YEAR

The list of Player of the Year awards that began following the completion of the 1966–67 season, as voted by the club's supporters, is as follows:

1966–67: Tony Book
1967–68: Colin Bell
1968–69: Glyn Pardoe
1969–70: Francis Lee
1970–71: Mike Doyle
1971–72: Mike Summerbee
1972–73: Mike Summerbee
1973-74: Mike Doyle
1974–75: Alan Oakes
1975–76: Joe Corrigan
1976–77: Dave Watson
1977–78: Joe Corrigan
1978–79: Asa Hartford
1979–80: Joe Corrigan
1980–81: Paul Power
1981–82: Tommy Caton
1982–83: Kevin Bond
1983–84: Mick McCarthy
1984–85: Paul Power
1985–86: Kenny Clements
1986–87: Neil McNab
1987–88: Steve Redmond
1988–89: Neil McNab
1989–90: Colin Hendry
1990–91: Niall Quinn
1991–92: Tony Coton
1992–93: Garry Flitcroft
1993–94: Tony Coton
1994–95: Uwe Rosler
1995–96: Gio Kinkladze
1996–97: Gio Kinkladze
1997–98: Michael Brown

1998–99: Gerard Wiekens
1999–00: Shaun Goater
2000–01: Danny Tiatto
2001–02: Ali Benarbia

POINTS

City's last two stays in Division One have produced record point hauls. In the 1999–2000 season a grand total of 89 points were gathered on the way to the Blues finishing runners-up to Charlton Athletic, while in 2001–02, Kevin Keegan's men went ten better with a new club record – one of many achieved that season – of 99 points from 46 games. The fewest points a City side has ever managed were 18 from 28 games in 1893–94.

POLLOCK, JAMIE – 1997 TO 2000

Appearances: 59 + 11 as a substitute
Goals: 5
Position: Midfielder
Born: Stockton-on-Tees

Jamie Pollock's time at Maine Road was not a particularly enjoyable experience for the player but he never gave less than his all during his time with the club. In the side one moment, out the next; installed as captain – a role that he seemed to have been born for – then demoted for disciplinary reasons – it was hard to keep up. Pollock's own goal against relegation rivals QPR in 1998 led to him being voted by the Rangers' fans as one of the most important players in QPR's history! Rangers survived and the Blues went down.

The tough-tackling former Middlesbrough and Bolton player also had weight problems and shed a number of pounds during City's Division Two days, but it wasn't enough for Joe Royle. He had targeted Alfie Haaland from Leeds United and his style was too similar to Pollock's for there to be enough room for them both. Royle sold Pollock to Crystal Palace in 2000 after the player had been part of a triumphant squad that won promotion back to the Premiership.

POWER, PAUL – 1973 TO 1986

Appearances: 430 + 9 as a substitute
Goals: 35
Position: Defender/Midfielder
Born: Manchester

Left-sided defender or midfielder, Paul Power was possibly one of the hardest-working City players ever to pull on a blue shirt. He captained City for many years and was one of the most respected professionals in the game. Though he wasn't a prolific scorer, he will always be best remembered for the wonderful solo goal he scored against AC Milan in 1978 and a most beautiful curling free kick against Ipswich in the 1981 FA Cup semi-final. These were two goals any top-class striker would have been proud to claim. His services did not go unnoticed by the club's supporters who twice voted him Player of the Year and he captained the Blues in three Wembley Cup finals – twice against Spurs in the FA Cup and once against Chelsea in the Full Members'. An intelligent and thoughtful man, he qualified in law after completing his studies in 1975. He was sold to Everton by manager McNeill in June 1986 and waited only 12 months before picking up his first League Championship medal with the Toffees. He now coaches the Academy youngsters at Maine Road and has lost none of his enthusiasm for football.

POYSER, GEORGE
Manager from 1963 to 1965
League Record: Games: 84 W: 34 D: 19 L: 31 F: 147 A: 128

The 80,000 miles spent scouting in one year as City's assistant manager obviously left a favourable impression on the board as they invited George Poyser to take over as manager from Les McDowall in 1963. He had been alongside McDowall for six years and seemed the obvious replacement but, popular as he was, Poyser could not arrest the club's alarming decline. Yet, things had looked promising at the beginning of 1964, with a League Cup semi-final against Stoke City and the Blues were also in a comfortable position in the League.

Exercising superb judgement in the transfer market, his two new signings Derek Kevan and Jimmy Murray would ultimately crack in 51 goals between them in the League. But a loss to Stoke in the League Cup, a third-round exit to Swindon Town in the FA Cup and critical defeats by promotion rivals Leeds United and Sunderland effectively ended the Blues' season as serious challengers on all fronts within a short space of time.

Poyser's second term at the helm again saw him invest wisely with Dave Bacuzzi and Johnny Crossan arriving at Maine Road, but with a long list of injured stars and home gates as low as 8,015, City had dipped to the lowest point in their history. Poyser resigned at Easter and the club finished 11th, while across the city, United were lifting the First Division Championship. They always rub it in, don't they?

PREMIER LEAGUE

The formation of the English Premier League in time for the 1992–93 season coincided with a downward spiral in the fortunes of Manchester City that have taken a full decade to put right. Peter Reid guided his team to a respectable ninth place after finishing fifth the previous two seasons in the old Division One but was then sacked the following season. Brian Horton found the going tough in his first season in the Maine Road hot seat, with City ending in 16th place and in the 1994–95 campaign, City finished one place lower, costing the unfortunate Horton his job. Alan Ball did worse still, managing the club during their first relegation from the Premiership by finishing one place lower still, in 18th. It was five seasons before Joe Royle took the club back to the top League but, alas, only for one season. Expectations are high following promotion back to the Premiership with Keegan's talented side, equipped for what every City fan hopes will be a long and fruitful stay.

PROMOTION

City have won promotion 12 times, going up as champions on seven occasions and once via the play-offs. The first occasion was achieved in 1898–99 when City ventured out of Division Two for the very first time after clinching their first piece of silverware and wing-wizard Billy Meredith scored 29 goals in 33 starts. Four years later, City were champions again of Division Two for the 1902–03 season following relegation the season before. They achieved the feat for a third time in 1909–10, winning the Second Division after being relegated the season before. The roller-coaster ride had begun barely 20 years into the club's life.

City's fourth second-tier championship was in 1927–28, they added a fifth in 1946–47 and in 1950–51 City were runners-up, by way of a change. Joe Mercer guided the team to its sixth Division Two title in 1965–66 and two years after they won the Division One Championship. Dramatic last days are nothing new to supporters of Manchester City and in 1984–85 the Blues needed a win against Charlton to fend off Portsmouth's late challenge. In a fantastic display, City had rattled in five without reply with just over an hour gone and the 5–1 final score ensured promotion. In 1988–89 City finished second with only a point needed from their final match. Trailing 1–0, Trevor Morley slid home the equaliser with minutes to spare and City were once more back with the big boys.

Yet more last-day drama with the penalty shoot-out win over Gillingham in 1999 and the 4–1 win at Blackburn the following season gave City back-to-back promotions for the first time in their history and 2001–02 gave them their most recent promotion and seventh second-tier championship.

PUBS

Travel to an away match to watch City and it's a fair bet you will see all pubs on the approach to the ground swamped with Blues enjoying a pre-match pint. The Blue Army is always happy to mix and chat with home supporters and the atmosphere is almost always friendly. For home games there are several particular favourite watering holes for City fans. The Gardeners Arms and The Osborne on Summer Place to the rear of the Kippax are two of the most popular, while The Claremont, The Welcome, The Beehive and The Friendship can be found full of home fans on match days. The Parkside is another favourite and is the closest pub to the ground.

Q

QUICKEST GOAL

Niall Quinn's goal after just 30 seconds against Bolton on 30 March 1996 is the quickest goal on record. The Premiership fixture ended 1–1.

QUINN, NIALL – 1990 TO 1996

Appearances: 219
Goals: 78
Position: Striker
Born: Dublin

The 'Big Irishman', as Niall Quinn came to be affectionately known at Maine Road, could hardly have played better during his six-year spell with City. He joined from Arsenal for a bargain £800,000 and was to become one of the most popular players to wear the No. 9 shirt for many years with a series of skilful and intelligent play that belied his size. Quinn's deft flicks, chips and cushioned headers were backed by excellent control and he was often a valuable extra defender at set-pieces and corners. One abiding memory of 'Quinny' was the time he took over in goals during a home match with Derby County after Tony Coton had brought down Dean Saunders.

The referee elected to send Coton for an early bath and Quinn put on the green jersey. With the whole of Maine Road willing him on, he guessed right and saved the penalty from Saunders! His two goals in the final match of the same season relegated Sunderland, the club he would eventually join in 1996. Now nearing the end of an illustrious career, he commendably donated the entire proceeds of his testimonial – believed to have been around £1 million – to charity. An excellent servant for Manchester City and Ireland, he continues to receive a warm welcome on his returns to Maine Road with Sunderland.

R

RANSON, RAY – 1976 TO 1984 AND 1993
Appearances: 233 + 2 as a substitute
Goals: 1
Position: Full-back
Born: St Helens

Ray Ranson enjoyed eight years in a sky-blue shirt before leaving for Birmingham in 1984. A product of the youth system, he signed as an apprentice in 1976 and made his debut in a 0–0 draw at Nottingham Forest in 1978. Ranson played through City's most turbulent period of the late 1970s and early 1980s and was an accomplished defender who won several England Under-21 honours while at Maine Road. Four years with Birmingham City was followed by another five with Newcastle United and, in total, there was a nine-year gap before he played for City again. Blues' boss Peter Reid signed him on loan from the Magpies and he made his second debut for the club in a 4–2 win at Chelsea. He stayed for five months, adding a further 17 League appearances to make a total City career record of 233 starts. He joined Reading following his loan spell at Maine Road.

REDMOND, STEVE – 1985 TO 1992
Appearances: 283 + 4 as a substitute
Goals: 7
Position: Centre-back
Born: Liverpool

Steve Redmond chose City ahead of his boyhood favourites Liverpool for his apprenticeship and was rewarded by seven seasons in the heart of the Blues' defence. Captain of the all-conquering 1986 FA Youth Cup-winning team, Redmond smoothly moved to first-team duties later that year and took over the captain's armband from Kenny Clements in 1988, becoming the club's youngest ever skipper in the process.

International honours followed for the ice-cool Redmond, captaining the

England Under-21s and earning 14 caps, and also winning the Player of the Year award in his first season as skipper. Though not the most towering of defenders, Redmond was excellent in the air and confident on the ground in a period when City were bouncing between divisions and he'd had more partners than most defenders have in a career – a tribute to his ability and attitude.

REEVES, KEVIN – 1980 TO 1983
Appearances: 157 + 1 as a substitute
Goals: 39
Position: Striker
Born: Burley

The signing of England international Kevin Reeves generated much excitement among the City supporters as the young striker was regarded as hot property at the time. Costing £1.25 million from Norwich City, Malcolm Allison had signed the Blues' second million-pound star and, unlike Steve Daley, City's first seven-figure signing, Reeves had a proven track record at the highest level. It was ironic that six months after arriving at City, his old boss John Bond would be appointed as manager.

Not the quickest forward City have ever had, he was good in the air and had excellent control and good skill. He led the front-line intelligently yet rarely had a regular partner. Reeves played a big part in the Blues' successful FA Cup and League Cup runs of 1980–81, playing in all 13 cup ties and scoring 5 goals. His last of the season was an FA Cup final penalty at Wembley that looked to have been enough to win the trophy for his side. He finished having made 52 starts and with 17 goals scored.

For the 1981–82 campaign he had the classy Trevor Francis alongside him in attack. The pair inspired City to top the table after a memorable 3–1 Boxing Day win at Liverpool and this was followed up two days later by a 2–1 win over Wolves. Reeves was an ever-present for that season and added 13 League goals to his career total. Bond left for Burnley in January 1983 and City were relegated some months later. Reeves followed his old boss to Turf Moor later in the year and the former England international later joined the Clarets' coaching staff.

REFEREES
There is a feeling among City supporters that, for some reason, referees don't like the Blues very much. Maybe all teams feel the same, but there have been several very poor showings by officials involved at City matches over the past 30 years. George Courtney was never the most popular referee

and Peter Willis once had a pie thrown at his head after sending off a City player at Maine Road. He later commented that he didn't mind because the pie was quite tasty! Alan Wilkie would have received few Christmas cards after awarding a ridiculous penalty in a fifth-round FA Cup tie at Old Trafford.

He accused Frontzeck of pushing Roy Keane when clearly nothing illegal had happened. Wilkie was the referee that had sent Eric Cantona off against Crystal Palace previously and many Blues felt that City were paying penance for his guilty conscience. Mark Halsey is probably the only official that all City supporters would happily buy a pint for if they ever saw him out and about. His decision to allow the correct amount of injury time in the play-off final against Gillingham allowed the Blues to salvage a draw and then win promotion.

REID, NICKY – 1978 TO 1987

Appearances: 250 + 6 as a substitute
Goals: 2
Position: Centre-half
Born: Manchester

Nicky Reid was a local boy made good who rose through the junior City sides to eventually become skipper of the club that he supported as a boy. Born in Davyhulme, Reid was part of a hugely successful youth-team set-up that, at one point, resembled a conveyor belt of talent from youth to senior squad. He added six England Under-21 caps before he left City for Seattle Sounders in 1982, only to return to Maine Road five months later to continue his career with the Blues.

Reid was a tough, uncompromising player who led by example with crunching tackles and no-nonsense defending. A strong runner – he enjoyed a dribble when given the opportunity – he was moved from defence to midfield when John Bond signed his son Kevin, also a centre-back. The City faithful had a sit-down during one game to highlight support for Reid, who they felt was being compromised for the manager's son. He ultimately won back his position at the heart of the defence before he eventually moved to Blackburn Rovers on a free transfer.

REID, PETER – 1989 TO 1993 AND MANAGER FROM 1990 TO 1993

Appearances: 100 + 14 as a substitute
Goals: 2
Position: Midfielder
Born: Huyton
League Record as manager: Games: 115 W: 48 D: 28 L: 39 F: 166 A: 145

There are many comparisons that could be drawn between Peter Reid and Stuart Pearce – honesty, integrity, the will to win and respect from fellow professionals are just a few on a very long list. Reid had the natural leadership qualities that City desperately needed during the late 1980s and early 1990s. Though he may have had his best years elsewhere, notably at Everton and Bolton Wanderers, the gutsy little midfielder never gave less than his all for City and the fans loved him for it.

Reid held together a young midfield and influenced a side headed for relegation into a tight, no-frills outfit. He arrived on a free transfer from QPR and was immediately installed as player-coach by Howard Kendall. Reid seemed the natural successor to the man who signed him when his boss returned to Goodison Park and he became City's player-manager by popular demand, guiding them to successive fifth-placed finishes in the League.

Things turned sour for Reid when, it is alleged, the board asked him to dispense with the services of his coach Sam Ellis. Reid refused to be forced into a corner and was sacked as a result, loyally standing by Ellis. The football being played at the time was neither attractive nor entertaining and a move for Reid was probably best for everybody. He became Sunderland boss not long after and returned to City for striker Niall Quinn and is still the boss at the Stadium of Light, though the pressure is beginning to mount on the likeable scouser.

RELEGATION

City have been relegated 11 times – still fewer than many other sides with similar ages, but they've been relegated 5 times in the last 20 years. The very first time was in 1901–02 and again in 1908–09 – on each occasion the club bounced back immediately after one season in Division Two.

Two cruel ironies coupled the next two demotions, proving that City are incapable of an average, run-of-the-mill disappointing season. In 1925–26 City lost 3–2 and missed a penalty on the final day to Newcastle United after requiring a point to survive, and the two clubs beneath, Leeds and Burnley, both won, sending the Blues down. With 89 goals scored during the ill-fated campaign, City still hold the record for the greatest amount of goals scored for a relegated club.

Even more dramatically, City won the First Division Championship in

1936–37 and then were relegated the next season! Again, this had never happened before or since. Only City! Other occasions when the Blues slipped out of the top flight were the 1949–50 and 1962–63 seasons. Twice in the 1980s City went down. The first occasion was in 1982–83 when a Raddy Antic goal five minutes from time spared Luton Town and City slipped into the bottom three for the only time that season. In 1986–87 the club failed to win any of the 21 away games, again losing their top-flight status.

In 1995–96, City had fought back from 2–0 down against Liverpool to level the scores 2–2. Needing a win for probable safety, City wrongly believed the point would be enough and began to time waste in the corners instead of charging forward for a winner. For many, it was unforgivable and manager Alan Ball found the thin ice he'd been skating on had all but melted away. Arguably, the lowest point in the history of Manchester City came when, despite the final day 5–2 win at Stoke City, the Blues were relegated to Division Two, now the third tier of English football, for the very first time. Within three years, the Blues had been relegated from the Premiership! The 2000–01 relegation was the last and 11th occasion, and many are hopeful it will be the last for a very long time, but, with Manchester City, you can take nothing for granted.

REVIE, DON – 1951 TO 1956
Appearances: 177
Goals: 41
Position: Forward
Born: Middlesbrough

Signed for what was a substantial fee in 1951 – £25,000 – Don Revie played as a deep-lying centre-forward and therefore difficult to mark in the role which was dubbed the 'Revie Plan'. He was able to make goals for others and confuse the opposition defence, most of whom had never experienced a system such as this. It meant that he was hardly a prolific scorer for City and he netted only 41 in 177 games – just under one every four matches – but so effective was he in this original and thoughtful position that he helped City to successive FA Cup finals in 1955 and 1956. It also brought him to the attention of England and he won six full caps. He moved to Sunderland in November 1956 for £24,000 and went on to become player-manager of Leeds United, helping to transform a struggling Second Division team into an excellent side that performed well in the top league and in Europe. He became England boss but could not repeat his successes at club level and resigned in somewhat controversial circumstances. He died in May 1989.

ROBERTS, FRANK – 1922 TO 1929
Appearances: 237
Goals: 130
Position: Striker
Born: Sandbach

The £3,400 that City paid Bolton Wanderers for Frank Roberts was a huge amount at the time but the talented forward proved to be worth every penny as he banged in 130 goals in 237 games. He won his first England cap two years after signing (he would win another three in total) scoring 32 goals in 39 League games in his third season with the club. He added a further nine goals during City's 1925–26 journey to the FA Cup final, eventually losing to Bolton Wanderers, Roberts' former side. He had proved that he was among the best strikers in the country at the time with a total of 30 out of the 89 scored that season. With Tom Johnson and Horace Barnes up front as well, City powered to the Division Two Championship in 1927–28, with Roberts adding a further 20 goals in 29 matches. He left in June 1929 for Manchester Central, having well and truly left his mark in the history books of Manchester City.

ROBINSON, MICHAEL – 1979 TO 1980
Appearances: 34 + 1 as a substitute
Goals: 9
Position: Striker
Born: Leicester

With barely over 12 months at Maine Road, Michael Robinson could justifiably say that he was never given enough time to settle with City and therefore unable to perform to the best of his ability. Malcolm Allison made the 21-year-old Robinson one of his first purchases following his return as manager. He paid Preston North End £765,000 for the youngster, who had averaged exactly one goal every three games for the Deepdale side.

The highlight of his brief stay was an excellent low drive in the Manchester derby to seal a 2–0 win over United but with a staggering 11 strike partners throughout the season, it's no wonder Robinson only hit nine goals in his 29 League starts. He moved to Brighton in July 1980 and later played for Liverpool, QPR and Spanish outfit Osasuna. He had won 23 caps for Eire in total and is now a well-known sports commentator on Spanish television. Scorchio!

ROSLER, UWE – 1994 TO 1998
Appearances: 165
Goals: 64
Position: Striker
Born: Attenburg, Germany

Crowd favourite Uwe Rosler – 'Der Bomber' – was, ironically, a typically English centre-forward whose bustling energetic style made his £500,000 fee from FC Nurnberg look like peanuts after finishing top scorer in three of four full seasons with the Blues. His partnership with Paul Walsh was particularly profitable, especially when serviced by a constant stream of inviting crosses by Peter Beagrie. Rosler was lethal in the air and went on to win caps for Germany after winning several from East Germany prior to his arrival in England. He returned home after City were relegated to Division Two but failed to repeat the heroics he showed while at Maine Road and recently had a spell with Southampton.

ROYLE, JOE – 1974 TO 1977 AND MANAGER FROM 1998 TO 2001
Appearances: 118 + 2 as a substitute
Goals: 31
Position: Striker
Born: Liverpool
League Record as manager: Games: 145 W: 61 D: 40 L: 44 F: 211 A: 160

Signed from Everton on Christmas Eve 1974 for £200,000, Joe Royle became an integral part of Tony Book's successful mid-1970s side, leading the line bravely and often being the foil for Dennis Tueart or Brian Kidd. He made his debut on Boxing Day, two days later, and was part of the side beaten 4–1 by Liverpool. He finished the season with just 1 goal from 16 games. The 1975–76 season would prove far better for the bustling forward as he scored 12 goals in the League and played a huge part in the Blues' successful League Cup campaign by scoring six goals along the way to the final.

Never a prolific striker, Royle ended with a total of nine goals the following term as City lost out on the First Division title by a single point. The arrival of Mike Channon from Southampton seemed to signal the end for Joe and he was loaned out to Bristol City. Just four days later, he made a dream debut by scoring an amazing four goals against Middlesbrough. If the Bristol club had needed any more convincing, then Royle could have done little more to oblige and the Ashton Gate side snapped him up for £90,000.

Royle later became manager of Oldham Athletic and turned them from annual Second Division strugglers into a team that became known for their giant killing acts at Boundary Park and featured in several exciting cup runs.

He took them into the top flight before being recruited by his former club Everton to help stave off relegation. Adopting the now famous 'Dogs of War' approach, Royle guided the Toffees to safety and an FA Cup final but couldn't take them any further in the League.

In 1998 he took charge of City and hopes were high that Division Two football could be avoided, but it wasn't to be. Though he seemed to have arrived with time to save the club, City were still relegated and Royle and his assistant Willie Donachie began to trim the unusually large squad and build a new one from the ashes. Gio Kinkladze was sold to Ajax for £5.5 million while the likes of Andy Morrison, Ian Bishop and Shaun Goater were all recruited for less than half a million pounds. Royle had the spine around which he could build a side.

City could only manage the play-offs and eventually overcame Gillingham to win promotion at the first attempt. Even better was to follow as the Blues made it back-to-back promotion for the first time by finishing runners-up to Charlton Athletic. Royle was a hero and could do little wrong in the supporters' eyes. With the likes of George Weah and Paulo Wanchope signed during the summer of 2000, the Blues faced up to life in the Premiership with confidence.

Nine months later and City had been relegated. The warnings had been there for all to see during the 2000–01 season but Royle's failure to read them led to questions being asked about his ability at the very top. Nobody could question his achievements in Division One but some of his judgements in the transfer market had been a little unconvincing. However City fans were willing to forgive the big man in lieu of how he had helped guide the club away from anonymity.

The City board were understandably disappointed that their manager had failed to keep them in the Premier League and at some of the dull football played during the season. After a meeting with City chairman David Bernstein, Royle was sacked – a difficult decision for Bernstein and a move that sent shock waves around football. Royle is yet to return to club management and is a regular commentator for televised football. A sad end for Big Joe, who it seemed could, at one point, do no wrong.

S

SAUNDERS, RON
Manager from 1973 to 1974
League Record: Games: 25 W: 8 D: 8 L: 9 F: 21 A: 26

With the persona of a somewhat dour individual it's hardly surprising that Ron Saunders never settled as manager at Maine Road, where a bright personality is almost mandatory to survive the role. His reign lasted just six months after he took over from Johnny Hart, who had to resign through ill-health, and though he took the Blues to the 1974 League Cup final, it had been Hart's side that had battled as far as the quarter-final stages. He'd arrived at the club just five days after resigning as Norwich City boss after an argument with Canaries' chairman Arthur Smith. With Hart stepping aside, Saunders couldn't have timed his departure from Carrow Road any better.

Saunders brought the exciting talents of Sunderland striker Dennis Tueart to Maine Road for a club record fee of £275,000 but his team played with little imagination and it became clear to many that the players he had inherited seemingly didn't want to play for the new manager. It was scandalous that a side containing Bell, Lee, Summerbee, Marsh and Law should fail to score in 10 of the 25 League games that Saunders was in charge. He was dismissed at the end of the season after what had been a forgettable reign.

SCOREBOARDS
In an interview in 2001, Bernard Manning said: 'We didn't have a scoreboard when I began going to watch City. They used to have this poor bloke who had to go around the ground with a board on his back. I always felt sorry for the poor bugger.'

Technology has come a long way since then but up until a few years ago, City fans could have been forgiven for thinking they had been passed by. The 'Scoreboard End', the terrace that once stood where the North Stand is now situated, earned its name from the 'ABC' scoreboard located at the back of the terrace. Fans would check the programme and next to each letter of the alphabet would be a match. For instance, at half-time 'A' might have read 1–0 on the board. A glance at the programme would reveal match 'A' was Arsenal versus Wolves, and so on.

Once the North Stand was finished, an electronic scoreboard was fitted at the back of the stand just under the roof. It worked well for several years but towards the end of its life it became the Norman Collier of scoreboards as various bulbs seemed to blow and not be replaced, and some scores and messages became almost a challenge to decipher.

Local brewery Greenhalls sponsored a lethargic electronic scoreboard for many years that sat in-between the Kippax and the Platt Lane stands. It seemed to die a death or just give up in the early 1990s and a smart new high-tech board was placed in the Platt Lane end just above the Family Stand. It occasionally goes haywire and overloads – usually after a goal is scored – but it's by far the best to date. State-of-the-art boards are planned for the new stadium but if asked, many would admit to missing the eccentric old boards – however useless they were.

SEAR, CLIFF – 1955 TO 1968
Appearances: 279
Goals: 1
Position: Full-back
Born: Rhostyllen

Cliff Sear was an amateur with City but was still based in South Wales, where he earned his living as a miner. He found the constant travelling too much to bear and concentrated on his life away from football. City realised the predicament the young full-back had found himself in and signed him on a professional basis soon after. Sear, a stylish defender with an incredible ability to slide tackle perfectly from a distance, would go on to play 279 games for the club and captained the Welsh Under-23 side in the late 1950s and won his one full cap against England in 1962. Sear had played in a turbulent period for the Blues but his consistency made him a popular player with the fans. After 277 games without scoring, he finally broke his duck in a 4–1 win over Bolton Wanderers. It was his last but one game for the club before joining Chester in 1968.

SENT OFF
Of the red cards shown to City players, some have been more memorable than others. In September 1962, Bert Trautmann was sent off for expressing dissent against West Ham at Maine Road. His dismissal saw the Blues collapse and lose 6–1. Ray Ranson and Tommy Booth were both sent off during a 'friendly' with Real Madrid in December 1979 and Mike Doyle once received his

marching orders for punching Leighton James. Perhaps the best, or worst of all, depending on how you look at it, was Kevin Horlock's dismissal for 'walking aggressively'!

SEQUENCES – LEAGUE

Every club has runs of League results, whether they are wins, draws or losses, that will be unearthed by the respective historians at times of greatness or misery. City are no different and we start with the more positive sequences. The record for successive League wins is nine set between 8 April and 28 September 1912. Eight successive wins in one season have occurred twice in 1904–05 and 1946–47. The record for consecutive draws is five, set in 1899–1900 and repeated in 1951–52. City's worst run of defeats was set in 1995–96 when they lost eight on the trot under Alan Ball. The club has also suffered six consecutive defeats a depressing five times in 1910–11, 1956–57, 1958–59 and 1960–61. The Blues went 17 games without a win in the 1979–80 season – a run stretching nearly four months. The greatest number of games played without a draw – 20 – was set in 1892, ending in 1893. The best is saved until last with the club's longest unbeaten run – 22 games set first in 1936–37 and repeated a decade later in 1946–47.

SHERON, MIKE – 1988 TO 1994
Appearances: 97 + 22 as a substitute
Goals: 28
Position: Striker
Born: Liverpool

A bright future was predicted for Liverpudlian forward Mike Sheron. Signed off a Youth Training Scheme by the Blues, the youngster soon earned a reputation as a cool, instinctive goal-scorer, even acquiring him the nickname 'Deadeye'. He made his debut in September 1991 in a 1–0 home defeat to Everton and went on to play in 29 games that season, scoring 7 goals. He also ended top scorer in the reserves in the same year.

He forged a good understanding with Niall Quinn and appeared 38 times in the 1992–93 campaign, scoring 14 times in all matches, 12 of which came during a 21-match period in League and cup.

Peter Reid's departure and Brian Horton's arrival were to spell the end for the likeable forward and, after another year and only six more goals, he moved to Norwich City for £1 million following the arrival of Paul Walsh and Uwe Rosler. He had won 13 England Under-21 caps during his time at Maine Road.

SILKMAN, BARRY – 1979 TO 1980

Appearances: 21
Goals: 3
Position: Forward
Born: London

There are dozens, perhaps hundreds of players who have made more appearances and scored more goals in their time at Maine Road, yet Barry Silkman is a footballer who left an indelible impression during his brief stay with the club. His appearance demanded that he was noticed – black curly shoulder-length hair, always tanned and a big gold earring, he could have been a forerunner of *The League of Gentlemen*'s character Papa Lazarou. Even his name is unforgettable!

A typical Malcolm Allison-inspired signing, the skilful forward arrived from Plymouth Argyle in March 1979 for £60,000 and played in all 12 of the remaining fixtures, scoring 3 goals. He was perhaps out of his time and looked as if he'd been caught in an early 1970s time warp. His style of play was more suited to the days of Hudson, Marsh and Best. Outrageous flicks and tricks galore, Silkman scored on his debut and added another on his home debut a week later. Quite a start but, unfortunately, not one he could maintain. The David Essex look-alike scored once more for City and played a total of 21 games before he left in January 1980 for Israeli club Maccabi Tel Aviv for £50,000. He failed to settle there and returned to England with Brentford in July, five months later.

SIMOD CUP

This competition had more aliases than an episode of *America's Most Wanted* during its brief efforts to become the elusive third cup competition in England. Crowd apathy was prevalent, attendance figures were often pitiful and, under the assumed names of the Full Members' Cup and the Zenith Data Systems Cup, it finally died a death in the early 1990s. For the record, City played in the tournament for two seasons. The first Simod tie, played in November 1987, saw City thrash Plymouth Argyle 6–2, just three days after hammering Huddersfield Town 10-1 in a Division Two fixture and, for the record, City striker Tony Adcock scored a hat-trick in each game. The Blues went out in the next round 2–0 at home to Chelsea. In 1988, a 3–2 defeat by Blackburn Rovers at Ewood Park signalled the end of City's days in the Cup.

SIMPSON, FITZROY – 1992 TO 1995
Appearances: 67 + 15 as a substitute
Goals: 4
Position: Midfielder
Born: Trowbridge

Live-wire Fitzroy Simpson became a City player in March 1992. One of several competitive midfielders signed under Reid's reign, the stocky former Swindon Town star cost £550,000 and made his debut in a 4–0 defeat at QPR. Energetic and a habitual collector of yellow cards, he also possessed good skills and was dangerous from dead-ball situations. Reid had obviously intended to groom Simpson to fill the considerable gap he himself would leave when he retired and even gave his new charge his No. 4 shirt. But Simpson never progressed in the way that had been, perhaps, expected. With the emergence of Garry Flitcroft and Steve Lomas, his selection became limited to injury cover and the occasional brief run of senior activity. He left in 1995 and shortly after became a 'Reggae Boy' for the Jamaican national side.

SIMPSON, PAUL – 1982 TO 1988
Appearances: 135 + 28 as a substitute
Goals: 24
Position: Winger
Born: Carlisle

Tricky left winger Paul Simpson became one of the youngest-ever players to appear for City when he made his debut aged 16 in a 3–2 win against Coventry City. He made a couple more substitute appearances but failed to start in any matches of the following campaign. Billy McNeill's decision to bring Simpson in for the run-in of the 1984–85 season proved an inspired move by the City boss.

With the Blues' promotion challenge wobbling badly, Simpson was selected to play in the final nine games and effectively replace Gordon Smith. He scored six times during the extended run and made countless others. His performance in the final game against Charlton Athletic established him as a firm favourite on the terraces. He was also a shining light in City's return to Division One with 8 goals from 30 starts.

He was sporadically used by Jimmy Frizzell in 1986–87 but then made 38 appearances as new boss Mel Machin took over the following campaign. Simpson's display in the 10–1 mauling of Huddersfield was wing-play of the highest quality. The popular forward was sold to Oxford United in 1988 before enjoying spells with Derby County and Blackpool, and is today player-manager of Rochdale.

SMALLEST PLAYER

Harry Anders is believed to be the smallest player to turn out for City. Standing 5 ft 2 in. high, the winger played for City from 1953 up until 1956. Shaun Wright Phillips, at 5 ft 6 in. is one of the smallest footballers to play for the Blues and was famously released by Nottingham Forest because of his size. The skilful utility player has proved the doubters wrong by becoming one of the most exciting Academy finds in years. Paul Dickov only stood at 5ft 5in. but his stature among City supporters was far higher.

SMITH, GEORGE — 1946 TO 1951

Appearances: 179
Goals: 80
Position: Inside-forward
Born: Fleetwood

George Smith actually began his career with City during the Second World War. He played 90 times and scored 45 goals – exactly one every other game. War records counted for little and he picked up his 'official' City career after the war and soon made up for lost time. He had served in the forces and sustained a gunshot wound to his hand but it didn't affect his instincts in front of goal. He scored 23 times as City won the Second Division and scored all five in the last game of the season – a 5–1 romp over Newport County. He left for Chesterfield in 1951 for £5,000, having scored 80 goals for the Blues.

SONGS AND CHANTS

City supporters have sung many songs over the years but it wasn't until 1990 that 'Blue Moon' became the fans' anthem. Both Peterborough United and Crewe Alexandra claim they serenaded their respective teams with the anthem first but, as the old adage goes, if you're going to take somebody else's song, make it your own. Mention 'Blue Moon' to anybody today and they think of Manchester City, not Crewe or Peterborough. Sorry, lads.

The 1970s were a great time for new songs and the Kippax favourites included the following: from the tune of 'Lily the Pink' came 'Colin the King' for Colin Bell; 'Sha-la-la-la-Summerbee' – self-explanatory; Dennis Tueart's song was 'Dennis Tueart King of all Geordies'; and 'Rodney, Rodney' for Rodney Marsh, who later admitted it gave him goosebumps every time he heard it.

There are more common and, in many cases, unprintable football songs heard at Maine Road but the ever-inventive Blues' fans were always coming up with originals like a customised version of the Oasis classic 'Wonderwall', 'I'm Dreaming of a Blue Wembley' and 'City 'til I Die'. The arrival of Shaun

Goater, though, has spawned two favourite fan songs: 'Who Let the Goat Out?' and possibly one of the best ever, 'Feed the Goat (and he will score)'. No doubt there will be many more to add to the list in future years.

SPONSORS

City have so far had five sponsors since club sponsorship began in time for the 1982–83 season. The first was Scandinavian car company Saab, who were unfortunate to be involved with the Blues at one of the club's lowest ebbs. Much the same could be said of Dutch electronic giants Philips, owners of PSV Eindhoven – City achieved little while wearing their name on the front of the players' shirts. Brother's ten-year relationship was fruitful for both parties, with the Blues in the Premiership for much of the time. Electronic games giants Eidos were sponsors from 1998 to 2002 resulting in a few personal visits from Lara Croft. First Advice, a new financial advice company based in Manchester, became sponsors in July 2002 for a period of at least three years and paid a record amount of money – believed to be somewhere in the region of £5 million – for the privilege. The full list is:

    1982–85: Saab
    1985–88: Philips
    1988–98: Brother
    1998–02: Eidos
    2002–present: First Advice

SPROSTON, BERT – 1938 TO 1950

Appearances: 134
Goals: 5
Position: Full-back
Born: Sandbach

Relocating as a footballer is not exactly a new problem but still causes footballers turmoil and loss of form. Such was the case for Bert Sproston. The young full-back had won his first England cap while playing for Leeds United but the cash-strapped Elland Road outfit were forced to sell their prized asset to Tottenham for £9,500. The youngster moved to London but was soon feeling unhappy and homesick. When City played Spurs in 1938, Sproston travelled with his team-mates to Manchester and promptly signed for City for £10,000, which was not far off the British transfer record fee. The next day, he played for the Blues against his former colleagues and helped his new club to a 2–0 win. After only 24 games with his new club, war broke out and when the League resumed in 1946, Sproston was 30 years old. He added another 110 appearances for the Blues before retiring in 1950, aged 35. He also won one England cap with the Blues.

STEPANOVIC, DRAGOSLAV – 1979 TO 1981
Appearances: 18 + 1 as a substitute
Goals: 0
Position: Defender
Born: Rekovac, Yugoslavia

Dragoslav Stepanovic – or 'Steppy' as he was affectionately known – joined City for £140,000 in time for the start of the 1979–80 season. The 34-times capped Yugoslavian international soon became something of a cult figure among the fans with his gentle eccentricities on the pitch, which meant a game rarely passed without him amusing the crowd with one thing or another. Steppy did his best to adjust to the trials of English football and made a solid debut in a 0–0 draw with Crystal Palace in August 1979. He played the first 14 games of the season, lost his place in the first team and then played only four more times. He became something of a regular for the reserves and would play one more game for City the following season – a disastrous 0–4 home defeat to Sunderland before eventually moving on the following summer when he returned to Wormacia in Germany.

STEWART, PAUL – 1986 TO 1988
Appearances: 64
Goals: 30
Position: Striker
Born: Manchester

Of all the signings Jimmy Frizzell made during his brief reign as manager of City, Blackpool striker Paul Stewart was his best and ultimately, a very profitable move for both the player and his new club. The arrival of Stewart for £200,000 signalled the end of Clive Wilson's career at Maine Road and – though he would stay on loan until the end of the 1986–87 season – it was the £250,000 received from Chelsea that financed the Stewart deal.

The former Tangerines' hit man was an instant hit with City supporters and though he arrived too late to stop the Blues being relegated from the top flight, he had done enough to suggest he would be a handful to Second Division defences the following season.

The Manchester-born striker was a revelation in his first full campaign at Maine Road. Quick, powerful and skilful, Paul Stewart had every attribute a good striker should have, and, with Paul Simpson and David White providing the ammunition, he fired in a total of 28 goals in all competitions, including a hat-trick against Huddersfield Town.

City had finished ninth and supporters were greatly disappointed when Stewart was sold to ease a worrying financial crisis. Of the many clubs monitoring the player, it was Tottenham who bid £1.7 million for him and in June 1988 he left for north London. His career continued to flourish and he won three England caps while at White Hart Lane. For some reason he dropped back into midfield when he moved to Liverpool and many City fans were mystified as to why such a talented striker should not play to his strengths.

STREET NAMES

Any south Manchester postman will be able to reel off the ten streets named after former City stars – the author should know, having delivered to most of them in the late 1980s! Manchester City Council made the decision to name several streets surrounding Maine Road after the heroes from yesteryear in 1977. It was a popular and vote-winning idea, though, in truth, it was more likely to have been the influence of some high-ranking City fan on the council. Good luck to them.

The list of names is:

Horace Barnes Close, Eric Brook Close, Tommy Browell Close, Sammy Cookson Close, Sam Cowan Close, Billy Meredith Close and Fred Tilson Close. There is also Frank Swift Walk, Billy Meredith Walk and Max Woosnam Walk. If there are plans for a Steve Daley Avenue, a Gareth Taylor Street and a Stuart Lee Drive, they've not yet been revealed to the general public.

SUBSTITUTES

The very first substitute for Manchester City was Glyn Pardoe for the first match of the 1965–66 season. He wasn't used in the game but three games later Roy Cheetham was and became the first City sub to actually play during a 4–2 win at Wolves. Paul Dickov holds the record for most appearances from the bench, with 57 introductions during various games. Several players have only made appearances as a substitute – Ashley Ward and Danny Hoekman both played one League game and two cup matches during their brief first-team histories and also from recent times are Terry Park (twice) and Ronnie Mauge (once). Ian Thompstone is the only substitute who scored on his only appearance – a late consolation in a 2–1 defeat at Ayresome Park, Middlesbrough. All will have dreamed about what might have been.

SUMMERBEE, MIKE – 1965 TO 1975

Appearances: 441 + 2 as a substitute
Goals: 67
Position: Forward
Born: Cheltenham

Mike Summerbee needs little or no introduction to City fans. One of the greatest wingers that has played for the club, he is still rightly held in reverence by supporters, both young and old. 'Buzzer' – as one and all knew him – was a vital member of the Joe Mercer side of the late 1960s and his contribution to the Blues' halcyon days was immense. Adored by the crowd, especially the Kippax, Summerbee played the game with good humour and was happy to entertain the Maine Road faithful with or without the ball, though his professionalism or will to win were never compromised in the least. With Colin Bell and Franny Lee, he was part of the Three Musketeers that inspired City to success after success.

Whether on the wing or as a forward, he wanted to play the game in a way the fans loved realising, perhaps more than most, that football is meant to be a form of entertainment for the paying public. He would terrorise the opposition, then have a laugh either with them or at their expense, and he even once pulled a 'moonie' at the Kop after standing in front of them conducting them like an orchestra! With Mike Summerbee, there was never a dull moment. Though far from a prolific scorer, he made many goals for others. He was also the first City star to be voted Player of the Year for two successive years in 1972 and 1973. Something of a fashion icon, this City legend was unfortunate to win only eight caps for England but became a successful businessman while still with the Blues. He was owner of a prestigious shirt-tailoring company supplying the likes of David Bowie, Michael Caine and Bruce Springsteen. Mike has returned to the club and is now part of the club's Corporate Hospitality team along with another legend, Colin Bell.

SUNDAY FOOTBALL

There are many people who believe Sunday football should be confined to the pub teams in the local parks up and down the country and there was a time when football on the Sabbath was strictly taboo. Nowadays, Sunday games are part and parcel of the season and only on Thursday's does domestic football seem to escape television coverage. Though Sky Television have played a huge role in games on Sundays, it was way back before the company was even a twinkle in Rupert Murdoch's eye that the Blues first played. With Britain in the grip of strike fever and a three-day working week imposed, the Football League announced a programme of Sunday football for 20 January 1974. It would be a week later, on the 27th, before City played against Nottingham

Forest in round 4 of the FA Cup and duly lost 4–1. It would be a dozen years before they played on a Sunday again, losing 5–4 to Chelsea in the Full Members' Cup final. The 2001–02 season in Division Two saw the Blues play a record number of Sunday games with ITV Digital seemingly keen to cover every game, and church attendances in south Manchester fell sharply.

SWIFT, FRANK – 1932 TO 1949
Appearances: 376
Goals: 0
Position: Goalkeeper
Born: Blackpool

Frank Swift's career spanned 17 years, a period in which he only ever played for City. He was the first goalkeeper to captain England and was the innovator of the long throw-out instead of a hoof up the pitch – he could also comfortably grip the ball in one hand. Swift had a run of four seasons when he was an ever-present in the team and would be likely to hold the record appearances for City but for the unavoidable break of seven seasons, due to the Second World War. Swift was a gentle giant and was much loved by the supporters and many older fans still talk of him in affectionate tones. Frank retired in 1949, making way for Bert Trautmann, and later became a journalist. It was after covering Manchester United's game in Yugoslavia that one of City's greatest ever players lost his life in the 1958 Munich air disaster – a tragic end to a hugely talented man.

T

TALLEST PLAYER

Before the 2002–03 season began, the holder of the tallest-player record at Maine road was Carlo Nash at 6 ft 5 in. Four other goalkeepers came within a fraction of Corrigan: Joe Corrigan and John Savage was half an inch smaller while Albert Gray and James Nichols were 6 ft 3 in. Michel Vonk were the same height, as was Niall Quinn. The signings of Peter Schmeichel and Sylvain Distin, however, are likely to give Carlo a run for his money.

TAYLOR, BILL

One of the finest and most respected coaches to work for Manchester City, Bill Taylor was Tony Book's right-hand man from 1976 to 1979. Joe Corrigan called him an 'inspiration' as a coach and his ability to get on with others had made him a very popular figure at the club and it was a former City player, Don Revie, who first introduced Taylor to the England coaching staff in 1974. The amiable Scot eventually became senior coach for England and was instrumental in helping the squad eventually qualify for the 1982 World Cup in Spain. The return of Malcolm Allison in January 1979 resulted in Bill Taylor resigning from his position. He stated that he was 'unable to work under the new arrangement', though it is hard to imagine he had envisaged leaving the club six months earlier when the Blues had finished fourth and second the year before that. Taylor moved to Oldham Athletic to become chief coach and assistant manager to future City boss Jimmy Frizzell. Tragedy struck in November 1981 when the Edinburgh-born Taylor died suddenly, aged just 42 years old, devastating the staff and players he'd worked with at City and England. A great loss to the game.

TAYLOR, ROBERT – 1999 TO 2000

Appearances: 14 + 2 as a substitute
Goals: 5
Position: Striker
Born: Norwich

Robert Taylor was known as 'Super Bob' at Gillingham, but he became known as 'Big Fat Bob' while at Manchester City. It was a term of endearment. Taylor had first come to the attention of City fans when he scored what should have been the goal that sent Gillingham to the First Division in the play-off final. He'd been a prolific scorer for the Gills but was somewhat injury-plagued, a pattern carried into his career at Maine Road. Signed in December 1999 for £1.5 million, he struggled to settle into the side despite occasionally showing his intelligence and predatory instincts. His biggest contribution for the Blues was to scramble a winner against Birmingham City to set up the thrilling promotion decider at Blackburn on the last day of the season. He left the club for Wolves in 2000.

TELEVISION

The very first televised game from Maine Road was on 15 December 1956, when City lost 3–2 to Wolves in front of just over 30,000 fans. The highlights were featured on BBC Television's *Sports Special* on the same evening. The result was symptomatic of the years ahead when for a long time the Blues seemed to freeze in front of the cameras, especially live broadcasts.

In what would be the first of many games televised live from Maine Road featuring the Blues, City lost 2–0 to Chelsea in 4 May 1984. The first live Monday night Premiership fixture on Sky Sports was a 1–1 draw between City and QPR – memorable for those who were there for Tony Coton's decision to ignore the new back-pass rule by illegally picking up the first back pass that came his way. The referee turned a blind eye and it was as if it never happened!

TESTIMONIALS

With many footballers in today's game on high wages and attractive bonus payments the testimonial game has all but disappeared – unless you play for Manchester United, of course, whose poorly paid stars need every penny they can get!

The last testimonial at Maine Road was thoroughly deserved and a crowd of over 25,000 turned out to pay tribute to Paul Lake, whose battle against injury stretched over five long years. United were the opponents and City repaid the favour at Old Trafford in 2000 for Dennis Irwin, though many Blues' fans stayed away in protest at what they believed to be an unnecessary game for an already wealthy United star.

Joe Corrigan had a benefit match on 7 November 1979 and must have been bitterly disappointed by the crowd of just 8,104 who turned up to see City beat Werder Bremen 4–0 at Maine Road. Paul Power, Mike Doyle and Colin Bell have all had testimonial games during the 1970s and 1980s but one of the biggest crowds for a tribute match was for Bert Trautmann. Around 48,000 turned out for the game in 1964 and Maine Road was jam-packed with people eager to pay homage to the legendary German goalkeeper who broke his neck helping City lift the FA Cup in 1956.

TEXACO CUP

Forerunner of the Anglo-Scottish Cup, the Texaco Cup was no more than a series of slightly more competitive friendlies than the usual pre-season fare. The very first games were actually played during the 1971–72 season and the Blues crashed out in round one. The tournament then became pre-season and the next time they entered, the Blues went out in the group stages. City fans have just had to live without the glory of a Texaco Cup triumph. The details are:

ROUND I
15 Sept 1971 City 2 (Mellor, Doyle), Airdrie 2 Att: 15,033
27 Sept 1971 Airdrie 2, City 0 Att: 13,700

GROUP I
3 Aug 1974 Blackpool 1, City 1 (Tueart) Att: 12,342
6 Aug 1974 Sheffield Utd 4, City 2 (Summerbee, Law) Att: 9,358
10 Aug 1974 City 2 (Lee, Tueart), Oldham Athletic 1 Att: 13,880

THOMSON, JOCK
Manager from 1947 to 1950
League Record: Games: 126 W: 38 D: 40 L: 48 F: 135 A: 166

Former Everton wing-half Jock Thomson didn't enjoy the best of times as manager of City after taking over from Sam Cowan in 1947. With the Blues just promoted to the First Division, he guided the club to a respectable tenth-place finish in 1947–48 – failure to win the final six games of that season prevented a more impressive start to life in the hot seat. The following campaign saw the Blues finish in seventh and yet again a poor run-in of five games without a win held City back from a higher placing. Things went badly wrong for Thomson and the Blues during the 1949–50 season, and City were, yet again, relegated – the sixth time in little over fifty years of competitive football – and Jock Thomson was replaced as manager by Les McDowall.

THORNLEY, IRVINE — 1904 TO 1912

Appearances: 204
Goals: 93
Position: Striker
Born: Glossop

In a scenario that might have been like Hillary Briss from BBC 2's *The League of Gentlemen*, Irvine Thornley was a Glossop butcher who saved his 'special stuff' for Hyde Road and his adoring fans. He moved from his hometown club to City and the FA later discovered 'irregularities' concerning his £800 fee but no mention was ever made of any directors' sausages changing hands. A hugely popular figure, he would become the first player to receive £1,000 from his benefit year. Controversy followed Thornley around and he had more than one disagreement with the authorities. He was sent off while captain in his comeback game after an eye injury but the supporters were still behind their hero, who was amazingly consistent from 1905 to 1910, hitting double figures for five successive seasons. He won an England cap while at Hyde Road and in 1912 he signed for South Shields and enjoyed several fruitful seasons with the Tynesiders.

TIATTO, DANNY — 1998 TO PRESENT

Appearances: 115 + 22 as a substitute*
Goals: 4*
Position: Defender/Midfielder
Born: Melbourne, Australia

Danny Tiatto has a determination and will to win that seems almost mandatory for all Australian sportsmen. He'd be the first to admit that he has had to tailor his aggression on the pitch to fit in with his lung-bursting runs and skill. His early days at Maine Road were a million miles from the coveted defender or midfielder that was a vital member of Kevin Keegan's championship-winning squad in 2001–02. Tiatto began life at City with nobody really knowing where he was best employed – including Joe Royle! In and out of the first team his frustration often boiled over and a plethora of yellow and red cards severely halted his progress. Today, Danny is a different player – still totally committed but more focused. A regular member of the Australian international squad, Tiatto's all-action style has deservedly made him one of the most popular City players on the current staff and he picked up the 2000–01 Player of the Year award as further proof.

TOLMIE, JIM – 1983 TO 1986
Appearances: 50 + 17 as a substitute
Goals: 19
Position: Striker
Born: Glasgow

Diminutive Scottish striker Jim Tolmie's career was revived by City boss Billy McNeill, who signed him from FC Lokeren in Belgium for just £30,000. The pint-sized forward went on to form a potent partnership with Derek Parlane and the duo netted 34 goals between them in their first season together. Tolmie had struck 15 times during the 1983–84 campaign, yet the following term was to be anything but fruitful, and he made only seven starts plus ten from the bench. His career at Maine Road was coming to a disappointing end, and the following season he played just one full game and made two sub appearances. He was loaned to Carlisle United in March 1986 before moving permanently to a Scandinavian club.

TOSELAND, ERNIE – 1929 TO 1939
Appearances: 409
Goals: 75
Position: Winger
Born: Northampton

Ernie Toseland joined City from Coventry in 1929 after scoring 11 goals in 22 appearances for the Sky Blues. The flying winger then went on to become a vital part of the Blues' championship and FA Cup-winning side of the 1930s. Unlucky to never win full England honours, Toseland was at his peak at a time of many other great wingers and it is for this reason alone that he never had the chance to shine on an international level. He rarely missed a game during his time at Maine Road and regularly hit double figures in the scoring department. He played in successive FA Cup finals for City in 1933 and 1934, scoring four times and playing in all rounds during the successful return to Wembley against Portsmouth. Ernie left for Sheffield Wednesday after ten successful years with the club.

TOURS
Though pre-season tours have become something that City rarely take part in, there are many tournaments and friendlies overseas from seasons gone by. The first overseas tour was of Scandinavia in 1910 and comprised four wins and one defeat. The second tour was in 1931 and was a great success with City winning all three games during a four-day French sojourn. They beat Racing Club 4–3, Red Star Olympique 5–0 and Les Diables Rouges 5–1.

A 1934 European tour pitted City against some of the cream of continental football. A 3–1 win over Racing Club was followed by a 3–3 draw with Fiorentina. AC Milan were too hot for the Blues and won 5–0 but City beat FC Admira Wacker 5–3 the next day and drew 4–4 with Marseille six days after that in an exhaustive spell of games and broken abacuses.

A 15-day trip to Austria and Switzerland brought three wins and two defeats and a total of 32 goals from the games. All things considered, the 1937 tour to Germany went fairly well with five tight matches in 16 days, one of which City won 3–2 with two more drawn.

The first of many trips to Ireland was in 1947 when City lost 4–2 to Shelbourne and drew 1–1 with Linfield. In 1949 the Blues played on European soil for the first time since the war with a six-match tour of Denmark, winning three, drawing once and losing twice.

In 1952 City landed in Spain for three matches and despite a 3–1 win over Real Zaragoza, both Sevilla and Barcelona thrashed the Blues 5–1. One year later and City returned to the newly formed West Germany and remained unbeaten in six games, including a first-ever clash with Bayern Munich that ended 3–3.

It was back to West Germany and France for the 1955 tour but the only success from five games in ten days was a 5–1 success over SV Eintracht Trier. The following year was back to what was now becoming a favourite destination and this time City left West Germany undefeated in six games scoring 17 times and conceding only five.

Spain and Germany were again the destinations in 1957 and another defeat to Barcelona, this time by 3–2, a 4–1 thrashing by Borussia Dortmund and then handsome wins over Werder Bremen (6–3) and the Spanish holiday resort town of Lloret de Mar (9–0) cheered up the tourists and restored confidence.

There were several bizarre scores during the 1958 visit to the USA and Canada including a 6–5 defeat by Hearts in New York and a 5–2 defeat to the same team in Vancouver. The Blues exacted some revenge on their touring partners from the UK with a thumping 7–1 win in Toronto before winding up the four-match series with a 6–0 defeat. City did manage to win all six of their other games but a 9–1 win over San Francisco All Stars won little credibility among the fans back home.

City made short trips to Germany, Austria and Italy in the early 1960s but it would be several years before the Blues returned to Europe with a 2–1 win over Eintracht Brunswick and a 1–0 victory over Standard Liège. It was back to the USA, this time with Dunfermline as touring partners and with City having just lifted the First Division Championship, but it was a dismal exercise and a pre-cursor of the disappointing season ahead. Three defeats to inferior American sides, players injured and sent off and four frustrating draws with Dunfermline left Joe Mercer saying 'Never again,' on his return home.

The Blues travelled Down Under to Australia for their 1970 summer holidays and delighted the ex-pats by winning six of their seven matches. The 1971 tours of Greece, Malta and West Germany ended with City failing to score in any of the four games. The year 1972 consisted of a tournament win in Sweden, an 8–0 win over Ope IF and two tough clashes with Greek giants Olympiakos (1–2 and 0–0). The following season City beat Panathinaikos 2–0 – the Blues' only game outside the UK that season.

The Blues flew all over the world in 1974 and 1975. There was another 3–2 defeat by Barcelona, a 2–0 success in Israel against the National XI and a 3–2 loss to Morocco. The Blues also travelled to Nigeria and beat two local sides, Shooting Stars (with no Vic and Bob involved) 1–0 and the Nigerian Forces 2–1.

A first-ever tour to the Far East included four wins over Japan, a 4–2 loss to South Korea 'B' and two wins over South Korea 'A' by 3–0 on each occasion. Spain beckoned in 1977 and Atletico Madrid won 2–0 and Real Betis held the Blues 1–1.

The year 1977 saw City undefeated in Belgium and Holland but the 1978 tour of Europe ended abruptly with a morale-sapping 5–1 loss to AZ Alkmaar. The 1980 tour to North America was almost as bad as the last time City played there, with a 3–2 loss to New York Cosmos, a 5-0 hammering by Vancouver Whitecaps and a 1–1 draw with Memphis. The tour ended controversially with a fine 3–2 win over AS Roma but Dennis Tueart was sent off.

A 1980 tour of Portugal and Holland ended undefeated but a return to Canada saw City again beaten by Vancouver Whitecaps, 2–0. John Bond must have wished he'd never decided to play any warm-up games in 1981 – City were crushed 8–0 by Werder Bremen only a couple of weeks before the new season. A collective team effort restored some pride with a 1–1 draw with PSV Eindhoven three days later.

City went to the West Indies for the first time in May 1982, beating Trinidad 2-1 and again 4–0. A poor City side lost five of their eight European tour matches in 1982 and the Blues were relegated at the end of the campaign. They still flew out to the States just a few days after the crushing last-gasp defeat to Luton Town and beat Tampa Bay 1–0 and Fort Lauderdale 4–2, though nobody was celebrating the successes too wildly.

By contrast, Billy McNeill's men had a fruitful stay in West Germany, winning all six games and scoring 26 goals in the process. An Irish tour and four games in Singapore yielded six wins and a draw the following year and, at last, a 1985 trip to the States with five wins and two draws – no defeats! It gave McNeill an excellent record of 18 wins out of 21 official tour matches under his leadership.

Almost a month in Switzerland and Spain for new boss Jimmy Frizzell yielded three wins, five draws and two defeats. The highlights were a 0–0 draw with Real Betis and a 1–1 draw with Barcelona – the first time City had avoided a loss to the Spanish giants. There was also an undefeated two-game break in the United Arab Emirates in November 1986.

Mel Machin's City side rattled in 10–0 and 12–0 victories within 24 hours on a trip to Scandinavia. They also won the other three games – this was the season City beat Huddersfield 10–1 in the League, incidentally. Machin enjoyed the trip so much that he repeated it for the 1988–89 pre-season and, once again, the Blues won all five games, scoring 22 and conceding just three. Machin's newly promoted side went to Norway for the 1989 pre-season. Three wins, including another 10–0 win, this time over Lervik, were followed by three draws.

With Howard Kendall now in command, the highlights of the nine tour matches in 1990 for the Blues were the 32 goals scored against five Swedish outfits and a 1–1 draw with Real Sociedad. City went to Hong Kong in 1991 for the first time and won once and drew the other game against local opposition.

Peter Reid's City played two games in Germany against Dynamo Dresden (1–2) and VfL Bochum (1–1). They also beat Irish opponents five times throughout the season. A 1992 tour against six Italian sides yielded only one victory, three draws and two defeats. City also travelled to Japan, beating J-League sides Mitsubishi and Hitachi by 2–0 and 1–0 respectively. A first-ever trip to South Africa saw the Blues play Cape Town and win 1–0. Kevin Keegan took his troops to Denmark in 2002, where they won a mini-tournament at FC Aarhus and also lost 1–0 to SV Hamburg a month later.

TOWERS, TONY – 1967 TO 1974
Appearances: 151+ 8 as a substitute
Goals: 12
Position: Midfielder
Born: New Moston, Manchester

Hardworking midfielder Tony Towers spent his City career moving positions to best suit the team during the late 1960s and early 1970s. He had to wait four years before Joe Mercer gave him a sustained run in the side, incredibly playing in 7 of the 12 numbered shirts that season. The 1971–72 campaign saw Tony have three runs in the side as the Blues finished fourth. When Malcolm Allison took over, Towers had his most fruitful run in the side yet, clocking up 35 games, mainly in midfield. Johnny Hart was the manager after Allison and he continued to use Towers in fits and starts. When Hart retired due to ill-health, Ron Saunders took the helm and two months later, Towers was on his way to Sunderland as part of the deal that brought Dennis Tueart to Maine Road.

TRANSFERS – MOST EXPENSIVE

Nicolas Anelka's £13.5 million price tag makes him the Blues' costliest player by a country mile – at the time of writing. Jon Macken is the next most expensive purchase at £5 million from Preston North End. Two more Keegan signings, Vincente Matias Vuoso and Sylvain Distin both cost £4 million each. Paulo Wanchope at £3.75 million was the previous record holder under Joe Royle's reign and Richard Dunne cost £3 million from Everton. Ali Benarbia, a free transfer, Shaun Goater at £400,000 and Eyal Berkovic at £1.5 million are proof that quality doesn't always have to cost the earth. The £5.5 million Ajax paid for the services of Gio Kinkladze in 1998 remains the largest sum paid for a City player.

TRAUTMANN, BERT – 1949 TO 1964

Appearances: 545
Goals: 0
Position: Goalkeeper
Born: Bremen, Germany

Bert Trautmann overcame virtually everything you could possibly imagine in his rise to becoming one of the most popular players ever to play for the Blues and probably the best-ever goalkeeper the club has had. Bert was a German paratrooper during the Second World War and was captured in Normandy and then made a prisoner-of-war. From the POW camp in Ashton-in-Makerfield, he tried his hand, pardon the pun, at goalkeeping. His training as a paratrooper had served him well, as he would later claim that it helped him to cushion the ball as he fell! There must be easier ways to learn the art.

He was released after the war and decided to stay in England, eventually finding work on a farm. He played for St Helens FC and shortly after married the club secretary's daughter. Word had spread of the German goalkeeper with huge promise and City soon signed him up, putting him straight into the first team. With the war still fresh in everyone's minds it is perhaps understandable that City fans were at first resentful of the German's presence in the team, especially as he was the replacement for the great Frank Swift, who had recently retired.

However, Bert soon won over the supporters, and they were quick to see him as a man with the heart of a lion. Incredibly, while helping City to a 1956 FA Cup final victory over Birmingham, Bert dived bravely at a Birmingham striker's legs and hurt himself badly. He had, in fact, broken his neck, yet he continued playing, despite the obvious agony he was in. Such heroism guarantees almost mythical status and at Bert's testimonial a huge crowd turned up to pay their respects. The word 'legendary' could have been invented for Bert, a giant of a man in every respect.

TUEART, DENNIS – 1974 TO 1978 AND 1980 TO 1983
Appearances: 259 +10 as a substitute
Goals: 107
Position: Forward
Born: Newcastle

Signed by City boss Ron Saunders in March 1974, Dennis Tueart became the club's record signing for £275,000 from Sunderland. Two days later he was making his debut in a 0–0 draw with Manchester United. He soon settled into the side and it wasn't long before he became a big crowd favourite. If he was popular going into the 1976 League Cup final against Newcastle, he became all but immortal to the fans after his spectacular overhead kick won the game 2–1.

Ambitious and keen to broaden his horizons, he left for New York Cosmos in 1978 and again became a hero to the vast crowds that crammed into the Meadowlands Stadium in the Big Apple. A Tueart goal would be welcomed by an electronic board message of 'Sweet Feet' or 'Do it, Tueart!'

Playing alongside some of the world's best players and living a life of luxury, complete with Cadillac, Dennis enjoyed almost two years in the USA before he rejoined City for £150,000 and came back to his adopted home of Manchester for good. Over the next three seasons, though beset by injury, he scored 22 goals in 66 starts. He left the Blues in 1983 as part of a wage-trimming exercise as the club faced up to life in Division Two. He is now a successful businessman and a City director, and has been on the board since 1997.

TWINS
Twins have been on City's books on only two occasions. Paul and Ron Futcher joined City from Luton Town within a few months of each other in 1978, and Nick and Anthony Fenton came through the club's youth policy, though Anthony never broke into the first team.

U

UEFA CUP

City began life in the UEFA Cup, formerly known as the Fairs Cup, in 1972–73 with a home leg against Valencia. The game ended 2–2 with goals from Ian Mellor and Rodney Marsh. The second leg ended the Blues' interest in the tournament with a 2–1 defeat by the Spaniards, with Marsh again finding the back of the net. Four years later in 1976–77 and it was *adios*, or rather *ciao*, in the first round, again despite a good home victory, this time over Italian giants Juventus. A solitary goal, courtesy of a Brian Kidd header, was never going to be enough against a cynical side and there were no surprises when the Blues lost 2–0 in Turin to crash out of the competition. The curse continued the following year when Polish side Widzew Lodz held City 2–2 in the first leg and 0–0 in the second, meaning that City were out on the away-goals rule.

The fourth and, to date, final UEFA Cup campaign in European football for City was also the best in 1978–79. It was perhaps no coincidence that the first time the club had played the away leg first resulted in success. The Blues ground out a tough 1–1 draw with Dutch side FC Twente and then completed the job with a 3–2 win at Maine Road. Belgian side Standard Liège looked to be heading home with a creditable 1–0 defeat with 85 minutes gone in the first leg of the second round. City, as only they can do, were rampant in the final five minutes with Kidd, Palmer and Hartford all scoring to make it 4–0. Liège found the mountain too high to scale and their 2–0 second-leg win hardly mattered.

The reward was a trip to Italy to face AC Milan in the third round. Fog meant the game was played the following afternoon to the scheduled date but when the action finally began, the Blues went sensationally 2–0 ahead through Power and Kidd. Milan fought back for 2–2, but the result was heralded as one of the best by an English side in Europe. City were inspired for the return game, racing into an unassailable half-time lead of 3–0. There was no further scoring on the night and with the scalp of Milan in the bag, many believed only one side could stop the Blues now and they promptly drew them in the quarter-finals. German outfit Borussia Monchengladbach earned a 1–1 draw at Maine Road and won 3–1 in the second leg, despite the goal of the game from Kaziu Deyna. The Germans would go on to win the UEFA Cup.

USELESS

A bit strong, maybe, but what the hell. There are many players from the past who could fit into the category 'useless' but here are a select few, who, to be fair to them, were probably far better players at clubs other than City. Gerry Creaney – arrived at the club from Portsmouth in exchange for Paul Walsh – World Cup legend that Allan Ball was, you had to wonder what colour the sky was in his world, sometimes. Creaney was a player who put the slug into sluggish and while there's no denying his pedigree at Celtic, it just didn't happen at Maine Road. Nigel Clough – the talented former Nottingham Forest star did nothing at all while at City and was so pedestrian that the ground staff recommended putting a crossing from one side of the pitch to the other for him. Robert Hopkins was signed in September 1986 and one month of sub-standard performances later he was on his way to West Brom in exchange for Imre Varadi. He is then supposed to have aired his views on the City fans and he wasn't too complimentary, either. Who cares?

V

VARADI, IMRE — 1986 TO 1988

Appearances 64 + 9 as a substitute
Goals: 29
Position: Striker
Born: Paddington

Imre Varadi made quite an impression for City during his two-year stay with the club and was signed to inject some much-needed imagination into a sterile attack. With only four goals in nine games, boss Jimmy Frizzell sold ineffective strikers Gordon Davies and Trevor Christie and made a straight swap, with the disappointing Robert Hopkins moving to West Brom and Varadi arriving at Maine Road. He made his debut in a 2–1 defeat at Chelsea, scoring City's only goal. With young scoring sensation Paul Moulden partnering Varadi, the pair inspired a four-match unbeaten run for the Blues. City still couldn't avoid the inevitable relegation back to Division Two.

Highly rated forward Paul Stewart was signed from Blackpool by new manager Mel Machin and emerging youth-team product David White was by now also knocking on the first-team door. Tony Adcock had also been signed during the summer from Colchester and, suddenly, City had several decent strikers vying for a first-team spot. With a return of nine goals from a dozen starts, the 1987–88 season started extremely well for Varadi, who was a huge hit on the terraces. Some say the chanting of his name led to an inflatable banana appearing at Maine Road for one home game and thus followed a chant of 'Imre Banana' – but, as with all legends, the source of the craze is unclear and probably not true.

He missed City's 1987, 10–1 thrashing of Huddersfield Town and found it difficult to break back into the side. When he did, it took him three months to score again. His City career was beginning to peter out but he still managed eight goals in 14 starts and finished the season with 17 strikes from 26 League games. He made just one full appearance and came on twice as substitute for the 1988–89 season, but new signings Wayne Biggins and Trevor Morley meant his opportunities would be, at best, limited. His former club Sheffield Wednesday made an acceptable offer and Varadi left for Hillsborough, aged 29.

VICTORIES IN A SEASON

The most wins recorded in a season is 31 during the 2001–02 campaign when City raced away with the First Division Championship, amassing 99 points in the process. The lowest amount is eight and this woeful statistic was recorded in 1893–94, 1949–50 and 1986–87. The Blues won only nine League games in Premiership seasons 1993–94 and 1995–96. No wonder we've all got grey hair.

VILJOEN, COLIN – 1978 TO 1980

Appearances: 35 + 3 as a substitute
Goals: 1
Position: Midfielder
Born: Johannesburg, South Africa

The £100,000 capture of South African-born Colin Viljoen was grandly announced in the later editions of the *Manchester Evening News* stop press in August 1978, just above 'Micky Miller's Late Night Selections' (some of you out there will know what I'm going on about!). The neat Ipswich Town player of 11 years made his debut in a 4–1 win at Chelsea. He was hardly a regular for the 1978–79 season but interestingly played in seven out of City's eight UEFA Cup matches as Tony Book made him an important member of the side that reached the quarter-finals. He was at the back end of his career when he arrived at City and a total of 35 appearances, including three as sub, were the sum total of his days at Maine Road. His solitary goal came in a League Cup tie at Sheffield Wednesday. He joined Chelsea in 1980.

VONK, MICHEL – 1992 TO 1995

Appearances: 96 + 7 as a substitute
Goals: 4
Position: Centre-half
Born: Alkmaar, The Netherlands

Michel Vonk joined City from SVV Dordrecht in March 1992 for £500,000. He became a popular figure among the fans, who sang 'Ooh, Vonkey, Vonkey' to the 6 ft 3 in. defender following any number of clattering challenges he made during a game. He made his debut a few days after signing in a 2–0 defeat at Nottingham Forest and remained in the side until the end of the season.

His partnership with Keith Curle was cut short by an ankle injury after just eight games of the new season and he missed the next four months as a result. Full-back Andy Hill switched to centre of defence as cover until he returned in January 1993 and played out the remainder of the season, adding three goals in total. He battled for his place with Alan Kernaghan the following term and never enjoyed the luxury of being an automatic choice for the remainder of his time at Maine Road. He finally joined Sheffield United in 1995.

VUOSO, VINCENTE MATIAS – 2002 TO PRESENT
Position: Striker
Born: Mar del Plata, Argentina

Vincente Vuoso joined City in the summer of 2002 and if the talent-spotters are to be believed, he has the football world at his feet. Regarded as a hot prospect in Argentina, the former Independiente striker was signed by the Blues for £4 million. An Under-21 regular for his country, Vuoso also played alongside Uruguayan international and Manchester United striker Diego Forlan for the Argentinian 'Red Devils' and scored 14 times in 64 games for them. He is the first South American to play for Manchester City.

WAGSTAFFE, DAVE — 1958 TO 1964
Appearances: 161
Goals: 8
Position: Winger
Born: Manchester

Popular local lad Dave Wagstaffe enjoyed six years with City and though it was an indifferent period for the club, 'Waggy' was very much a shining light, especially for the fans. A no-nonsense winger, he played in a direct fashion and his crosses were food and drink for the likes of Denis Law, Joe Hayes and Colin Barlow. He only managed eight goals in his 161 games – around one every 20 matches, but created plenty more for the strikers. He was sold to Wolves on Boxing Day 1964 for just under £45,000 and stayed 11 years at the Molineux club, making 324 appearances for them.

WALSH, PAUL — 1994 TO 1995
Appearances: 62
Goals: 19
Position: Forward
Born: Plumstead

The former Luton, Spurs and Liverpool striker Paul Walsh signed from Portsmouth in March 1994 for £700,000 and played a large part in City escaping relegation from the Premiership. With other recent signings Rosler and Beagrie, the diminutive striker instantly gelled and he soon became a firm favourite with supporters, due in no small part to his consistent all-out efforts on the park. In fact, Walsh, Beagrie and Rosler almost single-handedly kept the Blues up that season, scoring 10 of City's 12 goals between them on the run-in.

A little box-of-tricks, Walsh was lethal in the air and highly skilled on the floor and he gave everything for Manchester City during his time at the club. He was disappointingly sold back to Portsmouth after just one full season with the club, ending his Maine Road career, many felt, at least two years too soon. He'd scored 16 times in 53 Premiership matches and left behind an army of admirers.

WANCHOPE, PAULO – 2000 TO PRESENT
Appearances: 46 + 3 as a substitute*
Goals: 23*
Position: Striker
Born: Costa Rica

With elastic legs that confuse defenders and a will to attempt the impossible, Paulo Wanchope may have found his spiritual home at Maine Road. He has an excellent strike-record for City and scored a hat-trick on his home debut against Sunderland. An impudent back-heeled goal at Leicester in 2001 emphasised his skill and confidence to try something different. He has been at City for two seasons and played with various strike partners, including George Weah and Shaun Goater. Though he appears laid back and aloof, he is a hard-working team player with an abundance of talent. There is much more to come from the talented Costa Rican and his goal against Brazil in the 2002 World Cup finals highlighted his continuing progress. Only recurring injuries seem to be halting his impressive progress.

WAR, THE SECOND WORLD
There were many City players who proudly served their country during the Second World War. They are as follows:

ARMY
Sam Barkas, Harry Brunton, Alex Herd, William Hogan, James Hope, William McLeod, Sam Pearson, Harvey Pritchard, James Rudd, George Smith, Bert Sproston, Frank Swift, Eric Westwood, Thomas Wright and Lewis Woodroffe.

ROYAL NAVY
Albert Emptage and Joe Fagan.

RAF
Jackie Bray, Louis Cardwell, David Davenport, Peter Doherty, Maurice Dunkley, Wilfred Grant, Alf Keeling and manager Wilf Wild.

Several players were assigned wartime occupations other than the armed forces. Les McDowall was a draughtsman, Billy Walsh was a miner and Jimmy

Heale joined another set of boys in blue by becoming a policeman. Richard Neilson, John Milsom and Alex Roxburgh were all firemen who would have no doubt been first on the scene had Maine Road ever come under attack!

WARD, ASHLEY – 1987 TO 1991
Appearances: 0 + 3 as a substitute
Goals: 0
Position: Striker
Born: Manchester

Ashley Ward is one of a dozen young stars that left City as virtual unknowns to carve out impressive careers elsewhere. He very nearly came back to haunt the club in devastating style when the Blues played against Blackburn Rovers on the final day of the 1999–2000 season. A goal down, a second would surely have condemned the Blues to the play-offs when Ward made a neat turn and, with just Weaver to beat, measured a curling drive towards the far post. It hit the inside of the upright and bounced into Weaver's arms. The Blues would go on to win 4–1 and gain promotion.

Part of the FA Youth Cup losing finalists of 1989, Ward looked to be heading for a long and prosperous future at Maine Road and he finally broke into the first team – albeit as a sub – in a 2–1 defeat at Southampton. His next two games, again from the bench, were both against Millwall in the FA Cup when he replaced Clive Allen twice in nine days. Leicester City made a move for him in 1991 and he joined the Filbert Street side for several happy seasons. He has also played for Bradford City, Barnsley and Blackburn Rovers.

WARD, MARK – 1989 TO 1991
Appearances: 67
Goals: 16
Position: Midfielder
Born: Prescot

Former Everton, Northwich Victoria and Oldham Athletic star Mark Ward paid a heavy price for being part of a transfer deal that took crowd favourites Ian Bishop and Trevor Morley to West Ham United and brought Ward in turn to Maine Road. A skilful and hard-working right-sided midfielder, Ward had to work doubly hard to impress the disappointed City fans and was given a rougher ride than he deserved in the early part of his career with the club.

His efforts on the pitch gradually won over the more critical sections and as time went on, Ward, though never a player to have his name chanted on the Kippax, won the respect of the Blues' faithful by keeping his head down and getting on with his job. The highlight of his first season was successive goals at Aston Villa, Millwall and QPR – all spectacular and vitally important in the club's fight against relegation.

In fact, Ward almost exclusively scored long-range beauties and during his first full season with City (1990–91) he cracked in 11 goals in 39 games. With Howard Kendall gone and Peter Reid in charge, Ward's time with the Blues was already coming to an end. During a 5–1 win at Aston Villa, he was substituted and as he passed his manager on the touch-line he booted a bucket violently away.

Such petulance in full view of the 6,000 travelling fans and his boss was only going to end in tears. One can only imagine what was said in the dressing-rooms between two of the games fieriest characters and Ward was dropped two games later, never to pull on the light-blue jersey again. Three months later he had once again joined Howard Kendall, this time at Goodison Park, where his career had first begun as an apprentice.

WATSON, DAVE – 1975 TO 1979
Appearances: 185
Goals: 6
Position: Centre-back
Born: Stapleford

Man-mountain Dave Watson proved an inspired purchase from Sunderland in 1975 where he'd earned the unusual distinction of being a full England international without ever playing in the top division. The towering defender formed a successful partnership with Mike Doyle, particularly during the 1976–77 season, which very nearly won the old First Division Championship for the Blues.

He was 28 years old when he signed and, fortunately for City, the following four seasons would prove to be arguably the best of his career. Commanding in the air and crunching in the tackle, Watson went on to win a further 30 England caps while at Maine Road – second only to Colin Bell – before eventually being sold to German club Werder Bremen by Malcolm Allison.

WEAKEST LINK, THE
Anne Robinson's mega-successful quiz show was just about at its peak when City visited Ipswich Town in May 2001. The match, televised live by Sky Sports, was the Blues' last hope of avoiding relegation. City went ahead through Shaun Goater near the end but two quick home goals won the game for Ipswich 2–1 and relegated City. As the cameras panned the supporters, it focused on an Ipswich fan holding up a banner saying 'You are the weakest link

– goodbye!' It didn't go down too well with Blues' supporters and when the clubs met in an FA Cup fourth-round tie at Portman Road in 2002, City triumphed 4–1. Ipswich were later relegated themselves from the Premiership and their website was littered with 'weakest link' references. Revenge is sweet!

WEATHER CONDITIONS

The list of 'Abandoned Games' at the start of the book explains the end result of severe weather conditions that City have been actively involved in. One game you won't find listed was in 1906 when City finished the game with just six men having lost five players from heat exhaustion. With temperatures over 90 degrees Fahrenheit, it was no great shock that the Blues lost 4–1. Two days later, the drained players had to play again and went down 9–1 to Everton but gained revenge in the return at Hyde Road by winning 3–1 in cooler conditions.

WEAVER, NICK – 1996 TO PRESENT

Appearances: 178 + 1 as substitute*
Goals: 0
Position: Goalkeeper
Born: Sheffield

Nick Weaver wrote his name into the history books of Manchester City with a meteoric rise that took him to the verge of full England honours. Weaver played a vital role in City's successive promotions to the Premier League and became a household name as he saved the penalty that won the 1999 play-off final against Gillingham. His victory run would have probably seen him all the way back to Maine Road had Andy Morrison not decided he'd seen enough running for one day. A regular in the England Under-21 team, Weaver again played out of his skin as the Blues raced to promotion from Division One in 1999–2000. A dip in form during the ill-fated Premiership of 2000–01 saw the Blues buy Carlo Nash from neighbours Stockport County and the pair shared duties throughout the 2001–02 promotion campaign.

WEBSITES

The official Manchester City website is located at www.mcfc.co.uk. Another excellent source of information, unofficial, but long running, can be found at www.blueview.co.uk – the message boards rarely fail to raise a smile and it's an interesting place to hear other fans' views on events at the club. There are several links to other sites from Blue View. Several players also have their own sites and www.nicolasanelka.com is one of them. Alfie Haaland's can be located at www.icons.com.

WEMBLEY

The Blues have had their fair share of Wembley finals – probably more than many young supporters will realise. The very first time City went to the Twin Towers was in 1926 when Bolton Wanderers beat the Blues 1–0. Seven years later, City again lost, this time to Everton by 3–0. The Blues returned the following season to lift the trophy for the first time, with Fred Tilson grabbing a brace in a 2–1 win over Portsmouth. History repeated itself in 1955 when City first lost to Newcastle 3–1 then returned in 1956 to lift the Cup with a 3–1 win over Birmingham City. In 1969, the Blues beat Leicester City 1–0 with a thunderous strike from Neil Young. A year later and a 2–1 win over West Bromwich Albion secured the League Cup for the very first time.

In 1974 City lost 2–1 to Wolves in the League Cup final, but two years later in 1976, Dennis Tueart scored one of the greatest goals the famous old stadium had ever seen – an overhead kick – to clinch a 2–1 win over Newcastle United. City had been to Wembley an impressive four times in seven years.

In 1981 City played there twice in four days, drawing the FA Cup final 1–1 with Spurs and returning the following Thursday to lose 3–2 in one of the most exciting – but ultimately disappointing – finals ever. The only other two occasions the club has played on the lush, green north London turf was an amazing 5–4 defeat to Chelsea in the much-maligned – and unfortunately named – Full Members' Cup final in 1986. The 1999 play-off final against Gillingham was the club's last appearance at Wembley Stadium. For the record, City have never played an FA Charity Shield match there, either.

The total record for the Blues at Wembley is:

Pld: 13 W: 5 D: 2 L: 6 F: 21 A: 24

WEST GORTON

In 1881, after one year of being known as St Mark's of West Gorton, the club became West Gorton (St Mark's) and the humble beginnings of Manchester City were slowly beginning to progress. The team wore a black kit with a silver Maltese cross on the front – just about as far as you could get from what are believed to be the traditional sky-blue colours City would eventually become best known for.

It would prove to be the second of five names for the club and with no real home to call their own, the club's pioneers played matches at Clowes Street, Kirkmanshulme Lane Cricket Club, Queens Road, Pink Bank Lane and Reddish Lane. They stayed as West Gorton for three years before becoming Gorton in 1884.

WESTWOOD, ERIC – 1937 TO 1953
Appearances: 263
Goals: 5
Position: Full-back
Born: Manchester

Eric Westwood was an amateur at Manchester United before signing professional forms with City in 1937. A skilful defender whose career – like countless others – was interrupted by the Second World War. He was young enough to continue his career after the seven-year break and played successfully for City for a further seven years, winning a Division Two Champions' medal along the way. He won two England 'B' caps while at Maine Road before being given a free transfer in 1953 to Altrincham Town, aged 35.

WHELAN, TONY – 1973 TO 1974
Appearances: 3 + 3 as a substitute
Goals: 0
Position: Striker
Born: Salford

Every player who has ever pulled on a shirt for Manchester City is part of the history of the club and while researching for this book it has been fascinating to discover somebody whose career could have been completely different if certain events had never occurred. Tony Whelan was a young footballer who fitted into such a category perfectly. The former Manchester United junior joined the Blues after a month's trial on a free transfer in a deal that received little publicity. Two days after officially signing, Whelan made his debut against West Ham, filling in for the injured Rodney Marsh.

Instead of being overawed at his baptism, Whelan was City's star performer on the day, in a side that included Bell, Summerbee and Lee. He twice came close to scoring and would have done but for excellent work by the home goalkeeper Bobby Ferguson. After the game, Malcolm Allison couldn't resist giving the press his observations:

> The biggest tragedy with Manchester United is that over the years the youngsters haven't had a chance. I have known them to have four teams out and still have eight apprentices without a game – there's terrible wastage.
>
> I watched Whelan in the 'A' side and decided to take him on. There were times against West Ham when he could have been mistaken for Rodney Marsh – he showed that much skill. I think he will do a great job for me. It's significant all my senior professionals rate him very highly.

Whilst Whelan must have been floating on air after such a start to his City career, other events were shaping elsewhere that would dramatically change the youngster's path. He kept his place for the next two games before Allison walked out on the Blues. The man who had such belief in Whelan was gone and Johnny Hart was installed as the new manager. He axed Whelan from his first squad and he only made three more substitute appearances before being given a free transfer to Rochdale – had Allison stayed, who knows how things might have panned out?

WHITE, DAVID — 1984 TO 1994
Appearances: 328 + 14 as a substitute
Goals: 96
Position: Forward
Born: Urmston, Manchester

One of the most successful products of City's excellent youth system, David White was also one of the Blues' best modern-day forwards. Blessed with electric pace, the young right winger was part of the FA Youth Cup-winning team of 1985–86 and he also burst into the seniors the following season, playing on 24 occasions but scoring only once.

He'd been pitched in at the deep end into a struggling side heading for relegation and the experience did little for his confidence. Mel Machin decided to make White a regular as the club battled to return to Division One, and White would play 40 times, netting 13 in his first full campaign. His pace and finishing were a constant worry for opposition teams and he famously scored goal number ten in the victory over Huddersfield Town, completing his own hat-trick in the process.

An explosive player, he alternated between wide right and more central roles and became an important part of the Blues' side in the late 1980s and early 1990s. Rarely injured, White formed a deadly partnership with Niall Quinn and profited from the big Irishman's flicks in much the same way as Kevin Phillips has at Sunderland. He hit 15, 18 and 16 goals with Quinn alongside and City raced to successive top five finishes in 1991 and 1992. He won his one and only England cap in 1992 but failed to impress in a defeat against Spain.

In December 1993 White joined Leeds in a £2 million exchange that brought David Rocastle to Maine Road. He never repeated his heroics for the Elland Road side and later moved to Sheffield United. His most productive and exciting years, however, were undoubtedly spent with his hometown club and the 96 goals in excess of 300 appearances bear testament to the fact.

WHITLEY, JEFF – 1996 TO PRESENT
Appearances: 111 + 30 as a substitute*
Goals: 8*
Position: Midfielder
Born: Zambia

The younger of two brothers, Jeff Whitley also has proved the more successful. A full Northern Ireland international, though he could have played for the country of his birth, Zambia, Whitley trailed older brother Jim in the pecking order for midfield slots at Maine Road but continued to impress in the youth and reserve sides. He was given his chance, aged 17, at home to Barnsley but his poor back-pass led to a late winner for the Tykes. He'd done enough to earn Man of the Match honours but it wasn't quite the start he'd hoped for. His career was a stop–start affair and when he was loaned out to Wrexham during the 1998–99 season, a departure seemed imminent.

Whitley knuckled down and did well while in north Wales and on his return Joe Royle gave him the chance to show him what he could do. He impressed enough to become a regular in the promotion run-in from Division Two and played in the play-off final against Gillingham. He continued his progress into Division One and missed only four League games all season, scoring four times.

He was again a regular in the Premiership campaign of 2000–01 but Royle's departure was bad news for the harrying midfielder nicknamed 'Ratter'. Kevin Keegan gave the youngster a couple of outings as substitute but he broke his ankle in the second game of the season. He found it hard to break back into a midfield that now included Benarbia and Berkovic, and Kevin Horlock was in the form of his life. He was told by the club that it would probably be best to look for another club but he was still a squad member for the start of the 2002–03 season, as determined to return to first-team action as ever.

WIEKENS, GERARD – 1997 TO PRESENT
Appearances: 189 + 15 as a substitute*
Goals: 10*
Position: Midfielder/Defence
Born: Nordster, Holland

Fast approaching 200 games in City colours, Gerard Wiekens is the type of player whom managers love to have in their side. Solid and dependable, he plays a role not dissimilar to that played by Ian Brightwell during his City career, whereby, when asked, Wiekens comfortably slips into any position he is required to. Already in his sixth season at Maine Road, the quiet Dutchman has played midfield, centre-half and midfield anchorman – the latter arguably being his best position.

Kevin Keegan has used Wiekens along the back three in a five-man defence, or in the holding role behind the attacking playmakers. He doesn't score many, but when they do go in, they are usually spectacular – the goals against Stoke City and Leeds United spring to mind. Costing just £500,000 from FC Veendam, the hugely popular Dutchman represents a great piece of business for the club and he's even had a T-shirt dedicated to him – 'Walking in a Wiekens Wonderland' – after the supporters' song about him.

WILD, WILF
Manager from 1932 to 1946
League Record: Games: 297 W: 128 D: 61 L: 108 F: 572 A: 485

Typical that after championing the idea of a full-time manager at Maine Road without the added stresses of being secretary as well, Wilf Wild should be given the role as team manager as well as his secretarial duties. In spite of his concerns, Wild would show the dual role was not only possible to perform, but that it could be done with great success.

He was a hard-working and loyal servant to Manchester City and it was a just reward that his first two seasons in charge culminated with an appearance in the FA Cup final. The Blues were losers in 1933 but winners in 1934 for only the second time. However, there was even better to come. In 1936–37, Wild guided City to the League Championship for the very first time, inspired by the likes of Peter Doherty, Alex Herd, Frank Swift and Sam Barkas – all of whom Wild had brought to the club.

Whatever cruel deities watch over Maine Road ensured that Wild would suffer for bringing the City fans such happiness and the season after lifting English football's most glittering prize, City were relegated. The reigning champions had never before lost their top-flight status so quickly and, hardly surprisingly, it's never happened since.

Like Ernest Mangnall, Wild guided City through the war and when League football resumed in 1946, he began the season that would ultimately take the Blues to an unprecedented fifth Second Division title. He handed the team over to Sam Cowan in November 1946 and resumed secretarial duties once more, ending an exceptional period of management for the club. He died in his office in 1950 doing the job he loved.

WILLIAMS, ALEX – 1978 TO 1987
Appearances: 125
Goals: 0
Position: Goalkeeper
Born: Manchester

Alex Williams' City career was cut short by a back injury after he had finally dislodged the mighty Joe Corrigan from between the sticks. He looked destined for many years as the number one keeper for the Blues but an operation in the mid-1980s was the beginning of the end for the talented shot-stopper. Unable to regain full fitness, he was loaned out to Queen of the South before joining Port Vale in 1987. He retired two years later. One of the first black goalkeepers in Britain, Williams was very popular with the City fans and still works at the club today as Football in the Community manager. He was awarded the MBE in 2002.

WILSON, CLIVE – 1979 TO 1987
Appearances: 124 + 2 as a substitute
Goals: 11
Position: Midfielder/Full-back
Born: Manchester

City produced a plethora of talented black youngsters during the late 1970s. Roger Palmer, Dave Bennett, Gary Bennett, Alex Williams and Clive Wilson were local kids, but for skill and technique alone, Wilson was probably the supporters' favourite of the aforementioned quintet.

A capture from Moss Side Amateurs, the gifted midfielder made his debut in December 1981 in a 2–1 win over Wolves. Wilson acquitted himself well and the win took City to the top of the First Division. He made a couple more starts but City had fallen from top to tenth after winning just 3 of their last 16 League games. Wilson played none of the following season at all.

Under Billy McNeill, he began to establish himself and played 11 games of the Scot's first term in charge and the next was even more productive with 27 starts and 4 goals scored, mainly from his favoured position of midfield. By the 1985–86 season he was still not considered a first-team regular and played in 6 different numbered shirts, adding another 24 appearances and 5 more goals.

Paul Power's departure to Everton was the break Wilson had been waiting for and Jimmy Frizzell gave him the left-back berth for his own. Despite City's relegation, Wilson was an ever-present for the first time but failed to score any goals from his defensive role, yet his future had already been decided.

During March of that season, Wilson signed for Chelsea but was loaned back to the Blues until the end of the season – an unusual move at the time, but one that helped finance the Paul Stewart transfer from Blackpool. Wilson had finally broken through and was now on his way to London. He played for the Pensioners for several years before moving to QPR.

WIMBLYDON – CLUB CAT

Sometime during the summer of 2001, a stray ginger cat began visiting City's training ground at Carrington in search of scraps of food. The City backroom staff began leaving bits of meat and cat biscuits for the feline guest and before long the puss had made itself a new home. The players and Kevin Keegan would give it a pat on passing and it soon had its own bowl of food and milk by the reception entrance. One morning, Juan Carlos Osorio – City's South American conditioning coach – asked if it was 'Wimblydon' the Blues were facing on Saturday. Of course, he meant Wimbledon but pronounced it in such a way that he unknowingly found the name the staff had been looking for.

Wimblydon soon brought Kevin Keegan his first gift – a dead mouse – and laid it outside his office. His residence as City's official club cat was sealed when, after injuring a paw, he was picked up by the RSPCA. With nobody to pay a sizeable bill, director Chris Bird asked to have the bill sent directly to him. The *Manchester Evening News* got hold of the story and it was pasted on billboards all over Manchester – 'City's Purr-fect Signing' and such like. Wimblydon has since received fan mail and regularly appears in the official club magazine. A glamour puss, if there ever was!

WOOSNAM, MAX – 1919 TO 1925

Appearances: 93
Goals: 5
Position: Centre-half
Born: Liverpool

'Gentleman' Max Woosnam, who joined City from Corinthians in November 1919, was one of the great sportsmen of his era. A Cambridge Blue at golf, tennis and football, he also won a Wimbledon doubles title and an Olympic gold medal for tennis. Popular, and the perfect gentleman, hence the nickname, he even on occasion carried a handkerchief around the pitch to befit his image. Lucky for Max that there was no Stuart Pearce or Vinny Jones around in his day. Well-groomed, immaculately dressed and respected by all, Woosnam was a huge success with the City fans and this gifted man was also a powerful defender who captained both City and England. He was also a pioneer of amateurs being allowed to play with professionals increasing his popularity even more within the game, especially when he took a stand against the Amateur Football Association over the matter. He broke his leg on a fence that surrounded Hyde Road in 1922 and in October 1925 he left for Northwich Victoria, having made a lasting impression on the Blues.

WORLD CUP

City have had several stars represent the club in the World Cup. Colin Bell and Franny Lee were part of the 1970 England squad that was knocked out in the quarter-finals by West Germany. At Argentina 1978, Asa Hartford and Willie Donachie played for Scotland, who failed to progress beyond the group stages and went out on goal difference. Trevor Francis (England) and Asa Hartford (Scotland) were both involved in the Spain 1982 tournament but Sammy McIlroy (Northern Ireland) was the only Blue at Mexico 1986. Niall Quinn played for Ireland as City's sole representative during Italia 1990, while fellow countrymen Terry Phelan and Alan Kernaghan represented the Emerald Isle in USA 1994.

During the World Cup in Korea and Japan, all records were broken for City as no less than five members of the squad were chosen for their respective countries. Paulo Wanchope (Costa Rica), Niclas Jensen (Denmark) and Jihai Sun (China) all made selection while Richard Dunne (Ireland) and Lucien Mettomo (Cameroon) watched from the sidelines.

From the 'almost qualified' list are Cameroon star Marc Vivien Foe, who joined the Blues on a year's loan deal shortly after his country's exit; £12 million star Nicolas Anelka was part of the French winning team that won the trophy in 1998; Kaziu Deyna joined City shortly after the 1978 World Cup. City boss Kevin Keegan played against Spain in the 1982 World Cup. Colin Bell, at the very peak of his game, was devastated to be part of an England side that crashed out in the qualifiers to Poland in 1974 and he later admitted it was one of the greatest disappointments of his career.

Israeli Eyal Berkovic, Australian Danny Tiatto and Algerian Ali Benarbia would grace any side on a World Cup stage but, so far, their respective countries have never achieved qualification to the finals.

WORST START

The worst-ever start to a League campaign for City was in 1980–81 when 8 losses and 4 draws were recorded from 12 games. The run resulted in Malcolm Allison's sacking and accordingly the next game – unlucky 13 – resulted in a 3–1 victory over Tottenham at Maine Road. To the eternal credit of new manager John Bond, City ultimately finished in 12th position.

WRIGHT-PHILLIPS, SHAUN – 2000 TO PRESENT
Appearances: 49 + 15 as a substitute*
Goals: 8*
Position: Wing-back/Midfielder
Born: London

Talented adopted son of former England striker Ian Wright, Shaun Wright-Phillips joined City's Academy aged 15 after being released by Nottingham Forest, who told the youngster he was 'too small' to make the grade. His talents were honed in the City Academy and he was soon a regular in the reserve side. In 1999, manager Joe Royle gave the versatile attacker his debut and he played several games during the Blues' ill-fated Premiership campaign.

New manager Kevin Keegan soon made Wright-Phillips a first-team regular after a string of impressive performances and he ended the 2001–02 campaign as an invaluable member of the first team, scoring several spectacular goals and winning his first England Under-21 cap. He finished the season by being voted 'Young Player of the Year' for a third successive time – a club record equalled only by Steve Kinsey.

Y

YOUNG, NEIL — 1959 TO 1972
Appearances: 409 + 3 as a substitute
Goals: 108
Position: Forward
Born: Fallowfield, Manchester

Neil Young played a number of key roles in the City forward line before Joe Mercer gave him the No. 10 shirt for keeps and then contentedly sat back as the Manchester-born striker began to fulfil his considerable potential. Young possessed a cultured left foot and was at the heart of the Blues' halcyon days when the club swept all in its path. In fact, it could be argued that Young had a more substantial role than anyone else during the glory days, having scored crucial goals at times when important matches were finely balanced.

For instance, it was his left-foot cracker that won the 1969 FA Cup final against Leicester City. Young was, without doubt, a major influence in City's European Cup-Winners' Cup triumph a year later after scoring and then winning a penalty in the 2–1 win over Gornik Zabrze. He was also the top scorer when the Blues last lifted the Division One Championship trophy with 19 and bagged a couple in the final and deciding game at Newcastle United. He signed for Preston in January 1972 for £48,000 after 13 years at Maine Road. Recently honoured in a series of testimonial events organised mainly by supporters, Young was mystifyingly overlooked at international level, but his place with the heroes of yesteryear is guaranteed among all Blues followers.

YOUTH CUP
The club's youth team has won the coveted FA Youth Cup on only one occasion. In 1986 both City and United made it to the two-legged final. The first leg, watched by just 7,602, ended 1–1 at Old Trafford with Paul Lake scoring for City. The second leg at Maine Road was watched by 18,164 partisan City supporters, who roared the young Blues on to a 2–0 win, with goals from Moulden and Boyd. City had previously reached the final in 1978–79 and 1979–80 but on both occasions were losers to Millwall and Aston Villa respectively.

Z

ZAMBIA

Brothers Jim and Jeff Whitley were both born in the African country of Zambia. To add to the confusion, both players have Manchester accents and are full internationals for Northern Ireland. Jim, who has since left the club, is also a talented artist and his painting of Gio Kinkladze was made into a number of limited signed prints during the Georgian's stay with the Blues.

ZENITH DATA SYSTEMS CUP

It's an unfortunate fact of life that the Blues' awful decade from 1980 to 1990 saw the club enter some truly forgettable, awkwardly-named competitions that held little more than embarrassment for the City faithful. The Zenith Data was such a competition. In 1989 the Blues played three games in a bid to lift a trophy few were interested in, beating Middlesbrough 2–1 at Maine Road and then Sheffield United 2–0 away. Leeds United ended the Blues' interest 2–0 at Elland Road – just as everybody was getting excited! The following year City went out at the first hurdle in a 3–2 defeat at Sheffield Wednesday.